Masculinity after Trujillo

UNIVERSITY PRESS OF FLORIDA

Florida A&M University, Tallahassee
Florida Atlantic University, Boca Raton
Florida Gulf Coast University, Ft. Myers
Florida International University, Miami
Florida State University, Tallahassee
New College of Florida, Sarasota
University of Central Florida, Orlando
University of Florida, Gainesville
University of North Florida, Jacksonville
University of South Florida, Tampa
University of West Florida, Pensacola

Masculinity after Trujillo

The Politics of Gender in Dominican Literature

MAJA HORN

University Press of Florida
Gainesville · Tallahassee · Tampa · Boca Raton
Pensacola · Orlando · Miami · Jacksonville · Ft. Myers · Sarasota

Copyright 2014 by Maja Horn
All rights reserved
Printed in the United States of America on acid free paper

This book may be available in an electronic edition.

21 20 19 18 17 16   6 5 4 3 2 1

First cloth printing, 2014
First paperback printing, 2016

Library of Congress Cataloging-in-Publication Data
Horn, Maja, author.
Masculinity after Trujillo : the politics of gender in Dominican literature / Maja Horn.
pages cm
"This book is a part of the Latin American and Caribbean Arts and Culture publication initiative, funded by a grant from the Andrew W. Mellon Foundation."
Includes bibliographical references and index.
ISBN 978-0-8130-4930-4 (cloth: alk. paper)
ISBN 978-0-8130-5400-1 (pbk.)
1. Dominican literature—History and criticism. 2. Masculinity—Dominican Republic. 3. Masculinity in literature. 4. Gender identity—Dominican Republic. 5. Men—Dominican Republic—Psychology. I. Andrew W. Mellon Foundation. II. Latin American and Caribbean Arts and Culture Publication Initiative. III. Title.
PQ7400.5.H67 2014
860.9'97293—dc23
2013029228

University Press of Florida
15 Northwest 15th Street
Gainesville, FL 32611-2079
http://www.upf.com

This book is a part of the Latin American and Caribbean Arts and Culture publication initiative, funded by a grant from the Andrew W. Mellon Foundation.

*To my family
and to Miguel and Milagros, who made me family*

Contents

Acknowledgments xi

Introduction: The Politics of Gender in the Caribbean 1

1. De-tropicalizing the Trujillo Dictatorship and Dominican Masculinity 23

2. One Phallus for Another: Post-dictatorship Political and Literary Canons 50

3. Engendering Resistance: Hilma Contreras's Counternarratives 80

4. Still Loving *Papi*: Globalized Dominican Subjectivities in the Novels of Rita Indiana Hernández 102

5. How Not to Read Junot Díaz: Diasporic Dominican Masculinity and Its Returns 123

Conclusion 139

Notes 145

Bibliography 183

Index 193

Acknowledgments

This book is the result of my scholarly and personal engagement with Dominican culture and arts for the past ten years, which began with a serendipitous encounter with the Dominican writer, artist, and musician Rita Indiana Hernández. She insisted that I listen and learn about the Dominican Republic when I was primarily dedicated to thinking and writing about Puerto Rico and Cuba, and for this I will always be immensely grateful. Since then my scholarly work and life has been animated by the incredible generosity with which many Dominican writers, artists, and scholars have shared their thoughts and works with me, both in the Dominican Republic and here in the United States. I am greatly indebted to them.

The completion of this manuscript was made possible through a faculty research leave and research grant from Barnard College, as well as by a research grant from the Institute of Latin American Studies at Columbia University. Indeed, I have had the good fortune of writing this book while working at an institution that supports its faculty's research endeavors and surrounds me with colleagues and students who continuously challenge and stimulate my thinking. Since arriving at Barnard College in 2006, I have enjoyed the collegiality and support of my colleagues in the Department of Spanish and Latin American Cultures, including Orlando Bentancor, Ronald Briggs, and Javier Pérez-Zapatero, among others. My two senior colleagues Alfred MacAdam and Wadda Ríos-Font have, above and beyond the call of duty, dedicated their time and energy to supporting my work. This book has benefited both from Alfred MacAdam's painstaking help with phrasing my ideas in more succinct ways and from Wadda Ríos-Font's keen critical eye. Indeed, her probing question "What silences do you mean?" led me back to the Trujillo period and redirected my thinking in substantial ways.

One of the most crucial experiences in these past years, which has pushed my scholarship toward a broader Caribbean and African diaspora perspective, has been my involvement with the Africana Studies Program at Barnard College, where I now teach half my courses. Under the fierce leadership of Kim F. Hall, I became part of this scholarly community that has shaped my experience at Barnard in ways that I never could have anticipated and would never want to miss. Thank you, Kim. I am also immensely grateful for the ongoing support that other faculty in the growing Africana Studies program at Barnard continuously offer, especially Tina Campt, Celia E. Naylor, Yvette Christiansë, Monica L. Miller, Kaiama L. Glover, Paul Scolieri, and Abosede George. My participation in various interdisciplinary faculty initiatives has greatly enriched my time at Barnard, including the Difficult Dialogues Faculty Seminar and the Mellon Faculty Seminar of the Consortium of Critical Interdisciplinary Studies. I especially thank those colleagues who invested great time and effort in organizing these and who invited me to participate in them, including Janet Jakobsen, Neferti X. M. Tadiar, Monica L. Miller, and Jennie A. Kassanoff, among others.

I am also immensely grateful for the intellectual exchange and support that both current and former colleagues at the Department of Latin American and Iberian Cultures at Columbia University have offered in the past years, especially Carlos J. Alonso, Graciela Montaldo, Alberto Medina, Anke Birkenmaier, Maite Conde, Alessandra Russo, José Antonio Castellanos-Pazos, and Mark A. Hertzman. I furthermore thank the department's graduate students for their engaging discussions in my seminars that have helped me fine-tune some of my theoretical standpoints. At Columbia I also especially thank Frances Negrón-Muntaner, director of the Center for the Study of Ethnicity and Race (CSER), for inviting me to collaborate with CSER and for supporting (and teaching) my work.

Various interdisciplinary faculty work groups have discussed parts of this project over the years and helped me rethink, revise, and hopefully improve it. For this I thank the members of the Barnard Junior Faculty Writing Group, whose insights from history, political science, and theater greatly helped push my work into more interdisciplinary directions. I am especially grateful to the group's cofounder, Abosede George, who has become a close friend and neighbor and who ensures that my academic life never feels like a solitary or humorless endeavor. I thank the members of my Queer Reading Group: Hiram Perez, Lisa Estreich, Christine Cynn, Chi-ming Yang, and others for their good spirit, inspired readings, and thoughtful discussion of my work. The support and comments that I received when I presented this project to the Caribbean Studies Working Group at New York University helped me carry on with it at a crucial moment. I also thank the members of the Taller/Work in Progress group at the Columbia Department of Latin American Iberian Studies whose insightful comments on my second chapter were decisive for its final revision.

In the past few years my participation in the Transnational and Transcolonial Caribbean Studies Research Group (TTCSRG) has had a truly transformative impact on my scholarly and personal life. My ongoing exchanges with Kaiama L. Glover, Alessandra Benedicty, Kelly Baker Josephs, Christian Flaugh, and Nayana Abeysinghe and their many critical readings of my work have taught me so much about the value and importance of scholarly excellence, community, and friendship. Furthermore, my ongoing collaboration with my colleague Kaiama L. Glover at Barnard College in a team-taught course about the Dominican Republic and Haiti has been an eye-opening experience, and her intellectual energy, wisdom, and kindness are truly inspiring to me.

This book has greatly benefited from exchanges with various Dominican studies scholars, especially Carlos U. Decena and Miguel D. Mena; their scholarship informs this book in so many ways, and their encouragement and scholarly generosity mean more to me than I can express here. The thoughts, words, and scholarly example of Silvio Torres-Saillant and Lauren Derby were pivotal for this project, along with those of other Dominican and Caribbean studies scholars, including Lorgia H. García-Peña, Elizabeth S. Manley, April J. Mayes, Danny Méndez, and Celiany Rivera-Velázquez. This past year my conversations with two outstanding Dominican graduate students, Wendy V. Muñiz at Columbia University and Jennifer M. Rodriguez at Princeton University, have helped me calibrate various aspects of my analysis in this book; I look forward to many future exchanges with them.

I had the good fortune of discussing many of the ideas in this book with the Dominican artist Rider Ureña, which helped me hone my argument at a crucial time. I am also especially indebted to Carlo Concha Zea for the immense generosity with which he patiently corrected my translations of the many quotes (all remaining errors are, of course, mine). Parts of this book were edited with the help of Sonam Singh with his keen editorial and critical eye. This manuscript has also greatly benefited from the careful readings and the thoughtful suggestions of Ignacio López-Calvo and Emilio Bejel, and I thank them very much. I also thank Amy Gorelick, my editor at the University Press of Florida, whose quick response and interest in this project has made the publication process much smoother than I could have ever anticipated. I also thank my project editor Marthe Walters, my copy editor Lisa Williams, and the other members of the press's staff who have helped to ensure the timely completion of this project.

My scholarly path was initiated with the help and wisdom of a few key people to whom I owe many thanks. Marina Kaplan, my professor at Smith College, was entirely responsible for first fostering my scholarly interest in Latin American literatures and cultures. Debra A. Castillo, my dissertation adviser at Cornell University, has offered steady and continuing support that has helped shepherd me through any difficulties. I also am very grateful for the kind words of various professors and colleagues that at different moments helped me continue on with renewed enthusiasm. For this I thank Mary Pat Brady, José E. Muñoz, Jeff Rider, Daniel Balderston, Agnes Lugo-Ortiz, Dara Goldman, Ana Maria Dopico, Michael Kimmel, and Lawrence La Fountain-Stokes.

In the Dominican Republic, I was welcomed at FLACSO (Latin American Social Science Faculty) through the energetic support of the political scientist Jacqueline Jiménez Polanco, and I am immensely indebted to her and her many tireless efforts, including her suggestion that I develop a performance studies program at FLACSO. I thank Cheila Valera Acosta, then the director of FLACSO, for opening the institution's doors to me as a research associate and for allowing me to organize and teach my Performance Studies *diplomado* there in the summer of 2006. Teaching performance studies in the Dominican Republic to twelve students, many of them performance artists themselves, is one of my most cherished academic experiences. I am also immensely grateful for the collaboration of my inspiring coteachers Sara Hermann, the former director of the Museo de Arte Moderno, and the anthropologist Carlos Andújar, as well as for the support of Rafael Emilio Yunén, from the Centro León in Santiago, of Freddy Ginebra from Casa de Teatro in Santo Domingo, of María del Carmen Ossaye, from the magazine *Artes*, as well as of the Escuela de Bellas Artes.

My many conversations and exchanges with Dominican artists, writers, and friends inform all my thinking and writing about the Dominican Republic. For the generosity with which they welcomed me and shared their works and thoughts, I especially thank the artists Eliú Almonte, María Batlle, Fermín Ceballos, Caryanna Castillo, Patricia Castillo ("Patutus"), Mónica Ferreras, José García Cordero, Jaime Guerra, Laura Guerrero, Sayuri Guzmán, Arlyn Jiménez, Pascal Meccariello, MODAFOCA, Charo Oquet, Natalia Ortega, David "Karmadavis" Pérez, Rafael Pérez, Jorge Pineda, and last but not least Raúl Recio. I also want to thank the Dominican theater actors, dancers, and directors Orestes Amador (my former neighbor), Waddys Jáquez, Henry Mercedes, and Isabel Spencer, as well as the writers Frank Báez, Juan Dicent, and Homero Pumarol. I am also grateful for the friendship of Marianela Carvajal Díaz, Manuel Moreta, Manolo Rodriguez Vidal, and Andrea Bavestrello. Among all, Milagros Dottin and Miguel Peña have played, without doubt, the most important role in my many returns to Santo Domingo over the years. At their apartment, just across from the Universidad Autonóma de Santo Domingo (UASD), I have found the people, the conversations, the books, the music, and the food that have made Dominican culture come alive to me and almost feel like home.

In New York I had the good fortune of meeting the Dominican artist Gerard Ellis, who graciously gave me permission to have his artwork reprinted on this book's cover. I am also grateful for the open arms with which the Dominican American art collective Proyecto GRAFICA received me, and I thank all twelve members for their enthusiastic collaboration with me on an exhibit of their work at Barnard College in 2012.

Back at home in Germany, I especially want to thank my aunt Marion and her family, who helped make possible my studies at Smith College when I first came to the United States, and who I believe has much to do with my love of books and cats. Indeed, my cat, Babalu, though seemingly indifferent to his Dominican origins and (neutered) masculinity, has been the most loyal companion during the completion of this project. My longtime close friends Anne and Lisa have more than anyone else weathered with me the many ups and downs of undertaking this project, and my life would be much less joyful without their presence, love, and irreverence. Yet it has been the steady love and good humor of my family in Berlin, Germany—my parents Ellen and Rainer, and my siblings Mirjam and Nikolai—that has allowed me to make home in many different places over the years without ever feeling lost. Danke meine Lieben.

Introduction

The Politics of Gender in the Caribbean

The Dominican presidential campaign leading up to the 2012 elections littered the national landscape with political slogans. Among these was the presidential candidate Hipólito Mejía's ubiquitous "Llegó Papá" (Daddy's here). This slogan largely overrode more usual political promises, evincing the power of the discourse of masculinity in Dominican politics. The important role that gender plays in constructing citizenship and state power in the Dominican Republic demands a more complex understanding of hegemonic notions of Dominican masculinity, of the conceptions of femininity that they produce, and of their historical emergence. While such evocations of masculinity are usually rationalized as instances of centuries-old "traditional" Latin American patriarchal culture, *Masculinity after Trujillo* argues that today's hegemonic notions of masculinity were consolidated during the dictatorship of Rafael Leónidas Trujillo (1930–1961) and thus are in many ways a distinctly modern formation. In turn, Trujillo's own pervasively hypervirile discourse was, at least in part, a strategic response to the imperial and racialized notions of masculinity that accompanied the U.S. presence in the country, especially during the U.S. military occupation (1916–1924). Against the tendency to equate Trujillo's discourse of masculinity simply with that of a stereotypical Latin American "strongman," or *caudillo*, I point to the importance of accounting for how transnational and imperialist forces, including international political discourses of sovereignty and Euro-American racism, also shaped its articulation.

Indeed, the disappointments that postcolonial democratic politics have brought in the Dominican Republic, and in many other parts of the Caribbean, cannot be understood without accounting for how external forces have helped foster exclusionary forms of citizenship and corrupt state practices. In much of the postcolonial Caribbean, political reality appears to be stagnant and is met with citizens' disenchantment. The Caribbean critic David Scott, for example, speaks of "the acute paralysis of will and sheer vacancy of imagination, the rampant corruption and vicious authoritarianism, the instrumental self-interest and showy self-congratulation" that result in the "bankruptcy of postcolonial regimes" in the region.[1] The multitude of failures by postcolonial states has led many Caribbean citizens to relinquish hopes for political solutions for their societies' economic and social problems and has driven many toward migration. As the Dominican scholar Silvio Torres-Saillant notes, "although the region gave to the world some of the earliest instances of struggle for freedom and human rights, liberatory projects and discourses here seem to awaken increasingly less enthusiasm as the lives of people appear to revolve primarily around the business of material survival in dependent and declining economies that offer the Antillean person no social guarantee."[2]

It is in response to this reality that Torres-Saillant and other critics have expressed reservations about certain tendencies in Caribbean thought and letters of the past decades that are part of what Raphael Dalleo terms the "postmodern turn." Dalleo traces this postmodern turn, for example, in the later work of such writers and critics as Edouard Glissant and Antonio Benítez-Rojo, and associates it with their and others' embrace of pan-Caribbean paradigms to capture the region's specificity. Torres-Saillant critiques how it remains unclear how such pan-Caribbean paradigms (such as "creolization," "rhizomes," "rhythms," or "performance") contribute to addressing the dire material circumstances of many Caribbean people's lives and the political shortcomings of Caribbean postcolonial nation-states. Indeed, these pan-Caribbean paradigms are described by Belinda Edmondson as "iconic—clichéd, if you will—tropes of Caribbean discourse."[3] She terms these "Caribbean romances," because of how such tropes sustain "idealized representations of Caribbean society, of 'Caribbeanness,' both in hegemonic European-American discourses and, perhaps more important, in *intra*-Caribbean discourses."⁴ These "romances," Edmondson finds, problematically mystify "concrete ideological-political issues . . . into regional symbols divorced from their ideological context."⁵

This book contributes to a new wave of scholarship that addresses ideological-political issues and lasting inequalities in the Caribbean in their local contexts. Like other recent studies, such as Deborah A. Thomas's *Exceptional Violence: Embodied Citizenship in Transnational Jamaica* (2011) and Mimi Sheller's *Citizenship from Below: Erotic Agency and Caribbean Freedom* (2012), this study is dedicated to accounting for how inequalities in the region are sustained by current postcolonial Caribbean nation-states, together with the powerfully conditioning and constraining factors of colonial, imperial, and neo-imperial forces. What *Masculinity after Trujillo* shares with these studies is the concern with how local (rather than pan-Caribbean) forms of resistance—explored by Thomas in the form of "embodied citizenship" and by Sheller through the notion of "citizenship from below"—can challenge the political status quo and the hegemonic formations that help to sustain it.

The reference to "citizenship" in both Sheller's and Thomas's book titles suggests how national belonging and the nation-state continue to play a fundamental role in circumscribing Caribbean peoples' lives. While the Caribbean is rightfully looked at as a crossroads of the world that prefigured some of the forms of interconnectedness and mobility now associated with globalization, national imaginaries and states continue to play a decisive role in shaping Caribbean societies and citizens' lives and need to be an ongoing object of critical scrutiny. Dara E. Goldman also emphasizes the lasting importance of the literally and figuratively insular national context and insists that "despite the increasing translocality of Caribbean spaces," the insular nation continues to be a "central mode of self-representation."⁶ In fact,

> Hispanic Caribbean self-fashioning offers a compelling case study of local specificity and national persistence in the face of increasing transnationalism, neoliberalism, and geopolitical restructuring. . . . Accordingly, however retrograde it may seem, the attachment to political borders persists. The nation therefore remains highly crucial as the primary space of subject formation even as its precise position is radically redefined in an increasingly globalized world.⁷

Similarly, albeit focusing on the Anglophone Caribbean, Shalini Puri highlights the lasting and crucial importance of the nation in the postcolonial

Caribbean and remarks on the "prematurity of declarations of the demise of the nation-state."[8]

The case of the Dominican Republic also strongly suggests that despite the ever-increasing impact of outside forces associated with globalization the nation remains a primary determinant of national cultural identity, and the state continues to play a vital role in shaping its citizens' political and economic realities on the island. For example, the lasting role that the Dominican state plays in the (mis-)distribution of national resources is readily evident to most observers. Despite the notable growth in the country's gross domestic product since the 1990s, the state has insufficiently helped to ameliorate the inequities and hardships faced by the Dominican people. A cursory look at various World Bank surveys readily reveals the staggering failure of the government, regardless of the party in power, to translate economic growth into better living conditions for the majority of Dominicans.[9] In fact, the Dominican Republic is considered to have "one of the worst performing states in Latin America."[10]

The growth of the Dominican economy in recent decades has been based mainly on the tourism industry, remittances, and the output of free trade zones, where workers' rights and protections are minimal. At the same time the number of Dominicans who rely on informal employment to survive has grown exponentially. The percentage of Dominicans with "vulnerable employment," defined by the World Bank as "unpaid family workers and own-account workers as a percentage of total employment," hovers in the Dominican Republic around 40 percent.[11] The country also has the highest unemployment rate of all surveyed Latin American countries. In fact, despite consistently high rates of economic growth, the Dominican Republic has one of the region's highest percentages (50.5 percent) of people living below the poverty line (Bolivia, Honduras, and Guatemala have higher poverty rates, albeit with much smaller economic growth rates). The Dominican state's health expenditures are one of the lowest in the region, 5.9 percent in 2009 (only Bolivia and Peru spent less), and the country has Latin America's lowest expenditures on education, 2.3 percent in 2009. These numbers offer a glimpse at how state actions continue to determine in decisive ways the conditions under which Dominican lives unfold. Even as the "wholesale opening up of the economy" resulted in a loss of state capacity to "guide society," as the Dominican sociologist Wilfredo Lozano puts it, the state remains a "central actor" and a "fundamental instrument."[12] Understanding how the nation-state continues to determine the material, social, and political contexts of Caribbean subjects' lives, and how it can be prodded to work better towards greater economic and social justice, thus remains a crucial task.

Caribbean Cultural Agency and the Postcolonial State

Given the lasting significance of the Caribbean nation-state, this book hopes to help push Caribbean scholarship to think more consistently and thoroughly about how Caribbean cultural forces, including forces from "below" and in "embodied" forms, may evolve to challenge and reconfigure the political in its more conventional sense, that is, the postcolonial state apparatus and its forms of governance, to better address the needs of its citizens. My insistence on not forsaking the possibility of incisive political change is inspired in part by recent political and social reconfigurations in Latin America, both the so-called turn to the left, and the notable recent decrease in inequality in Latin America, counter to worldwide trends, which has been aided by state actions of both leftist and nonleftist Latin American governments.[13] It is in this context that John Beverley reminds us that, whatever the future of the state, at the current moment "the question of who controls the state—to the extent it means something to control the state—remains crucial to people's lives."[14] Serious proposals for social and political transformation then cannot sidestep the question of "how the state itself can be radicalized and modified as a consequence of bringing into it demands, values, experiences from the popular-subaltern sector ... and how, in turn, *from* the state, society itself can be remade in a more redistributive, egalitarian, culturally diverse way."[15] Beverley emphasizes here the importance and political significance of the forms that relations between society and the state take. Specifically, he highlights the ways in which popular-subaltern demands can evolve to reconfigure the state and thereby bring it to more broadly effect positive social change.

The pivotal question is, then, what kind of relations help incorporate subaltern and popular demands or demands "from below" into the state to pressure it to work toward redistributive processes and greater egalitarianism. This question has been consistently pursued in the work of Argentine political theorist Ernesto Laclau, whose work influences also Beverley's thinking. In *Hegemony and Socialist Strategy: Towards a Radical Democratic Politics* (1985), which Laclau coauthored with Chantal Mouffe, and then in later works, including *Emancipation(s)* (1996) and *On Populist Reason* (2005), Laclau assigns a key role to the types of relation or linkage that form between the state and the populace, as well as to the relations formed among the populace to express and put forth conjointly shared demands. His prime distinction is between equivalential and differential relations or linkages. Equivalential relations involve the horizontal coming together of peoples' various unfulfilled demands to articulate a collective will that can bring forth a successful challenge to the existing hegemonic formation. Alternatively, differential relations imply the absorption of demands "each in isolation from the others" by "the institutional system," for example, through clientelist arrangements.[16] According to Laclau, it is through the coming together of popular demands that an effective challenge to a hegemonic formation becomes possible. Such a reconfiguration of existing power relations then can lead to a redistribution not only of political, economic, and cultural resources, but also of less tangible "goods," including access to spaces of representation and to decision-making processes.

It is these kinds of specific ideological-political questions that the so-called postmodern turn in Caribbean thought has not always addressed. In fact, at times, its "Caribbean romances," as Edmondson calls these regional metaphors, rely problematically on unacknowledged gendered, sexualized, and racialized notions that reinscribe existing unequal power relations rather than challenge them. For example, Omise'eke Natasha Tinsley notes how neither the créolistes nor Glissant's Caribbean discourse address the gender of the Caribbean landscapes that they repeatedly evoke in their writings. Tinsley asks, "Does the mangrove retain the swamp's dangerous, sticky femininity? Does Glissant's frightening sea keep its conventional motherliness?"[17] She critiques how "gender and sexuality problematically remain nonissues" in their work, and how "the most renowned theorists of inclusive Creoleness often do not recognize how their very neocolonial rootedness in binary gender and sexual identities undercuts the complexity that they express as fundamental to their project."[18] Similar questions can be raised about the gendered nature of Antonio Benítez-Rojo's description in *The Repeating Island* of the Caribbean as "aquatic, a sinuous culture . . . [a] realm of marine currents, of waves, of folds and double-folds, of fluidity and sinuosity," and references to the Caribbean's "womb" and "vagina."[19]

Indeed, Vera M. Kutzinski strongly critiques Benítez-Rojo's unacknowledged gendered, sexualized, racialized, and classed connotations that underlie his celebration of an empowering Caribbean "certain kind of way." When Benítez-Rojo sets out to explain what he means by this "certain kind of way," he invokes the scene of two old black women passing under his balcony in Cuba during the Cuban missile crisis. He describes how "there was a kind of ancient and golden powder between their gnarled legs, a scent of basil and mint in their dress, a symbolic, ritual wisdom in their gesture and their gay chatter."[20] Seeing these two women and hearing their unconcerned "chatter" at this moment of extreme international tension convinces him that there will be no nuclear Armageddon. Kutzinski is rightfully wary of how, in this scene, Benítez-Rojo turns the singular "way" of the walking and talking of two black Caribbean women into "a scenario in which both the racial attributes of the two women and their lower-class status jointly contribute to the mysterious, 'magical,' inarticulateness and unself-consciousness" that "their 'chatter'" represents to him.[21] For Kutzinski, Benítez-Rojo re-creates here "a familiar voyeuristic scenario, one in which a male and usually white writer observes, in this case from the lofty heights of his balcony, the quotidian activities of racial Others who, more often than not, are figured as female because of the regenerative potential presumably inherent in their cultural 'performance' or 'style.'"[22] This scene, key for Benítez-Rojo's thinking about the Caribbean's repeating patterns, thus uncritically reiterates long-standing, unequal power structures.

Laclau's theoretical framework and conceptual tools would help us to ask, with regard to such a scene, about what forms of social relation would offer greater promise for a wider range of subjects, not only for the author on the balcony but also for the older, darker, female, and implicitly poorer fellow Cubans that he observes from above. Benítez-Rojo's evasion of racial, class, and gender differences in the scene he conjures hardly facilitates a potential "linkage" of the observer with the two black women and their coming together to articulate shared demands. His vertical and ultimately hierarchical positioning, rather, would seem to hinder the formation of the kind of horizontal relations necessary for forming the equivalential linkages that, according to Laclau, may rise to challenge and reformulate hegemonic formations. By allowing for the precise formulation of such questions, Laclau's theories help not only to consider how hegemonic formations may be challenged from below but, as I suggest, also to consider and understand in new ways the interstitial relation of gender, sexual, racial, class, and national imaginaries and their complexly imbricated political effects.

The fact that in many postcolonial Caribbean nation-states much-desired reconfigurations of hegemonic formations and of the political status quo that they help to sustain are not taking place raises the question of why unmet demands have not led to a coming together of peoples to form equivalential linkages and posit an effective challenge to hegemonic formations. A key factor for the success of such a process is, according to Laclau, "the unification of these various demands . . . into a stable system of signification."[23] For this "symbolic unification" to take place, the process of naming, of demands being brought and quilted together by a shared signifier (such as "anticolonialism," "justice," or "equality") is essential. Laclau's account of the rhetorical processes underlying processes of hegemonic reconfiguration offers a compelling way to think about the relation between Caribbean cultural and political processes and allows in particular for the highlighting of the role that cultural discourses, including literary ones, can play. We may ask, then, how literary and cultural discourses give voice to the various demands of heterogeneous subjectivities in a given Caribbean location. We may ask, furthermore, how literature and, more broadly, the Caribbean intellectual and literary public sphere can contribute to bringing forth ways of naming that help (or hinder) the coming together of these voices for the formation of a new collective will.

Laclau's conceptualization of hegemonic and anti-hegemonic forces and his account of processes of change are critical tools that can be fruitfully employed in Caribbean postcolonial contexts. These tools may help to consider more precisely what Caribbean configurations, including cultural ones, enable or hinder processes of social and political transformation and hold the most promise for posing a forceful anti-hegemonic challenge by helping to bring citizens' demands into the state and remaking the state in the process. I thus suggest that Laclau's work on hegemony offers a much-needed theoretical bridge between Caribbean scholars' scathing critiques of the "bankruptcy of postcolonial regimes" in the region (David Scott) and the compelling forms of Caribbean cultural agency that many scholars detect.

The Masculinization of Power

I want to briefly return to Hipólito Mejía's aforementioned slogan "Llegó Papá" to suggest how Laclau's conceptual framework can elucidate the ways in which cultural forces, and specifically gender discourses, structure relations between the political sphere and Dominican constituencies. The assurance that "Papá" had arrived and the apparent lack of any more explicit political content exemplify several facets of Dominican political culture.[24] The slogan speaks of the hierarchical conception of political leadership that predominates in the country, and how it is often naturalized through notions of masculinity. Notably, the hierarchical orientation of the Dominican political sphere, where the populace looks up toward "Papá" to provide solutions for their travails and demands, encumbers precisely the possibility of strong horizontal linkages forming among the populace. Instead, the individualizing solutions that are sought out tend to reinforce the pervasive practice of clientelism (and its close cousin corruption) in Dominican politics, irrespective of which party is in power.[25] This system of political relations, I argue, is continuously stabilized and sustained through notions of masculinity that naturalize them.

I here want to review briefly, then, some findings by scholars from various fields (anthropology, sociology, political science) that attest to the centrality of gender notions in structuring Dominican political, public, and private imaginaries. The most sustained engagement with notions of masculinity in Dominican politics is found in the work of anthropologist Christian Krohn-Hansen, first in his essay "Masculinity and the Political among Dominicans: The Dominican Tiger" and then in his book-length study *Political Authoritarianism in the Dominican Republic* (2009). In the latter, based on his ethnographic research in the country's southwestern region, Krohn-Hansen argues that "ideas of political life . . . were often closely interwoven with notions of masculinity."[26] This includes how "relations between leaders and followers, or patrons and clients, were given meaning in terms of ideas about masculinity."[27] Such gendered beliefs, Krohn-Hansen denounces, are often treated by scholars as merely "cultural" rather than properly "political" factors.

Yet recently some of the most important political scientists studying and writing about Dominican politics have taken note of the role that gender discourses play in Dominican politics. In a coauthored essay, Jana Morgan, Rosario Espinal, and Jonathan Hartlyn describe the notable effect that the return of a stronger "machista rhetoric" has had in Dominican politics in 2004 and thereafter. Previously, women had been making significant inroads in the Dominican political sphere. The strong internal push by Dominican women's organizations together with that of international institutions and agendas (especially after the 1995 Beijing conference on women) led to notable institutional gains. New laws were passed to ensure women's equality, a new state department for women's affairs was formed in 1999, and at the same time a women's quota was established for political parties' electoral lists.[28] These initiatives, however, did not result in as far-reaching changes as some had hoped or anticipated; instead, as Morgan, Espinal, and Hartlyn describe, in the early twenty-first century "this machista rhetoric and elites' deemphasizing of women's contributions undermined men's support for women in politics."[29] This loss of support leads them to conclude that "progress on women's issues is not unidirectional," and that "it cannot be taken for granted as the ineluctable consequence of broader socio-economic processes or of democratization, but is susceptible to elite influence and therefore requires continued activism and political leadership."[30] Their finding of how elite political discourses impact Dominican gender beliefs complicates the general assumption that democratic and socioeconomic development leads necessarily and straightforwardly to greater gender equality. Paying close attention to Dominican political discourses is therefore not ancillary but integral to any serious consideration of lasting gender inequities in the country and vice versa.

The fact that socioeconomic processes, such as the massive entry of women into the workforce and global impulses (e.g., the idea that "globalization brings openness and flexibility"), do not translate into unidirectional changes in gender norms in the Dominican Republic is also noted in a study of the Dominican public sector.[31] Jenny K. Rodriguez describes how organizational culture in the public sector is highly "masculinized," and "male and masculine are understood as dominant traits and thus have priority in the direction of interaction."[32] As a result, "when women participate in interactions initiated by men, they assume a passive role whereas men always assume an active role, whether or not they initiate the interaction."[33] The interactions themselves are "characterized by gender appropriate behaviors and tainted by sexualized innuendos," which for women means "modeling their identities to fit masculinized patterns, assuming a submissive passiveness and using sexualized femininity."[34] These dynamics structure relations between women and result in "criticizing/backstabbing each other based on the belief that they struggle with one another to be accepted by men, hence a feeling of competitiveness for male approval."[35] Interactions between men in turn are "based on expert knowledge and competitiveness: with practices that include challenging each other and references that link attainment to manhood or virility."[36] Thus, in male-to-male interactions men try to prove "that they are stronger/more manly than the other men, and at times resort to sexual innuendos with women in order to do so."[37] Rodriguez concludes that "sexuality seems to be a defining element in identity discourses of Dominican men and women in the public sector. It particularly relates to constructions that link sexualized ideas of bodies as important traits that define identity, individuality and what is understood as womanhood and manhood.... Both women and men have specific boundaries that are raised through language."[38] These boundaries are different for each gender. Namely, "whilst women are restrained by the prospect of doubts to their morality, men are by doubts to their manhood. Yet, in both cases operating patterns relate to strict meanings associated with sexualized roles."[39]

Many of these sexualized gender dynamics in the public sector have also been observed in Dominican society more broadly. Dominican sociologist E. Antonio de Moya suggests that in Dominican society there is a "consensus" that "(1) Men are the 'exact opposite' of women, whatever any or both of them could be. (2) Procreation is a necessary but insufficient condition for legitimizing masculinity. Homosocial relations among men are experienced as competitive gendered relations in terms of domination-subordination."[40] The work of other scholars—for example, Mark Padilla's *Caribbean Pleasure Industry: Tourism, Sexuality, and AIDS in the Dominican Republic* (2007) and Carlos U. Decena's *Tacit Subjects: Belonging and Same-Sex Desire among Dominican Immigrant Men* (2011)—concurs with de Moya's findings. Padilla and Decena both note the "investment in normative masculinity" among Dominican men who have sex with other men and their participation in "patriarchal gender dynamics."[41] These norms, then, not only apply to "dominant" heterosexual Dominican males but are widely shared by Dominican subjects of both genders and with different sexual preferences.

These shared hegemonic norms exist alongside a variety of Dominican masculinities and femininities, including a "multiplicity of (situational) masculine identities displayed by each man."[42] Drawing from Australian sociologist R. W. Connell's work on "hegemonic masculinity," de Moya notes how the majority of Dominican men do not necessarily embody this norm, but rather hegemonic masculinity functions as a "measure against which all men will compare themselves."[43] In Connell's own words,

> Hegemonic masculinities can be constructed that do not correspond closely to the lives of any actual men. Yet these models do, in various ways, express *widespread ideals, fantasies, and desires.* They provide models of relations with women and solutions to problems of gender relations. Furthermore, they articulate loosely with the practical constitution of masculinities as ways of living in everyday local circumstances. To the extent they do this, they contribute to hegemony in the society-wide order as a whole . . . [44]

Rather than the "normal" behavior of Dominican men, what this book is concerned with are precisely these gendered ideals, fantasies, and desires that structure relations in the private and public sphere, including in the political realm, and that, as I will show, contribute greatly to sustaining Dominican hegemonic formations and a troublesome political status quo.

American sociologist and prominent masculinities scholar Michael Kimmel foregrounds the importance of understanding hegemonic masculinity and gender more broadly as a relational construct that structures and is structured by the social (and, as I emphasize, the political). Kimmel critiques approaches that make "gender a set of individual attributes and not an aspect of social structure," which he finds ultimately "*depoliticizes* gender."[45] The studies I reviewed above all speak to the importance of addressing gender as a structural force rather than solely through the lens of individual identity in the Dominican Republic. They also speak to the need for more nuanced understandings of how local gender formations interact with what are thought to be the "modernizing forces" of economic development, democratization, and globalization. The massive entry of women into the workforce, new laws and political quotas, the impact of globalization, and generational changes have not reconfigured Dominican gender norms in easily predictable ways. Yet it is not only in the late twentieth and early twenty-first century that modernizing and outside forces have modulated Dominican gender formations; rather, as I argue, these have been mediated by outside impulses long before the age of globalization.

A more historically informed and nuanced understanding of these interactions and relations helps to illuminate the particular forms of political expediency that gender discourses have in the Dominican Republic, where having power and being powerless, domination and subordination, and being a leader or a follower are often phrased in gendered terms and through notions of virility. These sexualized forms of differentiation masculinize the political and public sphere, inscribe men and women in particular sexualized gender dynamics, and tend to divide women among themselves, while also entering men into a competitive relationship with one another. It is the divisive effects of these dynamics that, as I argue, constrain the formation of strong horizontal linkages among the populace that are so essential in the process of articulating potent challenges to hegemonic formations and the political status quo. Indeed, these gender discourses and their political effects in the Dominican Republic may not be unrelated to the challenges that collective organizing has faced in the country. Compared to many other Caribbean and Latin American countries, the Dominican Republic does not have a particularly strong history of social movements; there has been hardly any organizing around racial/ethnic identities, the women's movement has been important but intermittent, and Dominican labor organizing has been relatively weak.

This structural role and force of Dominican gender discourses and their changes and reconfigurations over time are missed by the prevalent diagnosis of Dominican "gender trouble," and of discourses like Mejía's "Llegó Papá," as a straightforward outgrowth of a pernicious "traditional" Latin American patriarchal culture with roots in the Hispanic colonial past. Such a diagnosis of Dominican gender and politics and the conceptual framework of tradition/modernity it hinges on has various problematic effects that ultimately obscure rather than illuminate the very real problems at hand. M. Jacqui Alexander addresses the effects of using the tradition/modernity binary as an interpretative framework and lens to speak of the "West" and its "Others." She asks, "How is tradition deployed within a hierarchically ordered West and its Others to construct a good democratic tradition . . . as over and against a bad barbaric tradition, whose agents require schooling or coercion to recognize its benefits? What kinds of patriarchies do different modernities require?"[46] With this last question, Alexander challenges the tendency to locate "violence in tradition only" and to give "modernity the power to automatically dissolve traditional patriarchy."[47] Indeed, the premise of this book is not to offer a denunciation of Dominican masculinity as "a bad barbaric tradition" that calls for proper "modern" schooling. Rather, this study suggests how modern Dominican gender mores have been and continue to be shaped also through the interaction with "modern" outside powers and their underlying patriarchal conceptions.

What kind of patriarchies Caribbean and Latin American *modernities* require is an important question as well that receives spotty scholarly attention—with some notable exceptions—in Caribbean and Latin American studies; of course, what kind of patriarchies Euro-American modernities require has received even less scholarly attention. It is true that Latin American and Caribbean gender formations have been significantly reshaped as women caught up with or even outpaced men in levels of education, entered the workforce in large numbers, and often took on the role as their family's main breadwinners and heads of household. Such changes led to widespread declarations of a "crisis of masculinity" in Latin America, and, similarly, in the Anglophone Caribbean the argument for "male marginalization" gained traction as much in academia as in popular and official sectors. More recently, scholars—including Matthew C. Gutmann in *Changing Men and Masculinities in Latin America* (2003)—have critiqued such arguments about the apparent demise of the power of masculinity and find that such declarations are at best premature, as gender inequalities have not disappeared, much less have been reversed. In fact, the *Americas Quarterly* special issue on "Gender Equality" (2012) in Latin America and the Caribbean finds that "women have achieved parity in access to education and healthcare, but have yet to attain political and economic parity."[48] This contemporary reality poses two critical challenges that this study helps to address: How and through what forces is the lasting power of masculinity in Latin America and the Caribbean sustained in the so-called global age? And how do globalizing impulses associated with neoliberalism, the international media, and migration interact with local gender formations beyond simplistic presumptions that these will inevitably "modernize" gender and lead to greater equality?

The Dominican Republic, where the state has long embraced neoliberal policies and other forms of opening itself up to outside influences, is an especially compelling context for studying how globalizing forces impact local gender formations in both predictable and unpredictable ways. Yet these cannot be accounted for through reductive references to a seemingly everlasting "traditional" patriarchal culture with roots in the colonial past that is stubbornly resistant to change. Rather I foreground how present-day hegemonic notions of Dominican masculinity historically evolved and the role of outside (and presumably "modern") forces in these processes long before the onset of today's globalization. Specifically, this book points to the need for a better understanding of the pervasive and largely misrecognized impact of U.S. imperialism on the country, including on its gender formations.

This study thus probes what Ronald L. Jackson II and Murali Balaji describe in *Global Masculinities and Manhood* as "the expansive gray area of how masculinity is communicated and practiced across cultures" that "has yet to be interrogated and articulated in depth."[49] More specifically, *Masculinity after Trujillo* contributes to answering what Gutmann notes is the understudied question of the U.S. role in defining "Latin" masculinity. As he states, "we still do not know enough about the role of the United States today and historically in helping to define and circumscribe 'Latin' manliness and its opposites."[50] In fact, in the future, with ongoing massive migrations from South to North America, the importance of a hemispheric approach to the study of gender, including Latin American and Caribbean masculinities as well as North American masculinities, will only become more urgent and relevant.

De-tropicalizing the Trujillato and Its Gendered Legacies

My emphasis on the transnational and imperial impulses that intervened in the process of forming today's hegemonic notions of Dominican masculinity complicates views of these as simply a straightforward expression of "traditional" patriarchy. However, more importantly, I throw a new light on how these notions help to sustain the present Dominican political status quo. As David Scott insists, finding answers to present challenges in the Caribbean region, including to its extraordinary levels of violence, corrupt state apparatuses, ineffective forms of governance, and steep inequalities, requires that we reconceptualize our understanding of these problems to conceive of true alternatives. In Scott's words, "the way one defines an alternative *depends* on the way one has conceived the problem. And therefore, reconceiving alternatives depends in significant part on reconceiving the object of discontent."[51] In the case of the Dominican Republic, "the objects of discontent" that critics continuously point to include clientelism and corruption in the political realm and misogyny, homophobia, and racism in the social realm. My argument that these "objects of discontent" have strong historical roots in the Rafael L. Trujillo dictatorship is in itself hardly controversial. In fact, many scholars as well as lay Dominicans frequently and readily assert that the Trujillato had a lasting and damaging impact on the country. Where I diverge is in my insistence that "Trujillo" should not be conflated too easily with Dominican political and cultural "tradition." Indeed, the Trujillato broke with many preceding Dominican formations or "traditions" in ways that were greatly enabled by the impact of U.S. imperialism on the country and on the personal trajectory of the dictator.

It is widely and rightfully recognized that the Trujillato and the notions of Dominican national identity it helped to ingrain cannot be understood without taking into account the country's often tense relation with its neighbor, Haiti, and the concurrent exaltation of its Hispanic colonial past. However, much less scholarly attention has been paid to how national configurations also cannot be understood without taking into account the imperialist presence of the United States in the country from the mid- to late nineteenth century. Indeed, there are relatively few scholarly considerations of U.S.–Dominican relations before the beginning of the massive migration of Dominicans to the United States in the sixties. The question of how the U.S. presence, including through two military occupations, from 1916 to 1924 and from 1965 to 1966, contributed to shaping Dominican national self-conceptions, including its gendered and racial self-understandings, remains vastly understudied.[52]

Many scholars have rightfully foregrounded how the Trujillato modulated Dominican national identity and anti-Haitian prejudices in incisive ways that imply a break with previous historical periods.[53] However, its equally fervent modulation of Dominican gender discourses is rarely addressed by scholars as constituting a similarly significant break with and reconfiguration of Dominican gender formations, with a few notable exceptions, including Lauren Derby's *The Dictator's Seduction: Politics and the Popular Imagination in the Era of Trujillo* (2009). I suggest that this elision is reinforced by how the Trujillato and its discourse of masculinity are seen as a continuation of "traditional" Latin American patterns. This view has been encouraged by Robert D. Crassweller's frequently cited and widely circulated *Trujillo: The Life and Times of a Caribbean Dictator* (1966). Crassweller's biography of the dictator, one of the first published after the end of the dictatorship, has shaped understandings of the dictator both inside and outside the Dominican Republic in significant ways. Crassweller's biography therefore has helped to give rise to certain lasting views of the Trujillato, as I describe further in my first chapter; however, here I want to briefly delineate two of these "tropicalizing" narratives (i.e., the "tropical" version of Said's orientalism, as coined by Frances R. Aparicio and Susana Chávez-Silverman) through which the regime and its raison d'être are apprehended.

Both scholarly and popular accounts of the Trujillato tend to rely on one of the following two plotlines or on a combined version of these: (1) that the dictatorship was an exceptional interim in the country's history driven by the exceptional (and often deemed as pathological) personality of the dictator; or (2) that it was the logical continuation of a long history of *caudillismo* and of a "traditional" political culture with authoritarian inclinations. As I will show, both of these interpretations pay insufficient attention to the regime's ideological premises and detract from important questions about how it instituted political, social, and cultural norms that have endured long past the actual lifetime of the dictator. The dominant focus on Trujillo's person and the definition of his regime as a "personalist," rather than an ideologically driven one, renders its ruling logics as mere personal whims of the dictator himself. They thereby become apolitical occurrences that are treated offhandedly as cultural phenomena and not as systematic social and political structures and discourses put in place by the regime to lasting effects. With regard to gender, the overall scholarly, literary, and popular tendency has been to focus on the hyperbolic masculinity of the dictator himself, with a particular kind of voyeurism with regard to his sexual appetite, rather than on the larger social and political implications and the lasting effects of his dictatorial discourse on Dominican gender formations.

The extent of these troublesome legacies of the Trujillato is evident in Dominican sociologist and cultural critic Miguel D. Mena's exclamation that "the General was executed, but his entire other body—*more of a body than just his physical one*—the bureaucracy, education, knowledges, practices, uses, disciplines, the styles of social and political life were preserved."[54] Mena hardly is a lone denunciatory voice. For example, the Dominican sociologist José Oviedo notes with similar exasperation that the tragedy of the twentieth century for the Dominican Republic is that "guidelines and values that come from Trujillismo . . . still operate as limits to our collective imaginary, still tell us how to be and what to do, what we are and what we are not . . . [and] survive in the common sense of many Dominicans, in their ways of living and interpreting what is 'Dominican' and in their perception of the state and politics."[55] Dominican historical scholarship since the 1970s and, more recently, scholars such as Silvio Torres-Saillant and Néstor E. Rodríguez have outlined and critiqued with great detail and care how the Trujillato thwarted commonsense understandings of *dominicanidad*, particularly with regard to Dominican racial and national identity. Building on their work, this book argues that the legacies of the dictatorship's deeply sexualized gender discourse, and especially the notions of masculinity that became hegemonic during its reign, need to be addressed with equal care and critical concern, especially given how they structure and constrain Dominican social and political relations until today.

Dominican Literature as Archive of the Authoritarian Past

As a literary and cultural studies–trained scholar, I take as my model for thinking about the contiguity of cultural and political discourses, and how gender tropes traffic between them, Doris Sommer's seminal work *Foundational Fictions: The National Romances of Latin America* (1991). In *Foundational Fictions*, Sommer suggests how heterosexual romance and matrimonial plots of nineteenth-century novels helped foster desires for national political unity in the newly independent Latin American countries. In a different but related vein, this book asks how today, in the twenty-first century, after the end of more straightforward equations of family and nation and vis-à-vis the waning significance of patriarchal family structures (and of male-headed households, formal marriage, and stable male–female unions), gender discourses traffic between cultural and political imaginaries and structure them. I consider my focus on the Dominican Republic to answer this question particularly appropriate, given that it was through Sommer's study of Dominican literature that she first rehearsed her seminal argument for *Foundational Fictions*, namely, in her much less known study *One Master for Another: Populism as Patriarchal Rhetoric in Dominican Novels* (1983). There Sommer suggests that the contiguity of patriarchal "family" and "nation" in Dominican fictions extended far beyond the nineteenth century and only gave way past the mid-twentieth century, for example, in the writing of Marcio Veloz Maggiolo, the foremost living Dominican novelist. *Masculinity after Trujillo* begins precisely where Sommer leaves off to inquire into the political valence gender discourses carry today in political and literary discourses in the Dominican Republic and into the traffic between them.

I consider it paramount to pay critical attention to Dominican literary production, not only because of its underestimated literary value but also because of the crucial role that literary and nonliterary texts have played in forming understandings of the Trujillato and of its legacies in Dominican post-dictatorship society. Writings of Dominican *letrados* in many ways function as a key archive of the authoritarian past, given the remarkable absence of official venues for remembering the dictatorship. Museums, memorial sites, or "truth commissions," which are commonplace in other Latin American post-dictatorship societies, have had relatively little importance in the Dominican Republic. Dominican letrados' role as record keepers and guardians of the country's collective memory of the regime in fact helps to explain why the Trujillo dictatorship, as Ignacio López-Calvo in *God and Trujillo: Literary and Cultural Representations of the Dominican Dictator* (2005) notes, is arguably *the* central theme of late-twentieth-century Dominican literature. Notably, López-Calvo points repeatedly in his study of this corpus to the troublesome sex-gender politics of many of the novels he analyzes. Taking López-Calvo's and other literary critics' observations—including those by Doris Sommer, Rita de Maeseneer, Nina Bruni, and Ana Gallego Cuiñas— about the troublesome misogyny and homophobia that often rear their heads in these texts, I ask what, beyond individual failings of the authors, the larger political and theoretical implications of the recurrence of these gender discourses are. My approach has much in common with Néstor E. Rodríguez's study *Divergent Dictions: Contemporary Dominican Literature* (2010 [2005]), where he places Dominican political and literary discourses in dialogue with each other to address some of the key discursive legacies of the Trujillato. However, if Rodríguez focuses on the Trujillato's racial and nationalist ideologies and their long afterlife in the Dominican Republic, I flesh out the equally tenacious afterlife of Trujillian conceptions of gender and their lasting implications.

My first chapter, "De-tropicalizing the Trujillo Dictatorship and Dominican Masculinity," begins by outlining the break that the Trujillato occasioned in the country's historical trajectory, including in its gender formations, and how this break was made possible by the long-lasting U.S. imperialist presence in the country, especially by the preceding U.S. military occupation from 1916 to 1924. For this, I draw from recent findings by various historians (Lauren Derby, April J. Mayes, Elizabeth S. Manley, and Neici Zeller, among others) about the impact that the U.S. occupation and its notions of racialized imperial masculinity (associated with Theodore Roosevelt's project of "manly" uplift of the darker and more "barbarous" races) had on Dominican gender formations. I suggest, then, that it was partly in response to this reality that the Trujillato's discourse of masculinity was able to take such hold in the country. Through a close reading of key speeches by the dictator and his main ideologues, especially Joaquín Balaguer, I outline the specific role and meaning of the Trujillato's discourse of masculinity. I highlight how it was the perfect vehicle for appealing to familiar patriarchal notions as well as for tapping into the international political language of sovereignty, which appealed strongly to the Dominican populace in the aftermath of the curtailing of the country's sovereignty by the United States. In summary, this chapter argues that while the Trujillato and its discourse of masculinity of course were not entirely "new," it is worthwhile to make the fine distinction between Trujillo as an outgrowth of "traditional" Dominican politics and culture and Trujillo's appropriation and, in the process, reinvention of Dominican "tradition," including of Dominican masculinity, for new purposes. The success of these discursive reinventions in turn was enabled by the strong nationalist sentiments that the U.S. occupation had produced, especially among Dominican letrados, who played a key role in these discourses' formulation and dissemination during the Trujillato.

My second chapter, "One Phallus for Another: Post-dictatorship Political and Literary Canons," begins by highlighting the lasting political role in the post-dictatorship period of a rhetoric of masculinity that continued to define and naturalize autocratic forms of political leadership and relations between political leaders and the populace, especially during Joaquín Balaguer's governments (1966–1978; 1986–1996). I then suggest how this rhetoric is problematically reinforced in the work of some of the country's most important post-dictatorship critical voices, politically leftist-identified Dominican letrados. While post-dictatorship Dominican letrados have been profoundly critical of the regime's racial discourses, including of its anti-Haitianism and of its conceptions of Dominican national identity, they often reiterate without much concern its hegemonic notions of masculinity. Through a critical analysis of two dictatorship novels, *De abril en adelante* (1975) and *Uña y carne: Memorias de la virilidad* (1999), by Marcio Veloz Maggiolo, today's foremost and most awarded novelist on the island, I show how the Trujillato's hegemonic notions of masculinity continue to remain alive and well. Maggiolo's highly self-conscious and often highly experimental writing rarely evinces the same critical consciousness when it comes to its representations of gender and sexuality. Specifically, the role that notions of masculinity play in perpetuating past political patterns—as I suggest throughout this book—is misrecognized in Maggiolo's writing. This critical "blind spot" is shared by several other (male) Dominican authors and, I speculate, is not unrelated to the fact that many remain tied up in relations of patronage and clientelism with the officialist Dominican political realm.

In the third chapter, "Engendering Resistance: Hilma Contreras's Counternarratives," I discuss the literary oeuvre of Hilma Contreras (1913–2006), which has been unjustly ignored by literary scholars, even after the author became the first woman to receive the national literary prize for her lifetime work, in 2002. Contreras's writing offers a several-decade critical preoccupation with Dominican gender formations, beginning with her first short-story collection, *4 cuentos* (1953), and her essay *Doña Endrina de Calatayud* (1955). Furthermore, Contreras's unstudied dictatorship novel, *La tierra está bramando* (1986)—a rare exception to the largely male-authored canon of Dominican dictatorship novels—explores more broadly the crucial question of how Dominican cultural practices, despite having been appropriated by the Trujillato for its ends, can still foster collective forms of action, horizontal relations, and anti-hegemonic alliances. Such questions, I argue, remain greatly relevant in the Dominican political and cultural landscape today.

In the following two chapters I consider how Dominican gender formations are impacted by globalizing forces today, including by those associated with neoliberalism, the tourism industry, global media, mass migration, and the diaspora. I address this question through the lens of a new generation of Dominican and Dominican American writers that emerged in the late 1990s. While this new generation has been accused of exhibiting a lack of political investment and postmodern laissez-faire, in part because of their disinterest in addressing the Trujillo dictatorship and political matters more directly, I insist that their writings in fact are profoundly invested in critiquing the hegemonic formations the Trujillato left in place, including its discourse of gender. However, unlike Contreras, this newer generation of Dominican writers does not foreground the possibility of recuperating aspects of autochthonous Dominican culture, but rather ponders the critical possibilities of new cultural repertoires that globalizing impulses are producing in the country.

Chapter 4, "Still Loving *Papi*: Globalized Dominican Subjectivities in the Novels of Rita Indiana Hernández," addresses the writing of Rita Indiana Hernández, the central figure of this new generation of Dominican writers, and analyzes closely her novels *La estrategia de Chochueca* (1999) and *Papi* (2004). Chapter 5, "How Not to Read Junot Díaz: Diasporic Dominican Masculinity and Its Returns," in turn, foregrounds the work of Junot Díaz, the most renowned Dominican American writer since receiving the Pulitzer Prize in 2008 for his novel *The Brief Wondrous Life of Oscar Wao* (2007), which I discuss along with his most recent short-story collection *This Is How You Lose Her* (2012). Both Hernández and Díaz suggest in their writing how global impulses have provided important alternatives to ingrained Dominican gender repertoires, especially for younger generations of Dominicans. However, both also highlight the lasting desirability of hegemonic notions of masculinity for Dominican men *and* women, which do not necessarily wane in the Dominican diaspora and with increasing globalization, but can at times be reinforced by these.

I conclude by making conceptual suggestions for the future study of Latin American and Caribbean gender formations, emphasizing the importance of a relational, or what some may call an intersectional, approach to studying these. Gender inflects not only identities but also social and political meanings and realms in key ways. This calls for accounts of local specificities that avoid freezing them into timeless "traditional" formations and that remain attentive to the forceful but never predictable impact of past, present, and future outside impulses.

Overall, this book hopes to help bridge and create stronger relations between scholarly debates in Latin American cultural studies and Caribbean studies that still intersect too rarely. This might give impetus, for example, to a broader and more systematic integration of gender into ongoing critical debates in Latin American cultural studies in ways that I see prefigured in recent work in Caribbean studies. In turn, ongoing debates among Latin Americanists, such as Alberto Moreiras, Gareth Williams, Jon Beasley-Murray, and John Beverley, about the concept of hegemony/post-hegemony in Latin American cultural theory (drawing often from Ernesto Laclau's theoretical work) can help illuminate key questions and challenges that Caribbean studies faces in the region, including how cultural forces from below and embodied can challenge and reconfigure hegemonic configurations and, ultimately, a political status quo that sustains lasting inequalities in the region.

1

De-tropicalizing the Trujillo Dictatorship and Dominican Masculinity

> He may be a son-of-a-bitch but he is our son-of-a-bitch.
> U.S. Secretary of State Cordell Hull

The century before Rafael L. Trujillo came to power tends to be described as a long period of political instability marked by constant battles between regional *caudillos* for power, the threat of Haitian invasions, and the voluntary ceding of the country's sovereignty to become a colony of Spain again, from 1861 to 1865. What historical accounts emphasize much less, besides these predominant historical plotlines, is the insistent meddling of U.S. forces and its lasting consequences. The United States began to have a notable presence in the country around the mid-nineteenth century, and it took on a preponderant role with the full takeover of Dominican customs operations "in progressive steps between 1904 and 1907."[1] Eventually, these events led to an eight-year military occupation of the country, from 1916 to 1924.

The effects of the long-lasting U.S. presence on Dominican society, politics, and national identity remain greatly understudied, especially in comparison to the attention scholars and writers have paid to the country's relations to its former colonial power, Spain, and to its neighbor, Haiti. Indeed, insistent foregrounding of Dominican–Haitian enmity, often represented as an almost inevitable struggle arising out of two nations sharing the same island, omits how outside forces—both U.S. and European—helped produce and foster tensions between them.² This chapter first addresses how the U.S. presence and intervention shaped Dominican national sentiments and gender formations in ways that facilitated not only Trujillo's rise to power but also Dominicans' embrace of his national-popular political rhetoric, including its hyperbolic language of masculinity. I then, through a close analysis of key speeches and discourses of the Trujillato, outline the specific ramifications of this language of masculinity and its lasting impact on Dominican social relations and political culture.

The Impact of U.S. Gendered and Racialized Imperial Ideologies

The United States began to play a preeminent role in the Caribbean in the nineteenth century and cemented its supremacy in the region with the onset of the Spanish-American War in 1898. In *The United States and the Caribbean: Transforming Hegemony and Sovereignty* (2005), Anthony P. Maingot and Wilfredo Lozano describe the precepts that underwrote the long-standing U.S. involvement in the region as a "Caribbean version of Manifest Destiny [that] was outright imperialism wrapped in a thick ideology with geopolitical and neoDarwinian racism."³ In fact, it was greatly in the interest of Dominicans, in their many-decade negotiations and dealings with the United States and its racist ideology, to signal their "worth" by downplaying their own blackness and emphasizing their racial difference from their Haitian neighbors.⁴

These racialized imperial dynamics firmly took hold when the United States, then under President Theodore Roosevelt, took over Dominican customs operations. This move was indicative of how during this period "U.S. diplomats moved from a position of influence to one of decisive authority . . . in the Dominican Republic and around the Caribbean."⁵ This takeover was accompanied by a host of political and cultural ideologies. As Emily S. Rosenberg describes, "in his *Corollary to the Monroe Doctrine* (1904), Roosevelt stated that when nations of the Western hemisphere conducted their economic affairs irresponsibly enough to raise the possibility of European intervention, the United States would assume the role of an 'international police power.' . . . The Dominican Republic became the first of what might be called dollar diplomacy dependencies (others would be Nicaragua, Liberia, and Haiti)."⁶ The "dollar diplomacy" doctrine was not just an intervention in a country's economic and financial affairs but was accompanied by an ideology that "blended discourses about manhood, race, adulthood, managerial expertise, and national interest into a program for spreading civilization."[7] Specifically, dollar diplomacy fused gendered and racialized notions in its civilizatory mission to provide "manly uplift to the darker-skinned peoples."[8] The countries on the receiving end of this "civilizing" mission thus figured as racially inferior and inherently less manly.[9]

In fact, the gendered implications of this civilizatory project emerge in this powerful comparison made by Rosenberg:

> The shared significations between dollar diplomacy and gender can be grasped quickly if one imagines turn-of-the-century bourgeois marriages as mini-domains of dollar diplomacy. Marriage, like dollar diplomacy, involved a *contract* in which the dominant (male) party promised monetary support (loans) and supervision in return for obedience and acceptance of regulation. Dollar diplomacy dependencies, like women in late Victorian bourgeois marriages, were coded as weak, irresponsible, irrational, and prone to excesses that needed to be brought under control. Contracts provided the masculine-coded mechanisms of control that positioned (and further differentiated) the status responsibilities of the unequal parties. Yet, also like marriage, the status inequalities were embedded in the controlled loan contracts of dollar diplomacy, even as the contracts tended to be culturally presented as freely negotiated and based on mutual attraction.[10]

The impact of these ideologies and how they shaped what may be called the psychological infrastructure of the country remain insufficiently understood.

The U.S. military occupation that began in 1916 offered, however, no longer the illusion of having been "freely negotiated." Scholars generally denounce this curtailing of Dominican sovereignty by the United States but also quickly move on to the occupation's often lauded "modernizing" measures, including infrastructure constructions (new roads and communication systems) and a more centralized governance system and police force, among others. One notable exception to this emphasis on the physical over the psychological impact of the U.S. occupation is the oft-noted Dominican nationalist fervor that awoke in response to the occupation.

Other important ways in which the U.S. imperial presence affected the country's collective psyche and national imaginary remain largely unexplored. However, more recently, various historians—including Lauren

Derby, April J. Mayes, Elizabeth S. Manley, Neici Zeller, and Melissa Madera—have begun to pay closer attention to how the U.S. military occupation and Dominican nationalists' reactions to it impacted Dominican gender formations. Their scholarship shows how some of the U.S. occupation's gendered discourses and policies were later perpetuated by Dominican governments, while others were strongly resisted by Dominican nationalists; however, in either case Dominican gender formations were shaped in lasting ways by the U.S. presence.

Melissa Madera, in her dissertation "'Zones of Scandal': Gender, Public Health, and Social Hygiene in the Dominican Republic, 1916–1961" (2011), describes how the U.S. occupation, as part of its civilizatory mission, implemented "'modern' public health and sanitary reforms" that "aimed to control female bodies in the Dominican Republic."[11] The occupation created an "official discourse against prostitution, and female criminality more generally, which was seemingly non-existent before the occupation, [and that] would become more prevalent throughout the 1920s and the Era of Trujillo."[12] One of the effects of this new public health discourse and practice was, according to Madera, that women were "increasingly pushed . . . into patriarchal relationships that served to help them [the occupation powers] control and watch over 'disorderly' women."[13] Thus, during the U.S. occupation and thereafter, "disorderly" women became a lasting concern of the Dominican state, while "orderly" woman were pushed back into more conventional gender roles. Women were enlisted into a patriarchal state project of controlling and denouncing "disorderly" women and thereby dividing women amongst themselves into "orderly" and "disorderly" or "good" and "bad" women. These kind of divisive processes and notions, as I describe in the introduction, remain alive today.

If some of the U.S. military government's gendered practices were adopted and perpetuated by the Dominican government later, there was also at the same time an ardent rejection by Dominican nationalists of what were seen as U.S.-style "modern" gender mores. As April J. Mayes describes,

> During the occupation . . . Dominican nationalists embraced José Enrique Rodó's extraordinarily popular work, *Ariel*, published in 1900, and its "stridently anti-democratic," inward-looking polemic that called upon Latin Americans to protect the Latin race and its high culture from Yankee imperialism, secular democracy, materialism,

and Protestantism. For their part, Dominican nationalists idealized the family and patriarchal authority as sources of *Latinidad*'s moral power.[14]

These idealizations resulted in a more conservative Dominican gender politics, as "Dominican nationalists constructed a nationalist mythology that removed women from the public sphere."[15] Their vision of modern Dominican nationhood, in response to U.S. imperialism, placed emphasis on patriarchal control of women and made motherhood women's principal role. In turn, "women who were deemed 'modern' were criticized for dressing provocatively and were viewed as unpatriotic" as "maternity and nationalism" became linked in Dominican "modernizing discourse."[16]

The U.S. presence also impacted Dominican masculinity and gendered the Dominican political imaginary in new ways. Neici Zeller, in her dissertation, "The Appearance of All, the Reality of Nothing: Politics and Gender in the Dominican Republic, 1880–1961" (2010), describes the gendered terms through which the curtailing of Dominican sovereignty by the United States was understood. According to Zeller, in accounts from that time period, "we can read a feminized but valiant 'la República Dominicana' resisting the male forces of 'los Estados Unidos.'"[17] Lauren Derby similarly notes how Dominicans sensed that "the nation had been violated, penetrated by an occupying force, and thus rendered passive, dependent, emasculated."[18] Derby thus speaks of a resulting "crisis of manhood" related to how "during the occupation, Dominican men had been deprived of their right to the National Palace, and their control over the home and the street had been compromised."[19] In response to the emasculating experience of the U.S. occupation, Dominicans felt that the nation and Dominican men needed to recuperate and reassert their virility.

Importantly, this view was not solely held by men but was also embraced and even vigorously policed by Dominican women. Zeller recounts, for example, the following anecdote of Ercilia Pepín, a renowned Dominican women's organization leader and schoolteacher: "Ercilia Pepín sent a skirt to a neighboring male teacher who had lowered the Dominican flag when the U.S. troops entered the town; a curt note asked him to stop wearing trousers since he clearly did not need them."[20] Cowardly behavior is here clearly (and problematically) linked to feminization, including by women themselves. Interestingly, Pepín's "dismissal of the male teacher as unworthy of his gender simultaneously cast her as virile, since she had kept the Dominican flag on its staff while the troops marched by her school."[21] This episode thus both points to the strongly polarized meanings of masculinity and femininity and reveals a certain transitivity that allows women to claim under particular circumstances this dominant position (vis-à-vis men)—a key issue addressed further in my fourth chapter.

The role played by women in policing Dominican masculinity as part of a nationalist defense is also evident in Madera's account of a contest held by a Dominican women's magazine. The magazine critiqued how Dominican men preferred to be clean shaven rather than sporting a mustache after the U.S. occupation. In response, "the magazine sponsored the 'perfect mustache' contest to try to recover this manly feature and 'Dominicanism,'" because of how "this new trend emasculated men and was unpatriotic since Americans introduced it to the country during the U.S. occupation."[22] The magazine contest reflects clearly how closely patriotism and masculinity had become linked in the Dominican national imaginary, and how this gendered imaginary was shared by men and women. As Teresita Martínez-Vergne insists, the "implicit maleness of the national character" of the Dominican Republic cannot be understood outside of how the dominant presence of the United States led to defensive stances in the Dominican Republic, where "to properly protect the virtue of the homeland, . . . virility was of the utmost importance."[23]

In summary, what this body of historical scholarship suggests is how the U.S. military occupation prepared the Dominican collective psyche and national sentiments—or what I term the "psychological infrastructure"—for the Dominican populace to embrace the Trujillato's political discourse of hyperbolic virile masculinity as part of a new nationalist project. However, this role that the United States has historically played is generally erased by predominant understandings of the Trujillo dictatorship, as discussed in the following section.

De-tropicalizing Trujillo

> One goes at night to a carnival. Lights of every color trace designs against the darkness. Outlandish noise, disembodied strains of music, screams of revelry, drift upon the air. Garish scenes appear and expand and multiply. Everything swirls in gusts of sensation until the imagination is overpowered and the real and the imaginary

blend into a general incoherence and delirium. Such is the spectacle of the Era of Trujillo . . .

Robert D. Crassweller

There is certainly good reason to describe the Trujillo Era, as Robert D. Crassweller's opening lines in *Trujillo: The Life and Times of a Caribbean Dictator* (1966) do, as a period of "general incoherence and delirium."[24] However, evocations of the regime's carnivalesque, outlandish, and garish aspects contribute little to a better understanding of how the Rafael L. Trujillo dictatorship lastingly shaped the country long past the end of this "delirious" period and well into the age of "rational" democracy. As I mention in the introduction, views of the Trujillato as an exceptional period, defined by the particularity of the dictator's persona that exceeds any simple form of classification, are widespread. For example, Crassweller asserts in the first pages of his book, "Rafael Trujillo is not an easy subject to reflect in biography. His instinctual nature had many facets, some of them quite contradictory, and the easy categories will not contain him. He was very much the product of Dominican culture and history, but he has also cut across an extraordinary number of unrelated epochs."[25] This declaration reflects precisely the two "tropicalizing" narratives that tend to underwrite representations of Trujillo:[26] (1) the emphasis on the exceptionality of Trujillo's persona, leading often to comparisons with far-flung rulers of antiquity or to oriental despots, and (2) the presentation of Trujillo as a "typical" Dominican character steeped in the country's Hispanic "traditional" colonial heritage and its presumably authoritarian-inclined political culture.

With regard to the "exceptionalist" story line, such views are aided by the Trujillo regime's oft-noted eccentricities and extravagances, for example, Trujillo's appropriation of entire national industries as well as vast amounts of land and cattle and an endless number of women, together with a taste for ostentatious uniforms and grand celebrations, and a penchant for naming many Dominican sites, including the capital of the country, after himself or his family members. Indeed, some of the dictator's now bizarre-seeming personal preferences and endeavors, including his performance of masculinity and his voracious sexuality, have provided great fodder for scholarly as well as literary texts. This centrality of Trujillo's persona is reinforced by scholars' definition of the dictatorship as a highly "personalist" rather than an ideologically driven regime. Crassweller's biography certainly encourages such interpretations of the Trujillato by asserting that "the life of Trujillo and of the government were intensely personal, intimate rather than official."[27] Moreover, Crassweller finds that Trujillo's "methods had a homemade quality, but the country was small and its traditions were not institutional but personal."[28] Trujillo is presented thus as a dictator "minus ideology."[29]

When efforts are made to define the Trujillato's form of rule more systematically, references to "oriental" forms of political leadership tend to emerge. For example, according to Crassweller, "if comparisons must be drawn, his essence and style found their closest parallel in the Oriental despots of ancient times—the rulers of Persia, India, and China."[30] Other scholars in turn often refer to Juan Linz's definition of "sultanistic" regimes to describe the Trujillo dictatorship, suggesting by its very name how the regime is placed outside the political logics and ideologies of the Western Hemisphere.[31]

At the same time Trujillo is presented as a profound connoisseur and, ultimately, as a reflection of the country's psychological makeup and, more broadly, of the "Latin soul." For example, Crassweller suggests that "the uses of vanity and pomp were among the many intuitions by which Trujillo glimpsed the Dominican soul, for he had a sure grasp of those sensitive areas of the national psychology that must be apprehended by the emotions rather than deduced by logic."[32] These "sensitive" areas and emotional propensities are, according to Crassweller, also those of the "Latin soul": "he projected individuality, and he appealed to the imagination and to the sense of the perfect and the extreme that is congenial to the Latin soul."[33]

This view easily slides into portrayals of the Trujillato as a continuation of "traditional" Dominican and Latin American political patterns. Crassweller speaks of Trujillo as beginning his regime as "a caudillo in the historic pattern," whose "psychological heritage had been that of the Spanish hidalgo and the New World caudillo."[34] Howard J. Wiarda addresses also this frequent identification of the Trujillato with caudilloism: "Caudilloism is the peculiarly Hispanic kind of traditional dictatorship. Present in the histories of both Spain and Portugal, it seems to be particularly prevalent in the Spanish colonies in Latin America. Caudilloism therefore merits special attention because the Trujillo regime is often considered to be a caudillo-like dictatorship."[35] Somewhat contradictorily, then, Trujillo is portrayed as a mirror or an echo of the Dominican or Latin American "soul" and political tradition, as well as a "personalist" dictator with no firm ideological underpinning, who at best evokes the idiosyncratic rule of "oriental despots."

One of the consequences of the emphasis on the dictator's passion-driven irrationality, his personal idiosyncrasies, and his "Latin" flair for drama is that the dictatorship's systematic belief system, including its conceptions of gender, remain ill understood. Another consequence is that views of the Trujillato as a perpetuation of "traditional" Latin American political patterns obliterates how the Trujillato cannot be understood without taking into account the impact of U.S. imperialism.

These two "tropicalizing" narratives about the dictatorship were greatly encouraged by Crassweller's biography of the dictator, which was immensely popular both on and off the island. This notable influence of Crassweller's account is recorded, for example, in a note published in a Dominican daily newspaper on the occasion of Crassweller's death in 2010: "In 1967 Crassweller became known among Dominicans in general with the first English edition of his book. . . . The book was translated into Spanish in 1968 and in many households became an obligatory reference about the so-called 'Trujillo Era.' . . . Pirated editions followed to such an extreme . . . that there is no known second 'legal' edition."[36] The "tropicalizing" views propounded by this biography and many other accounts of the Trujillato have become an important part of the Dominican collective memory of the dictatorship; yet these contribute to forestalling a much-needed better understanding of the incisive break that the Trujillato produced in Dominican hegemonic formations, in social and political relations, and in the country's national self-understanding.

Trujillo's Discourse of "Traditional" and "Modern" Politics and Gender

If one is concerned with the lasting hegemony of the legacies of the Trujillato (and there is good reason to be), close attention must be paid to its belief system and, yes, its ideologies. Neither the vision of the Trujillato as the result of the idiosyncrasy of an almost grotesquely "evil" individual, nor the view of it as a modern continuation of Latin American "caudillismo," help to elucidate how and why aspects of the Trujillato remain alive today in the Dominican Republic long after the consolidation of democracy.

Importantly, the latter view—of Trujillo as a modern-day *caudillo*—was strongly encouraged by the Trujillo regime itself. Indeed, we must ask how far Crassweller's influential biography reproduced the perspectives of one of his main informers, Joaquín Balaguer. Balaguer, of course, was one of the main figures responsible for crafting and disseminating the Trujillato's political discourse. During his regime Trujillo was consistently presented by his ideologues as a quintessential Dominican who was deeply immersed in the Dominican soul, and vice versa. As the massive celebratory publication for the Trujillo Era's twenty-five-year anniversary declares, "it is not possible to determine to what point this brilliant and predestined man is found immersed in the Dominican soul or to what degree, likewise, our people find themselves lovingly captured in . . . Trujillo's soul."[37]

Relations between Dominicans and the dictator were portrayed by officialist discourse as a veritable scene of seduction, with the *pueblo* swept away by the dictator's extraordinary persona. Indeed, Balaguer, in his well-known speech "The Principle of Alternability in Dominican History," addressed to a national audience in 1952, describes the Dominican "multitudes" as immediately "seduced by the arrogance of this man of arms or conquered by the prestige that already had begun to radiate from this Cesarean personality."[38] Notably, the attraction of the Dominican people to their leader is validated here by aligning Trujillo with other heroic historical leaders through the strategic evocation of Trujillo's "Cesarean" personality. In the same speech, Balaguer refers to Trujillo also as a "caudillo," thereby placing him within a long lineage of Latin American military strongmen, both strategies that are also echoed in Crassweller's biography.

Balaguer especially fawns over Trujillo's virile ardor in what now appear almost comical and certainly homoerotic terms: "The sole presence of Trujillo on the national stage, causes admiration from the first instance, and stimulates surprise, and lights up in his own enemies astonishing forewarnings, disconcerting everyone with his incandescent coldness and his icy violence. What an admirable human physiognomy and what an unprecedented historical profile is that of this hurricane-like caudillo . . . !"[39] The regime thus itself referred to Trujillo as a *caudillo*—though adding that he is a "caudillo moderno"—and thereby tapped into a familiar language of Latin American political leadership.

The strategic inscription of Trujillo into Latin American political culture effectively evades his close relation to U.S. military forces and ideologies.

Trujillo contributed in his own ways to his insertion into a political lineage of Dominican strongmen. He presented himself, at least indirectly, as heir to the previous Dominican dictator Ulises Heureaux (1882–1899). As Valentina Peguero describes, "On August 16, 1930, wearing a military uniform with golden trimmings and a hat that resembled those of Ulises Heureaux... Trujillo took his oath as president of the republic."[40] This lineage is also often invoked in scholarly accounts; as Peguero notes, "scholars have indicated that when Trujillo became president, he had Ulises Heureaux as a model."[41] Telling, for example, is that the renowned Dominican historian Bernardo Vega ventured even into the terrain of fiction to bring these two dictators together on the pages of his book *Domini Canes: Los perros del Señor* (1989) where he stages a fictional dialogue between them that gestures clearly to their close political affinity and historical relatedness.

However, what this historical lineage obscures is how, unlike with previous Dominican *caudillos*, Trujillo's rise was made possible largely by the U.S. imperial presence in the country. To begin with, U.S. officials themselves acknowledged the key role they played in Trujillo's rise to power: a 1931 memo from First Secretary Cabot to the U.S. State Department notes that "Trujillo was raised from the gutter by the Marine Corps and started toward this present position."[42] Beyond the key role that the United States had in Trujillo's personal trajectory and military ascendance, his path to power had been cleared by how the U.S. military occupation reconfigured Dominican power relations. As the Dominican sociologist Emelio Betances describes,

> The U.S. military government broke the back of the caudillo political system by restructuring society and disarming most of the population. Regional caudillo rivalries were crippled by the new road network and the sheer firepower of the military. The policies of this government strengthened the state apparatus but did so at the expense of the social structures, creating the conditions for the emergence of a new type of national military caudillo who would use state power to forge a new elite.[43]

Betances's references to both a "new type" and the "old" concept of the Latin American *caudillo* suggest how debates about whether the Trujillo regime was a continuation of or break with previous Dominican political tendencies are far from settled. For example, in contrast, Eric Paul Roorda concludes in less-ambiguous terms that the Trujillo dictatorship is "directly attributable to the U.S. Marine occupation of the Dominican Republic in 1916–1924."[44]

For the purpose of this study, I specifically want to address how U.S. and other international influences helped shape the Trujillato's performance and discourse of masculinity and the Dominican people's uptake of these. I thereby want to move into sight how the Trujillato constituted a reconfiguration and not simply a continuation of previously hegemonic notions of Dominican masculinity. To begin with, Trujillo's performance and discourse of masculinity were clearly in part informed by the U.S. military values that he had internalized from the U.S. Marines. This internalization is implicit in Roorda's description of how "the young officer's apparent assimilation into the culture of the U.S. Marine Corps, reflected in the approval of his American superiors, accelerated his rise in the Dominican ranks during the occupation."[45] Indeed, Peguero also emphasizes how "Trujillo assimilated the Marines' military culture well" and was described as being "'more Americanized' than any other Dominican."[46] Even after the end of the U.S. military occupation, Trujillo "always considered himself a Marine Corps officer."[47] As a result, "competence, organization, and discipline were inherent in Trujillo's military persona," which he constantly exhibited to the public through his extreme personal cleanliness, vigorous lifestyle, long hours of work, and incessant activity.[48]

In fact, Trujillo's close identification with the U.S. Marines and their ideology makes appear much less eccentric what is presented often as one of the dictator's idiosyncrasies: his desire to present himself (and the country) as mostly white. As Peguero describes, "the Marines arrived with a heavy cargo of prejudice and an anti-black attitude" and "viewed the Dominican Republic as a conquered land inhabited by inferior black people."[49] This makes it hardly irrational on Trujillo's part to describe himself on his application to join the new Dominican force organized by the Marines "as white when in fact he was mulatto."[50] U.S. racialized imperial ideologies, long present before the occupation, thus must be taken into account when trying to understand why "Trujillo wanted outsiders to believe that whites predominated among Dominicans," and why whiteness became important to present "'a better' image of the Dominican Republic abroad."[51]

If Trujillo's racial discourse was molded, at least in part, in response to the outside impulses and ideologies of U.S. imperialism, the dictator's discourse of masculinity cannot be understood outside of these influences either.

Trujillo's role as the country's patriarch, supreme macho, and virile savior was legitimatized and naturalized by the widespread sense that the Dominican Republic had been feminized and emasculated by the outside forces' domination and the curtailing of the country's sovereignty. This pervasively gendered nationalist rhetoric is reflected, for example, in the following description in the Trujillato's twenty-five-year anniversary publication: "The motherland was only a raggedy beggar who incited an offensive compassion and an insulting disdain. Trujillo restored her position and prestige, returning to her the appearance of a respectable and honorable nation."[52] The feminized and dishonored nation was uplifted and made respectable again by her supreme masculine defender, Rafael L. Trujillo. What this proclamation suggests is how the Trujillato inserted itself into a new narrative of the Dominican nation and the strongly gendered and sexual meanings inscribed in this plotline.

The Trujillato's emphasis on virility as a cornerstone of its political discourse in defense of the nation, however, was not merely a quintessential expression of "Latin" patriarchal masculinity. It was in fact very much in step with contemporary international political discourses at the time. For example, Michelle A. Stephens describes how a constituency that appears to be very dissimilar from Trujillo, namely, radical black (Anglophone and Francophone) Caribbean intellectuals, took recourse to similar discursive strategies at the same historical moment. Stephens notes how "the immediate years after World War I" were "a key conjuncture in constructing a new world order based on new forms of sovereignty and statehood."[53] These forms were embedded in a "masculinist rhetoric of sovereignty essential to both imperial and national visions of the state."[54] It is vis-à-vis this masculinist rhetoric of sovereignty that Stephens explains the investment of black intellectuals from the Caribbean and the United States in expressing "the *sovereignty* of both the self and of the state" through "highly masculine definitions of racial freedom, embodied in varying male figures and tropes for the black, revolutionary hero."[55] Trujillo similarly wielded his rhetoric of masculinity to signal the sovereignty of the self and of the Dominican nation-state after its curtailing by U.S. imperial powers.

This masculinist rhetoric of sovereignty is notably also at play in the Trujillato's justifications of its overstepping of democratic rules. Democratic procedures were presented by the regime as a "foreign abstraction" and ultimately as "un-Dominican" constraints that Trujillo, in a heroically manly act, rejects in a defense of Dominican sovereignty. As Balaguer reasons, democracy was ultimately only for effeminate "duds": "The principle of alternating (in power) . . . has then only had validity for those presidents who did not know how to wear the toga of virility on the throne. . . . For a titan like Trujillo, superior in political genius and in his ability to command to all his predecessors, the principle of alternation had to be forcibly reduced to an inoperative abstraction."[56] Trujillo was simply too much of a man for democracy. This passage tellingly indicates how the language of masculinity naturalized political leadership as an expression of "manly" ability. At the same time, any constraints placed on it, including by the rules of democracy, were denounced as an emasculating infringement of national sovereignty and the national self. Importantly, this language of masculinity was able to speak effectively to many Dominicans' sentiments in the wake of the U.S. occupation. On one hand, then, this masculinist language spoke to Dominicans' desires for modern sovereign nationhood, while at the same time it echoed a familiar "traditional" language of patriarchal power that helped to justify and naturalize Trujillo's grasp on the country. In this sense it was doubly effective.

To grasp why and how the Trujillato's legacies have continued to impact the country long after the dictator's death in 1961, one must better understand the paradox of how this language of masculinity naturalized a starkly hierarchical organization of Dominican society and politics that was overwritten by an emphatically egalitarian discourse. Indeed, the Trujillato created a powerful national-popular discourse that suggested that Trujillo had broken with ingrained Dominican hierarchies in key ways. For one, the Trujillato's officialist ideology presented the Dominican Republic as a racially homogeneous place where racial differences among Dominicans did not matter and racism was declared to be absent. For example, the regime's twenty-five-year anniversary panegyric emphatically states, "We repeat: we never have had the problem of racial discrimination."[57] At the same time, Trujillo, who was not part of the upper echelons of society and resented the Dominican elites for their initial rejection of him, identified himself insistently as the people's candidate (el candidato del pueblo). He was again and again portrayed as fighting against the abuses and privileges of the Dominican elite and claimed to have created a society where social class was not to matter much. As Balaguer insists, "Trujillo eliminated from Dominican life the old and secular principle according to which elected public positions ought to be passed on, because of a kind of hereditary privilege, to certain families of distinguished ancestry."[58] The Trujillato's national-popular discourse thus in many ways emptied of meaning racial and class differences and downplayed these as valid categories of differentiation among Dominicans. It is the lasting effects of this discourse of nominally egalitarian social and political relations that obscured profoundly hierarchical structures that I suggest would later, in the post-dictatorship period, greatly constrain the processes through which Dominicans could come together to articulate shared demands and posit an effective challenge to hegemonic formations. Specifically, the Trujillato's impact on Dominican social and political relations encumbered the kind of horizontal or, in Laclau's terms, equivalential relations that go into the articulation of a strong collective will. Furthermore, the Trujillato's appropriation of key liberal democratic terms, including "democracy," "equality," "liberty," and "justice," as well as antiracist and feminist discourses, would notably complicate Dominicans' rallying around these later as shared signifiers for their anti-hegemonic struggles.

Indeed, Trujillo's national-popular homogenizing ideology was wielded as proof for how the Dominican Republic was more democratic and implicitly more "advanced" than other countries, including the United States, as suggested in the following excerpt of Balaguer's speech.

> Neither the United States, with its racial discriminations, still prevalent in some states of the Union, nor Cuba, a country where society is still organized, as during colonial times, on the antagonism between blacks and whites and between whites and quadroons, has been able to give its democracy, in this eminently human terrain, the perfection that ours has reached under the presidency, without prejudice or aristocratic inclinations, of the one and only General Trujillo.[59]

Democracy, it is suggested here, is incompatible with class or racial differences that Trujillo is claimed to have successfully eliminated.

Trujillo also appropriated the language of gender equality and feminism for his ends to similarly signal the particularly "advanced" and even "liberal" nature of his regime. Both Neici Zeller and Elizabeth S. Manley discuss the seemingly paradoxical (self-) designation of the Trujillo dictatorship as a pro-woman and even feminist regime. Manley describes how the newly installed Rafael Trujillo officially recognized the formation of an all-women's organization called the Acción Feminista Dominicana (Dominican Feminist Action or AFD).... In this and several subsequent steps he aligned the regime with the concerns of women and took up the banner of this early feminist movement. In so doing he effectively suppressed many of their more pressing issues as he focused exclusively on granting women the vote and equal civil rights in 1942.[60]

Adopting the political goal of women's suffrage helped the regime erect its democratic facade. As Zeller describes, "the presence of urbane, articulate women in political gatherings gave the dictatorship the veneer of democracy and modernity it desired for local and international consumption."[61]

The term *feminism* was put to what now seem perplexing uses, not only by Trujillo but also by Dominican women's organizations themselves. For example, "in the heat of their involvement with the regime, during an assembly in April 1934, the AFD leadership all but renounced their feminist priorities by publicly asserting that their identity was that of 'FEMINISTS' (which meant *Trujillistas*).'... The phrase often repeated in the speeches of the day—'Trujillo, the feminist president'—perfectly embodied this change."[62] As Zeller notes, "the meanings assigned to the terms 'feminism' and 'feminist' within the dictatorship" would lastingly distort "the various meanings that Dominicans assigned to these concepts" long past the end of the dictatorship.[63]

The Trujillato did expand women's public and even political roles, albeit always within its own narrow scripts: "During the decade between 1940 and 1950, Trujillo and the *Partido* dictated the norms for women's political participation as citizens in ways that allowed new expressions of female autonomy without challenging traditional gender differences."[64] The Trujillato, in fact, further exacerbated gender differences, as Madera suggests in her discussion of the dictatorship's public health programs and how these "institutionalized maternalism."

> The discourse exalting motherhood existed in the late nineteenth and early twentieth century. However, maternalist discourse became more prevalent during the Trujillato, ... and with it a more highly publicized discourse of "non-mothering" or "bad mothers" emerged. The Trujillo regime publicized its own discourse concerning female behavior on a larger scale than Dominican society had previously experienced.[65]

Maternalist discourse, as well as the "social hygienic discourse and reforms carried out by the Trujillato dictatorship," thus "redefined gender roles, regulated sexual and reproductive practice, and brought the state into the domestic sphere."[66] Madera therefore rightfully speaks of the "gendered foundation of the modern Dominican state" that emerged under the Trujillo dictatorship.[67]

Given how discourses of racial and class difference were downplayed during the Trujillato (and thereafter), gender certainly took on a foundational role as a language for articulating differences among Dominicans, among good and bad women, and among men. In fact, the rhetoric of masculinity served as a principal and highly overdetermined signifier for apprehending political and social differences, where being more or less "manly" reflected on one's position in the social and political hierarchy where Trujillo, as the manliest, was at the very pinnacle of it.

Dominican Masculinity and Cultural "Tradition"

The masculinity enacted by Trujillo and officialized by him certainly relied on preexisting patriarchal concepts; yet he did not simply reiterate previous dominant notions of masculinity. Rather, Rafael L. Trujillo's performance of masculinity brought more marginal elements to the national stage to lasting effect. When Trujillo came into power in 1930, Dominican society was predominantly rural, and, as social scientist Michiel Baud describes, "patriarchal dominance was the one over-arching ideology" that was "shared by peasants and elite members alike."[68] In the "male world" certain prerogatives were shared across class lines, including the prevalent practice of having more than one family and mistresses. As anthropologist Malcolm T. Walker notes, "serial polygyny" was "the norm, the male moving from one woman to another throughout his life" and only rarely formalizing these relations through marriage.[69] Nonetheless, there were key differences between lower-class and elite forms of masculinity. Elite men hardly forsook the practice of *concubinato*, but they would, unlike lower-class men, have to publicly keep up a "proper" front, and they would be "legally married and, publicly at least, lead moral and respectable lives" with their "official" family.[70]

In fact, before Trujillo came into power in 1930, he also was compelled to comply with these elite norms. As Crassweller recounts, during his second marriage to a woman from the Dominican elite, Bienvenida Morel, Trujillo had a lover, María Martínez, who would later become his third wife. But beforehand, in 1928, "the liaison of the rising officer with the high-spirited young woman was open enough to produce social scandal" that the younger Trujillo could not simply ignore.[71] To contain the public scandal, Trujillo arranged "for the sake of appearance" a marriage for María "with a Cuban who never seemed to appear on the Dominican scene."[72] After Trujillo came into power, he certainly laid claim to key privileges of elite masculinity, including a church-blessed marriage with his third wife, María Martínez. He also demanded a constant national official adulation of his family members, especially of his mother, his third wife, their two sons (Ramfis and Radhamés), and daughter (Angelita). Yet Trujillo had secured for himself this veneer of elite masculinity in hardly traditional ways. Only by mandating changes in Dominican law was he able to marry with the Catholic Church's blessing his former concubine María Martínez and have his out-of-wedlock children formally recognized as his heirs.

Such maneuverings reflect how, as Lauren Derby argues, Trujillo did not represent primarily an elite model of "respectable" masculinity. Rather, Trujillo embodied an "underclass mestizo style of *hombría* or manliness forged through personal risk taking, bravado, and sexual aggression."[73] Trujillo himself was of lower-middle-class and mixed-race origins and was notorious for his many lovers and sexual exploits. As Derby insists, "the excessive nature of Trujillo's sexual avarice in terms of both quantity and publicity invoked the 'hypermasculine pose' of Dominican underclass masculinity, one that challenged the more controlled, respectable self-representation of the elite."[74] Trujillo thus broke with previous public mandates of elite Dominican masculinity by legitimizing and officializing this underclass version of masculinity.

These key reconfigurations of Dominican masculinity are greatly obscured by portrayals of Trujillo as a typical "traditional" Latin American patriarch. Yet of course the Trujillato itself, as suggested before, encouraged such interpretations through its strategic use of the language of "tradition" and of patriarchal rhetoric. These were central to how the regime appealed to the Dominican rural population, which was then still the large majority. As Richard Lee Turits describes, "Trujillo's hegemony in the countryside was founded not only on material support during a parlous period of land and agricultural commercialization but also on cultural factors, and specifically on the ways that the regime appeared to fashion state projects to reflect and reinforce peasants' own evolving cultural norms."⁷⁵ As Turits emphasizes too, cultural norms were not simply reproduced but were "fashioned" for the regime's ends. In turn, the appropriation and refashioning of traditional peasant practices and norms from above also reconfigured those below, amongst the Dominican populace.

The cultural traditions that the Trujillato appropriated included the widespread Dominican practices of patronage and co-parenthood (*compadrazgo*). Baud, in his discussion of pre-Trujillo agriculture in the Cibao valley—the area considered often as the cradle of today's *dominicanidad*—describes how "family labor alone was often insufficient to cope with the simultaneous work involved in the harvest, and this period was therefore the occasion to organize communal labor gangs, *Juntas gratuitas* or *Juntas de vecinos*"; through this "survival strategy . . . individual peasant households linked their fate to others" and "networks of friendship and social obligation were reaffirmed and consolidated."⁷⁶ These interdependent bonds and obligations structured not only horizontal relations among kin, but also the vertical and hierarchical relations between different social classes; "peasants and landowners were linked to each other by a complex arrangement of rights and obligations and patron-client relations proliferated in Cibao rural society."⁷⁷ Baud emphasizes the reciprocity principle embedded in this system of patronage: "It secured sufficient labor force and support for the *patron*. The peasant population was provided with security and a potential safety net in difficult times. Most importantly, landowners could give access to land and credit. The political and economic vulnerability of peasant production rendered protection and security in the shadow of a powerful member of rural society an important asset."⁷⁸ The prevalent practice of *compadrazgo*, asking a person of higher standing to be a child's godfather (or godmother), was another strategy for those of the lower strata of society to assure goodwill, protection, and possible favors from the rural elites.⁷⁹

Trujillo self-consciously took on the role as the country's principal patron and in this way linked the Dominican population to his regime through multifarious, pervasive, and sentimentally tinged kinship-like relations.⁸⁰ Scholars cite staggering numbers of Dominicans who became tied in one way or another to the regime. For example, Jonathan Hartlyn describes how Trujillo amassed properties and businesses, and how the rapidly expanded military and state bureaucracy resulted in "about 60 percent of the country's labor force depend[ing] directly or indirectly on him, 45 percent being employed in his firms and another 15 percent working for the state."[81] Added to the elemental material dependency of the Dominican people on the dictatorship were other, more sentimental familial and social ties. Peguero, for example, points to the centrality of such ties in the military, where "by 1952, according to one survey, 30 percent of the officers above the rank of lieutenant colonel were related to the Jefe by blood or marriage."[82] She also describes how Trujillo "developed a taste for *padrinazgos* and *compadrazgos*, a co-parenthood system he used for populist appeal."[83] He became "the best man at thousands of marriages, civilian and military, and the godfather of thousands of children" and generated strong ties of loyalty, since "one does not betray his or her godfather, godmother or *compadres*."[84]

This adaptation of the language of traditional peasant–patron relationships and peasant practices of patronage and *compadrazgo* (discussed with much more detail in Turits's important study *Foundations of Despotism*), however, did not simply reproduce these traditions. Rather, their transposition from local contexts (and face-to-face relations) to the national level reconfigured these in ways that are not always immediately obvious. Just as traditional local patron–client relations had granted peasants in the past a certain degree of protection and an ability to seek interventions in their favor, Trujillo, in a 1932 speech to Dominican peasants, assured them that "any peasant who feels harmed by the local authorities in his person or interests, can directly approach me with the assurance that he will be attended."[85] This seemingly harmless promise of "you will be heard" was part and parcel of a general call to keep a watchful eye out for any form of "misconduct," not only by officials, but also by other community members, neighbors, and even kin.

This imperative was inscribed in the "Cartilla Cívica" (1932), the notorious government civil primer assigned as mandatory reading in all schools. In this document the Dominican people were told that after many years of "disgrace" and "disorder," now "order is the most necessary condition for the Nation, and the Government is in charge of maintaining it."[86] In the last section, citizens are given concrete indications of what is to be done.

> If a man who wants to upset the order comes by your house, have him arrested: he is the worst of all wrongdoers. The criminal is in prison because he has killed a man or he has stolen something. The revolutionary wants to kill everyone he can and take everything he encounters: what is yours and your neighbors': he is your worst enemy.

That is why you should consider the soldier like a brother who defends what is yours. Help him. Guide him. Show him the way and accompany him to establish order, which is your guarantee.[87]

These calls to order tapped into peasants' traditional culture of *respeto*, described by Turits as a "culture of 'decency', deference, and mutual respectfulness in interpersonal relations and across social hierarchies."[88] Such relations always had been hierarchical, and peasants had been historically subordinate and generally subservient to their patrons. However, there was a degree of interdependency in their relation with the patron, who also relied on their work and loyalty.[89] In turn, while direct appeals could also be made to Trujillo, and many peasants and Dominican citizens did just that, this was no longer a relation of interdependence, and all hinged on the goodwill and whims of the dictator.

The Trujillato's evocation of the peasant language of *respeto* to rhetorically clothe its repressive practices and call to "order" did not reinforce or facilitate interpersonal relations within rural communities, but rather destroyed these. As the "Cartilla Cívica" clearly indicates, the Trujillato called on all citizens to enforce order by reporting on one another.[90] As Turits recounts, among peasants "most disconcerting perhaps was the knowledge that acquaintances, friends, neighbors, and even (former) spouses might denounce one, perhaps with false information, to gain benefits from the regime or simply out of personal jealousy or animosity."[91] The regime's watchful eye peered deep into Dominicans' lives and muzzled speech and imposed silence within the confines of private homes.[92] These "elaborate mechanisms of surveillance, and the potentially horrific consequences for even the smallest slip of the tongue," Turits concludes, affected and "mined even the average peasant's life."[93]

Indeed, Walker, who studied rural social relations before and after the Trujillato, detects a significant change that occurred during the Trujillato. He finds that "the 'Era of Trujillo' was also the time when families ceased to be cooperative and when interfamily and interpersonal relationships came to be marred by distrust and suspicion."[94] Rural society before Trujillo's dictatorship had been strongly hierarchical, but these social structures had assured an individual's place within the hierarchy and thereby offered a degree of certainty. Such certainties never existed during the Trujillo regime. Rather, as Krohn-Hansen describes, under the Trujillo dictatorship "the individual is kept in a state of uncertainty regarding fundamental social mechanisms, and this gives life to fear."[95] Favors could be granted but also revoked at any moment, and no Dominican citizen was secure in his or her social, political, and financial status independent of the regime and the goodwill of the dictator. Under these circumstances, "each individual is driven to live in a state of loneliness and secrecy" and is "governed by the principle 'one trusted nobody.'"[96] Inevitably, interpersonal relationships, communal and interdependent relations, which had been so central to rural Dominican society especially, deteriorated under these conditions.

The loss of all certainty and guarantees that an individual could expect from his or her social surroundings, from relations with kin, and from individual efforts resulted in an atomization of individuals that must have had far-reaching effects on the individual and collective Dominican psyche. These psychological effects are often evoked but rarely considered more comprehensively. A notable exception to this is the work of the Dominican psychiatrist Antonio Zaglul. As Peguero describes,

> the violent nature of his [Trujillo's] rule aroused anxiety, fear, and suspicion among Dominicans to the extent that the Dominican psychiatrist Antonio Zaglul diagnosed that by the middle of the 1970s, many Dominicans were suffering from some form of paranoia. Zaglul traced Dominicans' sense of systematic persecution and their insecurity back to the colonial period, as well as to the precarious political life from independence to the U.S. occupation, but he concluded that the psychological traumas the Dominican people suffered under Trujillo's militaristic state were the real cause of Dominicans' mental anguish.[97]

While such a collective psychological evaluation is perhaps questionable, Zaglul's diagnosis suggests nonetheless how deeply the Trujillato penetrated individuals' lives and, also, how this did not leave them psychologically unchanged.

Dominican political and social relations were thus deeply affected by the Trujillo dictatorship. Notions of political leadership, allegiance, and justice had become decidedly phrased in the language of masculinity that naturalized a strongly hierarchical, top-down system that was, however, obscured through a national-popular discourse of equality and democracy. In this system the "top" man hands down "rewards" and "favors" in the form of government positions and other spoils and expects in return unquestioning personal allegiance, loyalty, and obedience. While these are certainly practices that preexisted the Trujillo dictatorship, what is new is how at the same time horizontal relations among equals were also damaged by a deep distrust that isolated individuals.

The profound impact that the Trujillato had on Dominican society, subjectivities, and masculinity in particular, is attested to, I argue, by a form of subjectivity that consolidated during its time—the figure of the Dominican *tíguere*. In 1992 the Dominican sociologist Lipe Collado released a guide to this twentieth-century phenomenon, *El tíguere dominicano: Hacia una aproximación de cómo es el dominicano* (2002). While this type of masculinity had existed previously and elsewhere too, it was, according to Collado, in the capital during the Trujillato, when "the original tíguere . . . in the forties and fifties was able to place himself above the top of Dominican juvenile leadership in the few traditional barrios of the limited urban space of the capital."[98] Collado defines the tíguere as an urban figure who overstepped traditional hierarchies and inhabited a calculating individualism. The tíguere is described as a "social simulator," "a hero of all his battles . . . who appears at the center of the drama and manipulates the situation in his favor," and as someone who likes to "get his way," who is an "opportunist" and "a friend of lies."[99] But, on the other hand, in more positive terms, the tíguere is also described as a "protector of friends, people close to him, and family," who has strong ties to his immediate surroundings.[100] Thus, the tíguere does not represent a typical modern form of individualism but remains deeply embedded in kin and communal relationships that are the key stage for the enactment of his public persona. On the other hand, the tíguere constantly emphasizes his individuality and opportunism: he is the protagonist of all his stories, in which he always outsmarts the dominant system and its rules.

The tíguere emerged under the specific circumstances and constraints of the Trujillato and indicated "a change—that is, an example of transformation of a people's way of communicating about maleness."[101] On one hand, as Derby suggests, the figure of the tíguere offered a way for Dominican men to negotiate the many limits that the Trujillato placed on individual aspirations and male agency, and in this limited sense, he "was transgressive."[102] At the same time, the tíguere is not an individualist rebel outside social structures, but rather he is a pragmatist who knows how to navigate these structures to his own advantage. In this sense, Derby describes the tíguere as having "a form of power that is morally ambiguous, *tigueraje* offers a paradigm of upward mobility for anyone who is cunning and brave, yet it is a form that may involve chicanery and dirty tricks."[103] Importantly, the tíguere's "countercultural valence," as Derby notes, was one that "Trujillo officialized by bringing it into the corridors of power."[104] The tíguere is thus a transgressive answer from men "below" to the constraints of the Trujillato, but also an echo of the new hegemonic masculine scripts enacted from "above" by the dictator himself.

Indeed, I argue that the tíguere is best understood as a response to the profound "crisis of the subject" brought on by the Trujillato's reconfiguration of social relations in the country. As Miguel D. Mena argues, the dictatorship caused a "crisis" not only "of knowledge, but also of the subject, of his/her self-perception.... The tyrannical discourse did not only found a form of knowledge, but also an ethic, a corporality, a gesture, a form of expressing oneself."[105] One of the forms of subjectivity that reflected this new context is precisely the figure of the tíguere. Individuals in Dominican society historically had been deeply embedded in and defined by reciprocal (but also hierarchical) communal relations and a web of family, kin, and patron relations. The dictatorship's weakening of these ties, with its inculcation of distrust and uncertainty, created the conditions for a new type of subject. Individuals were atomized yet remained profoundly dependent on relationships that escaped their control during the Trujillato. In other words, the social structures that had assured an individual's place were profoundly undermined. However, these communal structures were not replaced by an ideology and material culture that promoted autonomy, self-sufficiency, and a meritocracy with tools for social and material agency. Rather, the kind of individuality and atomized subjectivity produced by the Trujillato offered no certain paths and tools of agency for anyone under its reign.

Dominican social relations were thus profoundly affected by the regime in manifold ways. The mistrust it sowed affected relations among equals as much as hierarchical relations with those higher up. Interdependent relations gave way to more atomized experiences in which survival or improvement of living conditions depended less on reciprocal relations than on favors or opportunities passed down from above. These hierarchical relations in turn were naturalized by and rationalized through the language of masculinity. As the Trujillato's homogenizing national imaginary erased meaningful differences within the national community, especially racial differences but also class differences, masculinity became the official ruling logic of differentiation. In this dispensation, political leadership, or any equivalent form of coming out "on top," was told through hegemonic notions of masculinity that continue to circulate in Dominican society and political culture today.

Dominican Letrados and the Legacies of the Trujillato

The long afterlife of the Trujillato's national-popular discourse and of the conceptions that underwrote it, including masculinity, has much to do with how the regime's propaganda was successfully spread and ingrained for over three decades with hardly any competing discourses. This discursive monopoly was made possible by the isolation that the dictatorship imposed on the country that, as Derby describes, created "a virtually closed society, sealing off Dominican access to passports and foreign travel and establishing tight control over the flow of information into the country."[106] Not only was the entering of information from abroad tightly controlled but so was all internal circulation of information. The print media as well as radio stations were at the service of the Trujillato, sometimes even owned by members of the Trujillo family. The vast Trujilloist propagandistic project also included innumerable public events throughout the country that required many Dominicans to participate actively for the first time in national political life.[107] This constant inundation by Trujillista propaganda was, as Derby and others argue, a key factor in how the regime "created acquiescence, if not submission, and compliance, if not belief," among the Dominican populace.[108]

In this process Dominican letrados played a key role as a fundamental conduit for the articulation and dissemination of the regime's ideology. Dominican letrados—orators and intellectuals at both the regional and national levels—fed and sustained the regime's massive propaganda apparatus and served as the regime's mouthpiece. The Dominican critic and writer Andrés L. Mateo, for example, insists emphatically that "intellectuals played a preponderant role" in instituting the new reality of the Trujillato.[109] Indeed, the extent to which letrados were drawn into the dictatorial government might be unprecedented in Latin America. The Spaniard Jesús Galíndez already claimed in the 1950s that "in some aspects Trujillo's tyranny acted in a similar mode to other Latin American dictatorships . . . but with difficulty will such an absolute abjection of the intellectual forces be seen in any other country."[110] Intellectuals under other Latin American authoritarian regimes, including in Brazil, Argentina, and Chile, in many cases played an important role in the opposition or at least distanced themselves from the regimes. In turn, in the Dominican Republic, as the Dominican critic and writer José Alcántara Almánzar points out, the dictator "had the support of a series of poets, narrators, art and literary critics, historians and jurists who, together with liberal professionals ... served as civil servants, diplomats and ideologues."[111] Indeed, there was hardly a Dominican intellectual whom the regime did not try to cull for its purposes, including the internationally renowned Dominican literary scholar Pedro Henríquez Ureña, who in 1931 briefly returned to the country to work in the education sector. Certainly, for those whose economic survival depended in large part on writing, publishing, teaching, and other related professions, there was, besides exile, hardly another choice but to fall in line with the monologic Trujillista discourse.

Despite an overwhelming complicity among Dominican intellectuals who did not go into exile, there were also known dissenters who remained on the island. While they could not publicly speak out against the dictatorship, they rejected it by not singing Trujillo's praise (one well-known example being the historian Américo Lugo). Dominican historian Bernardo Vega calls this group the "passive disaffected ones"—"those who did not conspire against the dictatorship but maintained a public position opposed to the regime's."[112] While the "desafectos pasivos" were not killed by the regime, they suffered another kind of death.

> If their rebellion did not lead to their deaths then they were considered inoffensive to a certain degree, and their critical view cost them the worst of exiles: a social exile, ostracized in their own homeland.... They remained for their security in their homes, they were not invited to social activities, they were not members of the official party and it was very difficult for them to find employment, even in the private sector. They lived, but they did not exist as social entities.[113]

All other intellectuals and letrados were in turn absorbed into the "emerging institutional apparatus" and greased, as José Oviedo describes, "a veritable chain of symbolic production and circulation, ... a chain that offered the necessary institutional web for the successful spread of the cultural myths."[114]

These "cultural myths" were "an inseparable part of the total defensive scheme" through which the Trujillato ensured the docility, if not the complicity, of the Dominican population for decades.[115] This defensive scheme was produced largely by the regime's own ideologues, both at the top and at the lowest social strata, with Joaquín Balaguer, Manuel Arturo Peña Batlle, and Emilio Rodríguez Demorizi as the regime's ideological figureheads. Néstor E. Rodríguez argues that it was the first two, Balaguer and Peña Batlle, who "were the most important defenders of the nation's archive. More than any other letrados of the time, they praised the works and the trajectory of the 'Era' even in its most despicable aspects."[116] The regime's massive propaganda system ensured, as Mateo describes further, how this

> discursive symbolism of the Trujillista regime inhabited magically the totality of citizen life. There was not one Dominican home where these symbols were not hanging on the wall as ritual signs of prevention and fear. There was not a single act in the life of social relations that was not mediated by the intimidating presence of the Trujillista myth-system.[117]

The designation of a "Trujillista myth-system" captures how this "mythical" discourse was not an accurate reflection of Dominican social reality as well as its pervasiveness and organization as a coherent "system." In fact, the Trujillato's deliberate and systematic use of misnomers for its practices, including terms such as "democracy," "equality," "feminism," and "liberty," and their impact on Dominican democratic politics and discourse remains little understood.

Though much is to be said about the Trujillato's seemingly more tangible remains, including its institutional legacies (such as the strengthened Catholic Church and Dominican military), it is the regime's discursive legacies and their effects that might have most lastingly affected the country. Among these legacies is the Trujillo regime's conception of national Dominican identity and the racial and anti-Haitian beliefs embedded in it, which have rightfully received much scholarly attention both on and off the island. However, as this chapter shows, the legacies of the regime's gender discourse—especially of its discourse of masculinity that naturalized the Trujillato's incisive restructuring of Dominican political and social relations—also deserve more scholarly attention. It is to these gendered legacies in the Dominican political and cultural realms that the remainder of this book now turns.

2

One Phallus for Another

Post-dictatorship Political and Literary Canons

> Trujillismo is still governing our country.... We are still being governed by *trujillistas* disguised as democrats, ... playing a democratic game they don't really believe in.... and so for us the thirty years of the Trujillo era are a national trauma, are a type of shell we have been unable to break out. We live painfully obsessed with those years. And that is why we continue to find in that era a fundamental narrative motif. We can't understand how we can continue to be what we are.
>
> Pedro Vergés, "Challenging the Silence"

The death of the dictator, who was assassinated in 1961, also ended his type of exalted public performance of hypervirile masculinity by Dominican political leaders. This did not, however, spell the end of the political significance of discourses of masculinity in the Dominican Republic. Notions of masculinity continued to be integral to structuring relations between the political sphere and the Dominican people, to defining notions of "good" and "bad" leadership, and to conceptualizing power relations more broadly. Post-dictatorship politics would ultimately further naturalize this politics of masculinity, and it became part of a widely shared Dominican "common sense." This, I argue, is reflected in how hegemonic notions of masculinity are often reiterated and reproduced by some of the country's most important critical and anti-hegemonic voices: Dominican post-dictatorship letrados. In this chapter I trace the problematic traffic of the Trujillato's gendered legacies in the body of literary works that has most insistently addressed the Trujillo dictatorship: the vast Dominican corpus of dictatorship novels. Specifically, I address this question through the lens of the narratives of the most renowned living Dominican novelist, Marcio Veloz Maggiolo. I focus on his novels *De abril en adelante* (1975) and *Uña y carne: Memorias de la virilidad* (1999), not only because of how they foreground the Trujillo dictatorship, but also because of how they capture the shifting relations of Dominican letrados with the political sphere and the state. Ultimately, I suggest that these novels help us understand why key critical and intellectual voices have not, despite their best intentions, been able to successfully revise some of the Trujillato's lasting discursive legacies in the post-dictatorship period.

Changes and Continuities in Post-dictatorship Political Culture

A period of turmoil followed Rafael L. Trujillo's assassination in 1961, as the role that his family members would assume remained unclear. The Trujillos finally left the country in 1962, and Trujillo's last puppet president, Joaquín Balaguer, who initially continued to head the Dominican government, also was eventually forced into exile. A year later, in 1963, the first post-dictatorship elections were held, the only truly democratic elections for over a decade to come. Juan Bosch, a well-known writer at the time, won the elections as the head of an opposition party he had formed in exile, the Partido Revolucionario Dominicano (PRD). Bosch's uncontested stature as a writer, however, would not translate into comparable political successes. His efforts to institute significant change, including through policies directed at reducing economic inequities and improving the lives of the majority of the people, were short-lived. After only seven months in power, his government was brought down by a military-led coup supported by business elites who saw their economic interests threatened. The impetus for the coup came from a rhetorical ploy familiar from the Trujillato, the accusation of harboring "communist tendencies," a charge adamantly levied against Bosch by the Catholic Church and business elites.[1]

As hopes for a political transformation from above were abrogated by the coup, Dominican sectors from below mobilized. Parts of the population, mainly in the capital, Santo Domingo, as well as some members of the military, began a revolutionary uprising in the spring of 1965 that called for the return of Bosch to the presidency. When the success of the rebellion seemed imminent, the United States again occupied the country, driven by the fear of another Caribbean foothold for communism forming alongside Cuba. Just as the prior U.S. military occupation had facilitated Trujillo's rise to power, the 1965 occupation led to a re-entrenching of authoritarianism in the country. As the Dominican political scientist Jacqueline Jiménez Polanco notes, "the military intervention of the United States once again became (as had happened during the Trujilloist prelude) the 'perfect' vehicle for a new movement toward authoritarianism."[2] After a transition government was formed at the behest of the United States, new elections were held in 1966. With the support of the United States and following a fraudulent election process, Joaquín Balaguer went on to head a civilian (but unmistakably authoritarian) government during his infamous "doce años" (twelve years) in power.[3]

Particularly during his first two terms in power, Balaguer, like Trujillo, availed himself of an arsenal of repressive mechanisms.[4] He was no less violent and ruthless than his predecessor when it came to rooting out perceived political threats, which was greatly aided by U.S. efforts to make Dominican leftists and opposition forces migrate to the United States to defuse political tension in the country. As during the Trujillato, the rhetoric of "order" and "social peace" provided a cover for the repression of any political opposition. Even if this repression was perhaps not as systematized as under Trujillo, and even though Balaguer himself feigned having no involvement with these crimes, the chilling effect on political participation was unmistakable. During Balaguer's "doce años," as political opposition was violently repressed, the general population had to satisfy itself with merely "a *ritual* guarantee of the right [of participation], sustained by fraudulent elections."[5]

The Balaguerato was not a democracy with some authoritarian leftovers from the past, but rather another authoritarian regime with a more convincing democratic facade. Certainly, Balaguer did not make a radical U-turn from views he himself had elaborated and propounded during the Trujillato. However, the civilian facade of Balaguer's government made him more readily appear, to outside eyes, as a modern democratic political leader. On the importance of this democratic facade, Jonathan Hartlyn argues that "the fact that Balaguer was a civilian figure who paid attention to constitutional and electoral formalities further facilitated the high levels of U.S. economic, military, and political support."[6] Indeed, the success of his pretense of a democratic opening is reflected in the copious amounts of U.S. aid that Balaguer's government received, which at the time was "the highest per capita economic aid in Latin America."⁷ The U.S. financial support helped boost the Dominican economy and facilitated Balaguer's ability to buy the support and acquiescence of Dominicans and to strengthen his grasp on the country. The Balaguerato was therefore yet another case in which the persistence of authoritarianism needs to be considered in light of the economic, military, and political interventions of the United States rather than as a latent "traditional" Dominican inclination toward despotism. The Dominican people themselves had, of course, chosen Bosch.

Dominican post-dictatorship politics were thus decisively shaped by two Dominican letrados: Juan Bosch and Joaquín Balaguer. Nicknamed "El Profesor" and "El Doctor" respectively, Bosch and Balaguer were considered erudite men of letters, and both figure prominently in any history of Dominican literature. In fact, in 1990 they received together the country's first national literary prize for their lifetime oeuvre. Yet the commonalities end here. Balaguer had moved in the highest echelons of power during the Trujillato, while Bosch had been one of the regime's most ardent critics in exile. Then, in the post-dictatorship period, the two faced off in six, mostly fraudulent, elections that resulted in Balaguer's two prolonged presidential terms that lasted a total of twenty-two years (1966–1978; 1986–1996), while Bosch governed the country only for the aforementioned few months in 1963.

Bosch and his abrogated presidency have come to represent in the Dominican national imaginary the country's best hope for a break with the authoritarian past. Balaguer's protracted reign in turn has become for many synonymous with the obliteration of these hopes and the perpetuation of a politics inherited from the Trujillato. Indeed, a strong sense of loss continues to attach up until to this day to Bosch's name and to what many think could have been a very different Dominican political trajectory. In the Dominican imaginary, Bosch lingers, as Miguel D. Mena describes, as "the prototype of what we should have been and might never be."⁸ There are thus, as outlined above, a host of reasons and forces—both national and international—that ensured that Balaguer would prevail over Bosch. Among these forces I argue is also the lasting political force of discourses of masculinity.

At first sight, Balaguer's political and personal image departed in significant ways from Trujillo's, especially with regard to his enactment of masculinity. In contrast to the masculinity embodied by Trujillo, Balaguer did not present himself as a virile military strongman, but rather as the more cerebral "El Doctor." His person was not centered on the physical performance of hypermasculinity, and he did without Trujillo's favored accoutrements: flashy uniforms, an immense fortune, innumerable lovers, and ostentatious pleasure in music and dance. Overall, Balaguer projected a civility and restraint that masterfully overlaid the authoritarianism of his government. Thus, the discourse of physical "virility" gave way under the Balaguerato to a more psychological notion of virility, centered on political savoir faire, strength of will, and decisiveness, including the willingness to overstep and ignore democratic rules.

Balaguer's conception of leadership is encompassed in the popular slogan "Only Balaguer can do it."[9] Such presumable political savoir faire in actual practice meant, as Silvio Torres-Saillant describes, that

> President Balaguer covered up crimes and scoffed at the law on numerous occasions. He broke promises and betrayed allies. That behavior, however, helped him sustain an absolute rule for various decades and magically usurp the admiration that power evokes in the soul of beings without greatness. . . . His inconstancies were elevated to the rank of political genius. In this way a public life filled with improbity became seductive as a viable model of political conduct.[10]

Thus, even if the particular enactments of masculinity changed from Trujillo to Balaguer, for both men individual cunning and not being beholden to anyone or anything (including democratic rules) became testaments of their masculinity. Torres-Saillant therefore rightfully speaks of "the phallic force of the Balaguer regime."[11] Indeed, Balaguer reiterated conceptions of political leadership and forms of relation to which the Dominican populace had become accustomed under the Trujillato. This included embedding strongly hierarchical relations in the seemingly benevolent language of paternalism that positioned the president as the strict father who knows best but is accountable to no one but himself.

Indeed, while various internal and external factors contributed to Bosch's downfall, notions of masculinity and their political ramifications played an undeniable role. Their lasting force is perhaps best captured in how the Dominican popular imagination also expresses Bosch's failure to hold on to political power through the language of masculinity, of him not having sufficient "balls" (cojones) to be ruthless like Balaguer. For example, a Dominican man interviewed by Christian Krohn-Hansen for his ethnographic study addresses the differences between Bosch and Balaguer in the following terms:

"Mario saw a basic difference between Balaguer and Bosch. He tied the difference to masculinity—valentía. Balaguer, he could laugh, was a 'man of the devil' (un hombre del Diablo). But Bosch, he said, lacked timing when he was put to the crucial test."[12] These remarks reflect prevalent understandings of what are politically suitable forms of subjectivity and how these are conceived through notions of masculinity as well as what type of links political leaders are expected to form with the Dominican populace, links that greatly lend themselves to reinforcing clientelist practices.[13] Krohn-Hansen describes how being "un hombre que comparte" (a man who shares), rather than being what in Dominican popular parlance is called a "un come solo" (a solitary eater), remains a defining characteristic of what is considered good political leadership in the country.[14] These sayings capture the common sense that political leaders are expected, in a typical clientelist mode, to hand out jobs and personal favors to their supporters, which Balaguer did prodigiously. Indeed, one of the reasons Bosch lost some of his initial supporters was his unwillingness to follow these clientelist patterns as he sought to create programmatic linkages with the electorate not based on doling out jobs and goods but on political programs and proposals.[15] Ultimately, neither Bosch's inability to hold on to power nor the post-dictatorship political landscape more broadly can be apprehended without also accounting for how notions of masculinity structure Dominican conceptions of political leadership in particular ways. The hierarchies that are naturalized by this masculinist political language in turn provide no scripts for enacting a broader program of social and economic justice, and they continuously forestall processes through which citizens can come together to articulate shared demands to challenge the political status quo. The political constraints produced by hegemonic notions of Dominican masculinity, I argue, are evident in the work of many Dominican post-dictatorship letrados, who despite their ardent desire for a forceful break with the past reiterate some of its key legacies.

Dominican Literature as Archive of the Dictatorship and Its Afterlife

The unfolding of events after the end of the Trujillo dictatorship, especially the revolutionary uprising of 1965, led to a widespread politicization of Dominican writers and artists. As the Dominican critic Soledad Álvarez describes, "the '65 revolution indelibly marked the writers and artists from the

'60s. Inside the city walls, besieged by the North American troops, poets, writers, and plastic artists clutched in one hand the shotgun and in the other the word."[16] When U.S. forces again occupied the country these euphoric dreams of a vastly different Dominican political and social landscape were shattered.

For some, the resulting political disenchantment led to a complete turning away from the creative field. As Alcántara Almánzar describes, "several insurgent writers from '65 entered into a long silence and abandoned publishing; a good-sized group entered the field of advertising, which partially or totally absorbed it; others dedicated themselves to university teaching."[17] Those who remained active in the literary field split into various, often feuding factions and literary groups (El Puño, La Máscara, La Isla, La Antorcha).[18] Yet, however fragmented and limited the impact of post-dictatorship letrados' oppositional voices on Dominican public and officialist discourses may have been, especially during the Balaguer years, they without doubt have ensured that the Dominican public sphere would never again be as monologic as it had been under the Trujillo dictatorship. Perhaps Dominican letrados' most important contribution is their critical accounts of the past Trujillo dictatorship, much needed after over three decades of propagandistic and panegyric discourse. More than any other Dominican medium—whether music, theater, film, or visual art—post-dictatorship writing, both fictional and nonfictional, took on the task of critically accounting for the dictatorial past. Given the relative scarcity of more officialist forms of memorializing the dictatorship, these textual accounts are one of the most readily available archives and records of the dictatorship for the general public.

Indeed, unlike other Latin American countries that in the aftermath of repressive regimes and violence formed various types of "truth commissions" to account for the past—including in Argentina, Bolivia, Chile, Ecuador, El Salvador, Guatemala, Haiti, Honduras, Panama, Paraguay, Peru, Uruguay, and most recently in Brazil—in the Dominican Republic such commissions have not played an important role. Also, only very recently, in 2011, was the Museo Memorial de la Resistencia Dominicana ("The Dominican Resistance Memorial Museum") created to specifically commemorate Dominican victims of political repression. It is not so surprising, then, that literary and nonliterary texts that recount the Trujillato have proven to be the exception to the often bemoaned absence of an avid Dominican readership. Literary and nonliterary works that rehash the details and cruelties of the dictatorship, often with telling titles, such as Lipe Collado's *Anécdotas y crueldades de Trujillo* (Anecdotes and Cruelties of Trujillo), are still very much in demand by Dominican readers.

Dominican literature has delved continuously into the memory of the Trujillato up until today, making it perhaps *the* central theme of Dominican literature in the late twentieth century. Bruno Rosario Candelier, a renowned literary critic in the Dominican Republic, in his essay "Tendencias, ciclos y valores de la novela dominicana," published on the website of the venerable Academia Dominicana de la Lengua, declares "dictatorship novels" to be the most recent of four novelistic cycles in twentieth-century Dominican literature, following "the cycle about the guerrilla revolutions," "the cycle of sugar cane novels," and "the cycle of biblical novels."[19] Rosario Candelier's evaluation is echoed by other critics, including Nina Bruni, who affirms that in the past few decades "the novel develops notoriously around . . . the dictatorship of Rafael Leonidas Trujillo (1930–1961)."[20] Rita de Maeseneer, in *Encuentro con la narrativa dominicana contemporánea*, in fact asserts that "surveying all novels related to Trujillismo would be equivalent to writing an almost complete history of Dominican narrative of the second half of the twentieth century."[21]

This surge of Dominican dictator novels strengthened rather than weakened at the end of the twentieth century. As Fernando Valerio-Holguín asserts, there was a veritable "'boom of the novel about the Trujillato,' especially since the 1990s."[22] Importantly, this boom in literature about the dictatorship in the Dominican Republic, then, cannot simply be adduced to a falling in step with the literary phenomenon of the Latin American "dictatorship novel." As the Spanish literary critic Ana Gallego Cuiñas points out, in Latin America, "the boom of the theme of the dictatorship takes place in the decade of the seventies. . . . In the eighties one observes a notable diminution that continues into the nineties. This does not happen in the Dominican literary panorama, which takes the opposite route, since publications about the Trujillo dictatorship would be *on the rise* and experience a genuine novelistic bloom in the nineties."[23] The Dominican "boom" in literary accounts of the dictatorship has been prompted thus primarily by impulses internal to Dominican culture, society, and politics, making it imperative to read these literary texts in their local context.

There are other important indicators of the particularity of this Dominican literary phenomenon that sets it apart from broader Latin American literary trends. For example, there is a telling paucity of one of the literary forms that according to Idelber Avelar, in *The Untimely Present: Postdictatorial Latin American Fiction and the Task of Mourning* (1999), predominate in Latin American post-dictatorship literature. Avelar detects a "primacy of the allegorical" in Latin American narratives that try to come to terms with past dictatorships.[24] He suggests that Brazilian, Argentine, and Chilean fictions "insistently confront the ruins left by the dictatorships and extract from them a strongly allegorical meaning."[25] For Avelar, "in these allegorical fables the entire text is subsumed under the logic proper to the tyrannies portrayed," but "paradoxically, then, it is precisely by circumscribing a world seemingly devoid of all otherness that allegorical novels *preserve* an outside—they preserve it at the price of being unable to name it."[26] However totalitarian the order that is allegorized may be, there is within these narratives a remaining knowledge of an "outside," of another possibility, a different potential political order, even if it has been defeated by tyranny. In more concrete terms, the authors of these allegorical fables write with the awareness, as Avelar says, of "the defeat of the political practices that could have offered an alternative to the military regimes" and draw from the experience of having lived under other, better political circumstances.[27] It is important to note here that the works analyzed by Avelar are from countries—Argentina, Brazil, Chile—with military dictatorships that date after the Trujillato and that these countries, unlike the Dominican Republic, had experienced prior periods of full democracy. In the Dominican Republic no long-standing positive political alternatives consolidated before the Trujillato, not least because of repeated foreign interventions, including by the United States. There was, so to speak, no compelling political alternative whose disappearance or depredation could be imaginatively recalled or mourned by Dominican writers, allegorically or otherwise.[28]

At the same time, the long afterlife of the Trujillato, most conspicuously in the protracted regimes of Joaquín Balaguer, also hindered the ability of writers—as Pedro Vergés suggests in this chapter's epigraph—to view the past with enough distance to abstract, allegorize, or otherwise symbolically encompass fully the "dictatorial system." However all-encompassing the Trujillato may have been, and however befitting allegorization according to Avelar's logic, its messy overlaps with the present, as well as the absence of strong past political alternatives, appears to have constrained the process of allegorical abstraction in Dominican fiction.

Dominican post-dictatorship literature neither is primarily allegorical nor tilts toward magical realism, the alternate major strand of modern Latin American literature that, according to Avelar, allegorical fictions were breaking with.[29] While some key Latin American dictator novels identified with magical realism, such as Gabriel García Márquez's *El otoño del patriarca* (1975), are cited as antecedents and models for Dominican dictatorship literature, this corpus is most often placed by critics under the rubric of "historical fiction" or of the "historical novel."[30] Doris Sommer, in *One Master for Another: Populism as Patriarchal Rhetoric in Dominican Novels* (1983), asserts that "what is significant about Dominican novelists is that so many of them write from a self-consciously historical perspective."[31] Ignacio López-Calvo, in *God and Trujillo: Literary and Cultural Representations of the Dominican Dictator* (2005), finds that "the realist approach is the norm among these works."[32] Such assessments suggest how these Dominican fictions are invested in a kind of verisimilitude, even when they are not written in a realist style. Notably, a few Dominican works have been considered at one point a "literary" work and at another point a "true" historical or testimonial account.[33]

These texts' endeavor and desire to convey a certain historical "truth" about the Trujillato reflects, I suggest, their self-consciously assumed role as arbiters of the country's past and collective memory of the dictatorship. However, these works' gesture toward verisimilitude (even if never quite full historical "truth") merits the same kind of caution with which Avelar considers Latin American testimonials. He notes that testimonials, though presumably the most denunciatory accounts of dictatorial trauma, can inadvertently reproduce some of the very same mythologies and discursive patterns of the oppressive regimes that they want to denounce. In his discussion of Miguel Bonasso's Uruguayan testimonial *Recuerdo de la muerte* (1984), Avelar argues provocatively that "the dictatorship achieved a fundamental victory, for the language in which its atrocities were narrated was, in its essence, the very same language it cultivated and promoted: macho militarism seasoned with pious Catholicism."[34] Despite the possibility of such discursive continuities, the question of how the discursive legacies of the dictatorship might impinge on the corpus of ostensibly antidictatorial Dominican works is hardly considered by literary criticism. Even as it is readily admitted in scholarship that legacies of the Trujillato continue to influence Dominican political and social realms, literature is somehow presumed to be inoculated from this ill.

Post-dictatorship literary works that claim to be written against or simply about the dictatorship are taken to automatically coincide with an anti-Trujillista stance, and criticism shows little concern with more closely analyzing the ideological subtexts of these works about the Trujillato.

The lack of critical attention to the textual politics of this key corpus and archive of the Dominican dictatorial past is aided by two facts: (1) that in the relatively small Dominican cultural sphere, everyone is already "in the know" about the presumable anti-hegemonic political stances and former leftist political sympathies of many of the authors concerned, a knowledge that grants their writing a kind of political alibi; (2) the problematic injunction of Dominican literary critics for the country's literature to "catch up" with the more "advanced" literary developments in Latin America and in the world, in part by embracing modernist writing styles. As a result, the works that Dominican leftist intellectuals and writers are mainly renowned for today—including their writings about the dictatorship—are not the works produced under or inspired by the revolutionary euphoria and political mobilization of the 1960s. As Juan José Ayuso, a member of this revolutionary generation, describes, these earlier works had followed the "idea of social and committed art and the idea of popular freedom and justice."[35] However, they did not leave much of a trace in the national literary canon, largely because their political commitments could be read off them so readily, resulting in their broad dismissal by Dominican critics. As Álvarez attests, "few literary generations are as stigmatized as the one of the sixties."[36] Given the political expediency of many "officialist" literary works under the Trujillato, when literature was forced to express its adherence to the regime's tenets, the general weariness with the mobilization of literature for political ends is understandable. Yet, the resulting "anti-ideological" post-dictatorship imperative, I find, has had its own ideologically troublesome side-effects.

In the post-dictatorship period, "good" literature has generally come to be defined as writing that follows modernist paths. This often has led to an embrace of formal experimentation and to the rejection of more explicitly political commitments or engagements. As Torres-Saillant describes, Dominican writers fear that their work "will be denied its worth because of its 'political' nature, which, according to the official aesthetics' credo, is accepted in the yard as a synonym for poor artistic quality."[37] This credo is implicit, for example, in Álvarez's conclusion that "there were many postwar books. None of them has remained as a significant title, with the exception of

Los ángeles de hueso (1966) by Marcio Veloz Maggiolo.... *Los ángeles de hueso* is a precursor of the *modern novel* in the country."[38] Álvarez specifically locates this laudable literary modernity in how Veloz Maggiolo "uses typographical possibilities, the overlap of temporal planes, interior monologue, spatial displacement, the interweaving of different viewpoints and various narrators, and verbal dislocation."[39] This comment suggests how the "modernness" of Veloz-Maggiolo's fiction is thought to "rescue" his work from the pitfalls that other, more explicitly political, writing from this time period falls into.[40]

My concern is how the prioritization of formal experimentation and of "modernist" literary expression leads critics to read and treat such texts as if they were devoid of any ideological content. This tendency is reinforced by the "political alibi" granted to many authors on account of their known prior political stances. Such presumptions have had troublesome consequences for the critical evaluation of Dominican post-dictatorship literature, given that it exempts "modern" Dominican fictions from a critical interrogation of their textual politics and underlying ideologies. Yet the important role that these fictions play in the production of the country's collective memory of the Trujillato makes this interrogation an important critical undertaking, which I pursue in my following analysis of two of Veloz Maggiolo's key dictatorship novels.

Marcio Veloz Maggiolo's Modern Fictions

Marcio Veloz Maggiolo is arguably the most important contemporary Dominican novelist, a standing attested to by the innumerable national literary awards that he has received in past decades.[41] Maggiolo is also often credited with "modernizing" the Dominican novel, and many of his writings take up the theme of the Trujillato. Born in 1936, he began writing under the Trujillato, at first using religious allegories to address the Dominican political context.[42] After the end of the dictatorship, he was tied to the emerging leftist cultural groups, and he is generally considered to have been close to the politically engaged Generation of the '60s (though some critics place him more squarely with a previous generation, the Generation of '48). Among his earlier works, his novel *De abril en adelante* (1975) is considered an important turning point in Dominican literary history. The novel's thoroughgoing formal experimentation makes it for several critics the work that marks the moment when Dominican literature became recognizably "modern." Also, the novel's revisiting of the dictatorial past is thought by some to have spearheaded the insistent turn to the Trujillato as the principal literary theme in late-twentieth-century Dominican fiction. Beyond Veloz Maggiolo's pivotal role in the Dominican literary landscape, his works are considered here because of their self-reflexive chronicling of the generation of letrados from the 1960s. His writings help to trace how the Dominican intellectual sphere shifted from revolutionary fervor to political disenchantment and, in some cases, to an eventual accommodation with the powers that be.

Indeed, Veloz Maggiolo's narratives often employ narrators who are themselves writers, giving his fictions strong autobiographical overtones. For example, *De abril en adelante* (published in 1975, but completed in 1970) describes the time when the new authoritarian political reality under Balaguer has settled in, but the revolutionary fervor is still a recent memory for young Dominican leftist letrados. At this specific historical juncture, the novel describes how Paco, an aspiring writer and one of the text's main narrative voices, crisscrosses the capital, Santo Domingo. As Paco meets various friends, mainly members of a literary group with leftist political inclinations, he repeatedly brings up a novel he intends to write about the dictatorship and past revolutionary uprisings to address why past Dominican resistance movements have failed.

Though Paco appears to be the main narrative voice, the narrative's perspective changes throughout the text, and the identity ascribed at first to various central characters, including Paco, is put into question later on. These multiple and changing narrative perspectives are often found in Veloz Maggiolo's works and make it almost impossible to pin his texts to any single stance or authorial viewpoint. Indeed, such shifts are at the heart of the author's "modern" style that also engages in a relentlessly metafictional bent. *De abril en adelante*, for example, recurrently refers to the writing process, shifts narrative perspectives, intercalates stories, and repeatedly confounds what is presented as "real" and "literary" in the text.[43] This experimentation is reinforced through various strategies, such as the work's self-description as a "proto-novel" (protonovela) and of various chapters titled as "proto-chapters" (proto-capítulos), alluding self-consciously to the contingency of the process of writing.

Unlike some Dominican critics who find this experimentalism gratuitous, Doris Sommer and Ignacio López-Calvo argue in their discussions of the novel that it productively serves to highlight the constructedness of literary representation, as well as, more importantly, the impossibility of arriving at any definite historical "truth" about the past.[44] For example, López-Calvo notes that "Veloz Maggiolo opts for a more experimental approach in which fragmentation and polyphony contribute to explain the difficulties of producing objective historical discourse."[45] The main narrator's ongoing dilemma over how "best" to represent history certainly gestures toward the difficulty of speaking coherently and comprehensively about the dictatorial past that in its aftermath seems almost "unreal." Paco, for example, worries about how a historical episode that is "very true" (bien cierto), even though it appears as too eccentric to be believable, can be turned into literature—"How to represent it in a novel in a truthful way, that is a whole other thing."[46] Sommer thus suggests that "historical truth" and its literary representation are among the novel's principal concerns; she states, "As I read it, the fundamental challenge in this book is how to make history believable."[47]

Without doubt, readers are consistently and even quite heavy-handedly presented with reflections on literary representation and historical truth throughout the novel and with an express desire for approximating verisimilitude (though not through straightforward "realism"). Yet I find that another concern poses itself with at least equal if not more urgency, namely, the male group dynamics of the leftist letrados in which the narrator Paco is embedded. The emotional core of the text is the relations and infighting of this loosely connected group of mostly male writers, artists, and intellectuals in Santo Domingo. They bond and argue over one another's literary talent, liaisons, political stances, and past positions during the dictatorship. Throughout the novel, Paco is deeply concerned with what the other group members say or think about him, and he remarks with keen self-awareness that "you can't live without the opinion of the other; you can't do anything without the other assenting; you can't even feel sure of yourself if the other is not assuring you."[48] These competitive, often divisive, and at times petty group politics are central to the narrative, a fact that the protagonist himself acknowledges even as he actively participates in these. A jab such as the following is typical of their conversation: "I look at Samuel. He had let his sideburns grow; he likes tight pants and big buckles.... I can't explain to myself how one can preach revolutionary ideas dressed like a bourgeois little gentleman."[49] Paco's ongoing concern with what his male peers think of him leads to an acute paranoia, and he speculates: "They will arrive at Juan's place and there they will return to this issue, against me. They will continue to critique me."⁵⁰

The posturing and bickering of this "juego snob" (snobbish game) extends to these men's literary ambitions as well as to their political convictions. Though the novel declares politics to be a serious matter, and this group's shared leftism is what brings them together, there is a notable emptiness when it comes to their political proclamations, evident in the off-handedness with which these are treated. One of the narrative voices declares, for example, "I tell Paco to cut this communist crap, to be cultured one need not be a communist."⁵¹ Ideological allegiances appear more as superficial posturing than as deeply felt or organically developed commitments. This is reflected in the at times seemingly opportunistic switching of political stances and in how these are rarely accompanied by serious reflection or engaged action (unlike, presumably, in their past, during the revolutionary uprising). The novel thus attests in many ways to the decline of the political Left during the Balaguerato. However, it also demonstrates how identifying with the "Left" remains a strong basis for group allegiances in the Dominican cultural sphere during this time period.

In fact, their shared leftist political convictions give the characters a political alibi that, in their eyes, protects them from the taint of the recent dictatorial past. It is taken for granted by the narrative that they all share an anti-Trujillista stance and a generally anti-hegemonic position that extends automatically to their literary projects, including Paco's much-debated novel-in-the-making. As a result, all members of the group seem to be able to draw a very neat line between themselves and the recent Trujillista past. For example, the Trujillato appears in Paco's narrative project primarily as a writerly problem that he wants to broach through the figure of Coronel Aguirre, a Trujillo loyalist who committed many crimes and cruelties in the name of the regime. He also happens to be Paco's father. These family ties to a brutal military leader cast suspicion on Paco in the eyes of several friends, who note how he has "so many wealthy friends and ties to the past tyranny."⁵² However, the narrative suggests that their judgment and suspicion of Paco is ultimately unfair, as it remarks emphatically on how Paco is now clearly aligned with a leftist ideology and foregrounds his estrangement from his father. In this way, the novel sidesteps the question of how the dictatorial past may continue to act upon the present and on these characters in ways that are less conscious and less explicit, and despite their own best intentions.

The narrative avoids considering such overlaps by positing a deep chasm between father and son. This chasm is deepened by addressing Paco's relationship to Coronel Aguirre as primarily a literary concern—Paco repeatedly declares Aguirre "is a formidable [literary] theme"—rather than as a personal one with an emotional purchase on the narrator.[53] The novel, whether it poses the Paco–Aguirre family relation as "true" or "fictional" within its narrative world (given that the text repeatedly puts into question the identity it establishes for Paco and for Aguirre), does not imagine a more complex and emotionally meaningful relation between the two, particularly on the part of the son. The complexities that such a relation would have introduced into the rendering of Paco, and more broadly of his generation, is avoided by neatly severing them from the Trujillato, with no messy or too-personal connections to the recent past. Instead, the Trujillato mainly functions as a problem of the past for writers to use as literary material, rather than having a tangible bearing upon the present lives of this group and generation. Indeed, the various imagined outcomes for Coronel Aguirre—including that he joined the anti-Trujillo battle at the end or committed suicide out of guilt—further suggest an unwillingness to consider more insidious connections between the Trujillato and the present. The outcome that remains simply unimaginable is what most likely would have been the case: Aguirre having peacefully retired, comfortably living in the same house, perhaps even on friendly terms, with his son Paco.[54]

This dissociation from the dictatorship is further reinforced by how the narrative focuses, as do most other Dominican (and non-Dominican) literary works about the Trujillato, on the seemingly outrageous and grotesque acts of the dictator as an irrational and cruel madman.[55] Many literary works about the Trujillato center on representing extreme acts of violence or sexual "perversions" committed either by the dictator himself or by his followers.[56] The literary commonplace of the dictator's excessive sexuality and the accompanying scenes of violence are part and parcel of a broader tendency toward the grotesque in works about the Trujillato. In fact, the inclination toward such grotesque representations is one of the few common traits and preponderant tendencies in the disparate writings about the dictatorship not only in the Dominican Republic but in other Latin American works as well. As López-Calvo notes, "a feature common to the Novel of the Dictator, the Trujillo cycle, and cultural production in times of tragic institutional crisis is the use of the grotesque as an evocative way to describe the ineffable and satirize behaviors that are considered inhumane."[57] Various critics, including López-Calvo, Gallego Cuiñas, and Neil Larsen, note how such grotesque "evocations" can function very ambivalently and can lead to a reductive portrayal of the dictator. In the process of portraying the inhumanity of the dictator, many texts end up mythologizing him.[58] One of the earliest critiques of this tendency is Larsen's 1988 essay "¿Cómo narrar el trujillato?" where he critiques how the Trujillato is represented "in the best case, as a great number of sensationalist anecdotes inserted into the dictator's own biographical thread."[59] Furthermore, "Trujillo is presented, on one hand, as an almost comical madman. . . . On the other hand, as a giant and Dantesque Satan."[60]

These tendencies are also evident in Veloz Maggiolo's novel. The narrative refers, for example, with notable glee to the depravity of the Trujillato's "fiestas," in which "sex and licentiousness destroyed the notion of private propriety in those who called themselves his staunchest defenders. This was the Generalissimo's experiment, in which month after month Santo Domingo's high society partook."[61] One of the acts presented as exemplary of the Trujillato's depravity is an episode when Trujillo's brother forces two young socialites to wed two lower-class men, and he himself has sex with the brides in front of the wedding guests. The shock value that this scene wants to produce relies notably on evoking sexual transgressions whose outrageousness is deeply wound up with an overstepping of class and racial boundaries and thus with an affront to the moral values of Dominican "high" society.[62] The novel problematically relies on such scenes and their gender, sex, and class connotations, as well as the implicit racial dynamics of presumably "darker" lower-class men raping upper-class and presumably lighter-skinned women, to critique the vileness of the dictatorship. A certain unease is thereby revealed on the part of the text with the confounding of racial and class boundaries that is associated with the Trujillato, especially when this involves what is considered here inappropriate access from men "below" to the bodies of elite women.

However, the scandalized tone with which the dictatorship's sexual "desenfrenos" and uses of women are described in *De abril en adelante* vanishes when it comes to describing the sexual "desenfrenos" of the narrator and his male circle. Paco, for example, is involved sexually with two women, a cousin and the girlfriend of one of his friends. At one point he exclaims gloatingly, "I think of Matilda last night, awesome! . . . three times. And Melissa the night before that, sensational."[63] The text emphasizes here a virile masculinity that is further enhanced by "taking" women from other men, even supposedly close friends. The competitive relation between men and the deep divisions between men and women in the text, as well as the inevitable sexualization of their relations, are particularly evident when women endeavor to participate as peers in this group's literary gatherings. These efforts are recurrently demeaned in the novel. In one case, when a woman poet comes to the meeting, the narrative voice recounts how "the thing about who would sleep with her began.... In short, within a week Alberto had cuckolded her husband and since then her poems appear every Sunday—with whorish persistence—in the [newspaper's] supplement pages."[64] It is repeatedly suggested that the women in the group get published mainly because of their sexual entanglements with male members of the group (pun intended). In general, the women who attend these meetings are represented as sexual objects and hardly as equal intellectual contributors. Given this gender matrix, it is not surprising, then, that *the* greatest trauma in the novel is a distinctly gendered trauma, namely, the fact that an older female novelist, Zinia, was a finalist in an international literary competition.[65] Her success is presented as the main reason for Paco's desire to write his own novel, egged on by his friends: "Come on you shit, write a novel. Don't you see that Zinia says that she was a finalist?"[66] Zinia's being a finalist in a literary competition is mentioned over thirty times in this novel of fewer than three hundred pages. Tellingly, this trauma of a woman's greater literary success is not treated with the same self-critical and self-mocking tone that these men's political beliefs, literary endeavors, and social behaviors are otherwise addressed with in the narrative.[67] Despite the narrative's hyper-self-consciousness throughout, it is generally devoid of any critical consciousness when it comes to the dynamics of gender and sexuality it represents.

Doris Sommer also remarks on the problematic gender politics of *De abril en adelante*. Most of the women in this novel, she notes, "lack the men's particularity and capacity for complementary creativity and for debate," and "their only function seems to be to distract the men from important functions and to trivialize their lives."[68] Sommer furthermore finds that in Veloz Maggiolo's novel "the difference between the author's treatment of complex men and simple women is revealing," and that his "overall treatment of women does not evince any serious preoccupation with the general issue of sexism or with the particular situation of women in the Dominican Republic."[69] However, in the following paragraph she tempers this conclusion by suggesting that "Veloz's anti-*machismo* is more self-conscious in his short but meaningful treatment of homosexuality."[70] She further adds that "when the narrator introduces Teddy, who is gay, the description is almost condescending. But it quickly turns into an empathetic remark about how Teddy's newspaper articles have been censored."[71] This latter empathy thus appears to correct the previous homophobic condescension in the text. More broadly, this empathy appears to be sufficient for Sommer to correct Veloz Maggiolo's misogynist representation of women, allowing him to still be considered an "anti-machista," despite the textual evidence that suggests otherwise, as Sommer herself notes.

Sommer's consideration of the novel's gender and sexual politics as ancillary to its larger narrative project is surprising, given the larger argument she makes in her study about the political valence of Dominican literary representations of gender and sexuality. The language of family, matrimonial union, and attendant notions of gender and sexuality mobilized by populism, Sommer argues, are reproduced in Dominican literature—as her book's subtitle *Populism as Patriarchal Rhetoric in Dominican Novels* clearly proclaims. "Populist ideology," according to Sommer, maps family paradigms onto the political and becomes a vehicle for imagining the Dominican nation: "Populism 'captures' . . . the traditional patriarchal relationships of an agricultural economy for a political discourse suggests and identity between familial relationships and national history. The result seems more like a natural given than an ideological construction because of the way family structure tends to be taken for granted."[72] Populist contiguities of the private and the public are a common feature in Dominican literature, according to Sommer. In contrast, however, Veloz Maggiolo's *De abril en adelante* is the literary work that Sommer finds "breaks most radically with the populist rhetoric."[73]

The novel certainly forgoes evoking the patriarchal family that is often employed by populist rhetoric as a blueprint for its imagining of the national community; however, I argue that the novel does not forgo all ingrained gender narratives. Most crucially, the novel insistently echoes notions of masculinity officialized by the Trujillato and forms of social and political relations reinforced by it. This masculinity, as discussed in the previous chapter, is not principally identified with the patriarchal values and structures of the traditional agricultural community. Rather, it is a distinctly urban masculinity that is closely linked to the figure of the tíguere, centered on virility, and exemplified by the ability to outsmart everyone to secure one's individual advantage, without regard to legal or ethical codes.[74] This masculinity is reflected, for example, in the novel's characters' constant jockeying for position and struggle for being the "top dog," so to say. This chapter's title, "One Phallus for Another," thus is a play on Doris Sommer's book title *One Master for Another*, that points to how hegemonic notions of virile masculinity have carried over from the Trujillato.

The hierarchical orientation of these notions of masculinity is reflected in the protagonists' continuous concern with their personal standing vis-à-vis others. At the same time, their fear of "el que dirán" attest to how the controlling force of gossip and the deep distrust among equals that were ingrained by the Trujillato still remain. These forms of relation ultimately determine the characters' group politics more than any other more explicit political ideology, and their collective leftist political convictions appear superficial in comparison to their profound concern with their social standing among their male peers. Veloz Maggiolo's novel describes with notable critical self-awareness and with plenty of irony these group politics of the Dominican Left, segmented by continuous infighting. Yet where the novel lacks critical self-awareness, as Sommer and other critics have noted too, is in the notions of gender and sexuality that it reproduces. Specifically, I argue that the narrative fails to perceive how these notions inherited from the Trujillato are integral to delimiting these characters' relations and undermine the critique the novel purports to articulate.

Now, Marcio Veloz Maggiolo is hardly the only Dominican writer whose representations of gender and sexuality have been deemed problematic. Critics have repeatedly observed how misogyny and homophobia are troublesome features in the works of other prominent authors of Dominican dictatorship novels, such as Efraim Castillo and Diógenes Valdez (also associated loosely with the generation of the '60s).[75] Gallego Cuiñas, in an exhaustive study of Dominican dictatorship novels, suggests that, broadly speaking, "machismo has reverberated in the novel about the Trujillato."[76] Similarly, Fernando Valerio-Holguín describes the "narratives of the Trujillato" as "machista art."[77] Rita de Maeseneer points out, for example, how in Efraim Castillo's *El personero* "some very conservative structures in the relation between men and women are corroborated in the entire novel."[78] López-Calvo, on the other hand, notes how homophobia emerges in "several Trujillato narratives," and finds that "the fact that they were written during the 1980s and 1990s, when the sentiment against this type of intolerance had become widespread, makes this issue even more problematic."[79] Thus, "the apparently conflicted ideology of some of the implicit authors creates appalling contradictions," when "texts of resistance that a priori condemn the dictatorship's intolerance and oppression are sometimes tarnished by their latent homophobia."[80]

These texts' underlying gender beliefs and sexual prejudices often emerge in their descriptions of the purportedly outlandish sexual behavior and supposed virility of the dictator.[81] Even while these works present Trujillo's insatiable sexual appetite as grotesque, they can nonetheless display a not-so-hidden admiration for his virility. According to López-Calvo, "the Generalíssimo's legendary sex drive . . . probably enhanced his image as a patriarchal macho figure that many uneducated male citizens (and judging by some of the passages in the Trujillo cycle, perhaps also some Dominican intellectuals) secretly or openly admired."[82] More pointedly, López-Calvo notes how Diógenes Valdez's novel *Retrato de dinosaurios en la Era de Trujillo* (1997) reflects the "author's apparently conflicted ideology with respect to the Trujillo family's male chauvinism . . . his phallocentric discourse shows a hidden pride or admiration for the *machismo* and the international sexual exploits of the most notorious Dominican playboys."[83] The politics of gender and sexuality in the writing of these Dominican letrados thus remains at times embedded in some of the Trujillo regime's very own ideological parameters, specifically its hegemonic notions of masculinity. As I suggest in the following section, these reiterations ultimately constrain the vision of anti-hegemonic politics that they can imagine.[84]

Marcio Veloz Maggiolo's Virile Memories

The constraints that these gender and sexual ideologies place on visions of political resistance and, more broadly, on the emergence of strong anti-hegemonic impulses in Dominican society, is suggested in another, more recent, novel by Marcio Veloz Maggiolo, *Uña y carne: Memorias de la virilidad* (1999). This text was declared by the author upon publication to be his most trenchant literary confrontation with the Trujillo dictatorship to date. The novel also offers a critical reflection on the trajectory of those from the Left who had once challenged the political status quo, such as the group chronicled in *De abril en adelante*, and describes their increasing accommodation with the powers that be. This rapprochement of formerly oppositional voices with the political status quo is given voice in the text through Nicasio, a former radical leftist. Yet, in that moment, in the 1990s, when Balaguer had returned to power for a second time (1986–1996), Nicasio ridicules his past political inclinations and admits how he has very comfortably accommodated himself with the politics of the president "Verdaguer" (a more-than-obvious allusion to "Balaguer"). As the protagonist states, "I slowly distanced myself from my initial political ideas. They weren't necessary. . . . I got fed up and directed my world toward a calm life, beyond romantic notions."[85] Nicasio is now a valued adviser of Verdaguer, a member of his reformist party, and firmly entrenched in the government's clientelist politics that provide him with a lavish lifestyle. As Nicasio states, "I was no longer a follower of any Left, but rather a reformist delegate, with a diplomatic passport, a penthouse, three Mercedes cars, and a pleasant life that I wanted to hate at first, but which I got used to."[86]

Much has changed, then, in the two decades since the more immediate post-dictatorship period portrayed in *De abril en adelante*. While in *De abril en adelante* the political defeat of the Left was strongly felt and mourned by Dominican writers, artists, and intellectuals, their leftist political affiliations (however hollow in some ways) nonetheless remained relevant to their beliefs and social interactions. In *Uña y carne* such political inclinations, as well as the literary and intellectual groups that had formed around them, have given way entirely to individualist cynicism, self-absorption, and an interest in material benefits, with a notable absence of any group formations or collectivities in the text.[87]

The novel is clearly critical of the political reality created by Verdaguer, but it insists on the overriding importance of returning to the Trujillo dictatorship, given that the Dominican Republic is "a country without memory."[88] This lack of memory is, according to the narrator, precisely what cements the power of the current regime. Nicasio says: "During the previous governments in which I participated, oblivion has been one of the fundamental politics of various regimes. The peace of these times is built upon oblivion. . . . Produced and manipulated amnesia brings political results and encourages wealth and well-being."[89] The foregrounding of the dictatorial past and the recuperation of memory is presented by the novel therefore as an important challenge to the present status quo. However, what does this challenge consist of, and how effective is it ultimately in destabilizing the present?

Large chunks of this fragmentary novel are dedicated to reminiscences about the Trujillo period. The apparent occasion for the return to the past is the imminent arrival of the dead body of a friend of Nicasio's, a former Dominican dissident who had to go into exile in France. The fact that the current regime would rather have his body disappear than give him a dignified burial in his home country creates a certain conundrum for Nicasio and occasions his delving into memories of the past dictatorship period, when he and his friend Daguerre are said to have been as close as "uña y carne" (an idiomatic expression similar to "like two peas in a pod"). His reminiscences about the past via the friend's dead body clearly reach far past the personal and are portrayed by the novel as a critical gesture and a narrative settling of scores with the Trujillo period.

In this critical return to the past, as the subtitle of the book *Memories of Virility* (Memorias de la virilidad) makes plain, virility plays a key role: "Something that has a lot to do with this story is virility."[90] In fact, the secondary plot, one that actually takes up more space than the dilemma surrounding the friend's corpse, centers on maneuverings during the Trujillato to secure for Trujillo, "El Jefe," a cure for his failing sexual prowess. The narrative insistently suggests that El Jefe's supposed virility never lived up to the myths surrounding it. In fact, there are more than thirteen references to Trujillo's not-so-impressive member, often voiced in the novel by women who presumably had sexual relations with him. One is quoted remembering how "he achieved a somewhat forced erection that I silently laughed at."[91] Another woman proclaims that "what El Jefe had was 'nothing but an insignificant little dove.'"[92] Another lover found out that "El Jefe's virility was tiny, short-lasting."[93] And, "it was said that the beloved Jefe had a short and weak prick," and that "the big shot with the most powers in the Caribbean 'had one like a little dove.'"[94] In the end the novel thus proclaims that "all this show about him being very sexually potent is just a story."[95] The main recipe for this text's anti-Trujillista critique is hard to miss here: the Jefe's virility, a key source of his power, is a myth that needs to be dismantled. Very straightforwardly and heavy-handedly the narrative links the question of the dictator's sexual prowess to his political power. This is seen in statements such as that "his virility was the beloved Jefe's principal political and social force," and that "the formula for virility is also the formula for remaining in power."[96]

While in relation to the dictator politics and phallus are neatly linked, there is again a notable lack of critical awareness in the text when it comes to the representation of the protagonists' virility. Concerns with sexual conquests and personal standing again overtake any sustained address of political issues in the narrative. Though both Nicasio and Daguerre are declared to have been political dissidents, their political beliefs remain entirely without content, since the reader learns little about their specific political stances, beliefs, or acts; rather, the narrative is taken up mostly by their sexual trysts. Moreover, even though Daguerre and Nicasio are supposedly as tight as "uña y carne," the nature of their friendship receives hardly any treatment in the novel. For the most part, rather than portraying their presumably strong friendship bonds, the text mainly contrasts one with the other, representing Daguerre as a "dud" and Nicasio as the "stud." The narrative repeatedly suggests that Daguerre was a bit "damaged" because of his homosexual proclivities, just like his brother. As the narrator describes, "Daguerre had his fag side that he hid . . . ," and "his *faults* . . . ran in the family, since his brother Boni, a doctor, was also a little faggot."⁹⁷ This candid recognition of homosexuality, which might superficially bolster the narrative's progressive credentials, treats homosexuality primarily as a mark of inferiority and as indicative of an insufficient and subordinate masculinity.

Though Veloz Maggiolo often broaches the topic of homosexuality in his writings, this orientation tends to diminish the masculinity of his characters. In a collection of essays about Veloz Maggiolo's narratives, *Arqueología de las sombras: La narrativa de Marcio Veloz Maggiolo*, various critics remark repeatedly on this tendency. Soledad Álvarez, in her discussion of his novel *Materia prima*, mentions how one of the characters is described disparagingly as "a perfumed fag" (marica perfumado).⁹⁸ She more broadly notes how "the novel's masculine characters reproduce the ideology of the period."⁹⁹ Valerio-Holguín notes in turn how in the novel *Ritos de cabaret* there is an ambivalently gendered character (Caminati-Iriarte) who is not negatively portrayed; however, in the case of the two main characters, a father and son, the possibility of the son having homosexual inclinations results in his father encouraging his son's own mother to have sexual relations with him to "save" the son's masculinity. Incest, as long as it is heterosexual, is favorably represented as assuring the son's manhood and rescuing him from the "blemish" of homosexuality.¹⁰⁰

The degree to which homosexuality is thought to "blemish" male subjects is made clear in *Uña y carne* when it is revealed why Daguerre was forced into exile. It is not primarily his political activities but the "denigration" of a violent sexual act that became public knowledge that forces him to leave. Namely, during an arrest Daguerre was violated by his guards with a "plantain" (plátano), and the social implications of this incident devastate him, as he exclaims, "over, there are no more chances, I have nowhere to work. They will laugh at me in the streets, when the rumor spreads they will see me as the ridiculous one, sodomized with a miserable vegetable and turned into a caricature. . . . My brother Boni has told me again that I have no way out. He wants me to leave as soon as possible to wherever."[101] His worry over the public disclosure of this forced sodomy—an act of subordination that effectively destroys his social standing as a man—rather than his political beliefs, is what leads him to flee the country.

Nicasio, in stark contrast to the subordinate masculinity of Daguerre and the failing phallus of El Jefe, is endowed with an infallible member. Nicasio "during a few hours could sustain inexhaustible contact," and his "virile member" was "immense and hot like a paraffin-spilling burning stick," a "mallet of sparkling fire."[102] Nicasio is such an exemplary stud that he allows a male friend, Jardiel, to watch him having sex: "We had bet that I would show him how to make love during an entire night. It was not the first time."[103] Indeed, the novel produces a starkly homosocial world—not devoid of homoerotic undertones—where men compete over their masculinity via women, and in the end those who come out alive and on top are those with the most sexual prowess, the most manly being Nicasio. In turn, those who cannot muster such phallic prowess are presented at the losing end of things: Trujillo is fading from power and almost impotent with a laughably small phallus, and the suspiciously effeminate Daguerre returns to the country in a coffin and is discovered to have had his genitals cut off.

Along with the downgrading of those "tainted" with effeminacy, insufficient virility, and non-heteronormative sexual behaviors in the novel, women are profoundly, and often also violently, marginalized. Women are mainly presented as goods of lesser value to be consumed by men and at times killed off, at least in the male character's fantasy. Notably, Nicasio, the virile superhero, is surrounded by dead women or women he imagines killing. Quite dispassionately he recounts how his decision to betray his political allegiances to accept an offer to collaborate with "Verdaguer" was utterly devastating to his "partner" (compañera) Dorila: "My offer was a sort of bomb in my recent emotional life. Dorila opened her eyes as if going mad. She let herself fall onto a cane rocking chair and began to cry, and cry. I knew that the effect would be like this. Two days later she was hospitalized, she aborted a purple and yellow fetus, and wasted away in a bed of the Altagracia clinic... I decided not to see her anymore. Someone paid for her treatment and even her funeral."[104] His apparent complete lack of emotional involvement with his suffering "compañera" is echoed in scenes in which Nicasio appears to suggest that he killed other female lovers: "There was nothing new about Muriel's death. It was a sole slash on the neck and an ocean of blood on the plastic-covered mattress," and "the firemen and police... found me navigating in an ocean of blood and with the beautiful body of a woman with a slit throat."[105] The narrative eventually reveals these deaths to be mere fantasies when it refers to "the imaginary deaths of Muriel or of Sadia."[106] The retraction of these femicides as mere fantasies is a characteristic textual "innovation" in Veloz Maggiolo's narratives, a move that together with the shifting narrative voices makes it hard to identify one definite perspective endorsed by the text, which makes the novel a moving target for any critique, including this one.

Nonetheless, a persistent problematic pattern crisscrosses this and other dictatorship novels that similarly critique Trujillo by questioning his supposed virility, either through allusions to his impotence or other presumably "anti-masculine" frailties, including certain homosexual proclivities. Given that the Trujillato was deeply anchored in the role of the dictator as the supreme "macho" of the nation, Maggiolo's and other authors' novels seem to be justified in deflating his hyperphallic patina. *Uña y carne*, for example, with its repetitive statements about the dictator's unimpressive phallus, appears to suggest that had Dominicans only known about this reality, the dictatorship would not have had the same power and could have ended much sooner. Yet the novel does not ultimately transcend the myth of phallic power so much as it displaces it onto the main protagonist. The impotence of the dictator contrasts tellingly with the hyperpotency of the protagonist; while the narrative insists on the problematic political valence of the dictator's phallus, the protagonist's exaggerated sexual prowess appears as merely a private and apolitical matter. The auspicious confluence of Nicasio's phenomenal phallus with his privileged political and social position, and conversely the confluence of Daguerre's flawed masculinity with exile, poverty, and death and of Trujillo's small phallus with political decline, however, belie their discreteness and suggest how the narrative remains caught up in the very same phallic politics it wants to decry. In merely redeploying this rhetoric and displacing it from one phallus to another, the much more profound ramifications of the political mobilization of the language of masculinity under the Trujillato and its ongoing social and political implications are missed and uncritically reproduced.

Uña y carne: Memorias de la virilidad continues to trade throughout in the Trujillato's masculinist discursive political economy that limits the novel's visions of resistance and its ability to imagine what is politically thinkable, offering ultimately an impoverished vision of anti-Trujillista and anti-hegemonic politics in general. Of course, it is hardly only Veloz Maggiolo's work that misrecognizes the political import of gender and sexual logics. In various ways and to differing degrees, texts by such canonical Dominican authors as Efraim Castillo, Diógenes Valdez, Armando Almánzar Rodríguez, Pedro Peix, José Alcántara Almánzar, and Avelino Stanley, among others, reiterate and reproduce the very same masculinist ideology officialized and popularized by the Trujillato. Emasculating the supreme patriarch and the country's most virile member, in both senses, becomes a gesture of resistance to his rule of the national family. Their shared tendency to reduce the problem to the figure (or the phallus) of the dictator himself, however, ultimately offers little insight into how and why the Trujillato would impact the country long past the actual death of the dictator.

The Political Limits of Dominican Letrados' Critique

Notions of gender and sexuality are ancillary neither to Dominican dictatorial and post-dictatorial politics nor to Dominican cultural politics. These notions and the political and social relations that they naturalize are also at work in the lasting relationship of Dominican intellectuals and writers with the political sphere and the state. Despite the incisive changes that the cultural sphere underwent after the end of the Trujillato, the material dependency of Dominican letrados on the state has remained remarkably consistent. The effects of this on the Dominican intellectual sphere began to be interrogated by Silvio Torres-Saillant controversially in the 1990s. In a series of articles published in the Dominican Republic, he questioned the ability of Dominican letrados to inhabit a critical stance while being economically dependent on the political establishment. He finds that "the fear of closing doors for oneself hinders the writer in making genuine incursions into the critical field."[107] Torres-Saillant decries how

> the community of letters is ... mediated by the need for harmony with politicians, businessmen, generals, and prelates of power ... for the sake of an official position, a consulting job with the armed forces, or a public relations position in a bank or as the director of the Colonial City trust or one of the other public or private institutions where the clergy has influence.
>
> On the affability with which the learned community interacts with those in power depends who receives the privilege of a literary prize whose cash amount is sufficient to pay their home renovation. Add to this the obtaining of financing for the publication of the next book, the access to newspapers and electronic media to stay relevant in the public sphere and collecting economic resources to support cultural projects or television programs.[108]

There is thus good reason to ask difficult questions about the presumed critical perspectives of Dominican intellectuals and writers who have entered in closer relation with the Dominican state apparatus through government-sponsored positions, prizes, and publication opportunities.[109]

The urgency of asking these questions became widely evident during one of the bigger scandals to reverberate throughout the Dominican cultural sphere. In fact, Torres-Saillant, in a slim volume tellingly titled *El tigueraje intelectual*, addresses extensively this 2002 scandal. The book's preface, by Dominican sociologist Franklin Franco Pichardo, summarizes the affair.

> In April 2002 one of the most unheard-of and unprecedented events took place in the history of Dominican intellectual life. A book edited in 1990, *The Decline of the Dominican Nation* authored by Manuel Núñez, was awarded the National Book Fair Prize, sponsored by the E. León Jimenes company, and, by this virtue, declared "Book of the Year." ... The news of the award of this prize hit like a bomb in national intellectual circles. ... Both Torres Saillant and Avelino Stanley and this author critiqued the awarding of the prize to Núñez's book ... fundamentally, because they considered that the essay in question was profoundly racist with an overload of anti-Haitian prejudices.[110]

Torres-Saillant himself describes Núñez's work as "a work clumsily devoted to vindicating the ideological schemes promoted by the Trujillista historiography."[111]

What was perhaps the most astounding aspect of this cultural drama was the jury that had awarded the prize: three letrados associated loosely with the '60s generation and with leftist political views who had previously critiqued in their own writings these very same ideologies. These writers, who "served as the jury as part of the personnel of the Ministry of Culture," were Marcio Veloz Maggiolo, Andrés L. Mateo, and Carlos Esteban Deive.[112] As Torres-Saillant notes,

> if they in fact participated in the decision, validated with their signatures, one has to interpret their decision as a public retraction of their previously held views.
>
> By rewarding the thick volume of *The Decline of the Dominican Nation* (1990, 2001) by Manuel Núñez, an author known for his anti-Haitian, hispanophile and conservative ardor, the aforementioned colleagues are saying to us that they regret having subscribed to the causes they had formerly defended.[113]

Néstor E. Rodríguez expresses a similar consternation with the fact that "three of the most notorious critical voices of the post-dictatorship era" honored Manuel Núñez's problematic work.[114] He notes how "by awarding the prize to *El ocaso de la nación dominicana*, these intellectuals bestowed recognition upon a work that repeats the same ideas about Dominican cultural identity that they had proposed to dismantle years before."[115] Rodríguez then cites works by these letrados to definitively demonstrate how their writings challenge the very premises of the book that they awarded the national literary prize. This apparent ideological turnaround leaves both Torres-Saillant and Rodríguez, two of the foremost Dominican literary critics and experts, thoroughly stunned.

I want to suggest, however, that what this scandal mainly speaks to is how in the country's political culture and in its cultural politics there are forms of relation and linkage that provide much more binding ties than political positions of the "Right" and the "Left" or any specific ideological stances. Even if without doubt the jury members have moved away from the more radical leftist political beliefs they presumably once held, I doubt that they have gone so far as to align themselves with the Trujillista notions of racial and national identity endorsed by Manuel Núñez. Instead of looking for clues for these authors' "true" political ideologies in their decision, we may do better focusing on the political and social relations that the jury members found themselves in the end more strongly beholden to, namely, the politics of patronage and clientelism in which they are also embedded. As I argue throughout this book, it is imperative to better understand these hierarchical relations that cut across Dominican political, social, and cultural realms and that greatly constrain the kind of horizontal (or equivalential) processes that, according to Laclau, lead to the articulation of strong anti-hegemonic challenges that may reconfigure the social order and the political status quo. These relations' starkly hierarchical orientation in turn continues to be naturalized through the language of masculinity. Dominican letrados' reiteration of these hegemonic notions, not surprisingly, limits their visions of political resistance as much in their fictions as in their interventions as public intellectuals.

This reality helps to explain also why, as Torres-Saillant affirms, even after the end of the Balaguerato and the country's supposed entry into "full" democracy in 1978, "the conservative sector . . . has had the power to name reality and render the opposition mute, which has put serious limits on what the new generation of Dominican scholars has been able to do for their people. . . . There is no question as to who really has the last word."[116] As a result, homogenizing conceptions of Dominican national identity and the racial prejudices underwriting these continue to inform officialist political discourses.[117] As Rodríguez points out, "forty years after the physical disappearance of the tyrant *dominicanidad* is still theorized following this theoretical mold" that relies on "a unifying 'European' *dominicanidad*."[118] Why the often virulently critical and avowedly anti-hegemonic voices of Dominican intelligentsia have not been able to wrest the last word from more conservative voices of *dominicanidad* (and its erasure of Dominican blackness and concurrent anti-Haitianism), I suggest, is related in part to how they themselves remain tied up in political and social relations phrased and naturalized through notions of gender and sexuality, specifically of masculinity and virility, that the they help to continually reproduce. An incisive anti-hegemonic critique of Dominican officialist political discourse and of dominant conceptions of Dominican national cultural identity thus will, by necessity, have to involve a serious interrogation of this gendered rhetoric, as the authors studied in the following chapters strongly impress upon us.

Engendering Resistance

Hilma Contreras's Counternarratives

> In a phallocracy nothing offends as much as the insubordination of women given that it threatens some of the power structure's essential strata.
>
> Silvio Torres-Saillant, *El retorno de las yolas*

In the 1980s new impulses emerged in Dominican literary culture at the same time as long-awaited changes were taking place in the political sphere. As Dominican political "canons" were being dismantled, a new body of literary works was also challenging many of the canonical tendencies traced in the previous chapter.[1] In 1978 Balaguer reluctantly stepped aside and the country experienced a democratic opening that led to the emergence of new cultural, social, and political voices. The literary sphere, for example, saw the emergence of a new group of women writers, including Chiqui Vicioso, Ángela Hernández, Carmen Imbert Brugal, Martha Rivera, and Ylonka Nacidit-Perdomo, among others. It is the latter who is greatly responsible for bringing the reclusive Dominican writer Hilma Contreras (1913–2006) to public attention again in the Dominican Republic.[2] In fact, Contreras's withdrawal from public life in the post-dictatorship period resulted in her moniker "the silent writer," and it was only after becoming the first woman to win the Dominican national literary prize in 2002 that she was catapulted into the public eye and introduced to a wider Dominican audience.

The fact that Contreras was at the time a little-known writer is not only due to her self-imposed isolation in later life, but also, I suspect, the result of her remoteness from the two literary generations that predominated in the Dominican literary sphere at the time: the then dominant and largely male generation of writers of the '60s and the more recent generation of the '80s, in which women played a significant role for the first time.[3] This chapter turns to Hilma Contreras's oeuvre, rather than to the work of this new generation of woman writers, for several reasons. One is that despite Contreras's prominence in the country's literary history after receiving the national literary prize, her work remains vastly understudied. Particularly, her dictatorship novel *La tierra está bramando* (*The Earth Is Roaring*, 1986) is ignored by all aforementioned studies of Dominican dictatorship novels.[4] More importantly for my purposes, Contreras's sparse but several-decade-spanning oeuvre from the late 1930s to the mid-1980s offers a rare persistent engagement with Dominican notions of gender and sexuality, from her earliest published works, including her essay *Doña Endrina de Calatayud* (1955), to her short-story collection *Entre dos silencios* (*Between Two Silences*, 1987), Contreras's most well-known publication.

This chapter thus pays much-needed critical attention to this writer's literary works and suggests how they challenge some of the Dominican literary canon's problematic tendencies discussed at length in the previous chapter. Beginning with Contreras's earliest writings, published during the Rafael L. Trujillo dictatorship, I flesh out Contreras's ongoing and evolving grappling with Dominican gender and sexual formations, including the impact of the Trujillato on these. I then discuss how her critically neglected dictatorship novel, *La tierra está bramando*, ponders, more broadly, the key question of how Dominican cultural practices (including practices of *compadrazgo*/kinship and *chisme*/gossip) that the Trujillato appropriated for its politicized ends may be recuperated to inform new strategies of political resistance.

Hilma Contreras's Modern Fictions

Contreras's oeuvre, while generally thought to be deserving of a prominent place in the country's literary history, remains difficult to place.[5] One adjective that is frequently employed to describe and define Contreras's writing is its resolutely "modern" character. As described in the preceding chapter, Dominican critics often embrace a "modern" literary style as a commendable and progressive feature of Dominican literature. Yet critics' evocations of "modern" can also signify in more ambivalent ways, namely, to indicate that something is not "traditionally" (and properly) Dominican. It is the latter meaning, and the suspicion of foreign influence that motivates it, that in some cases lies behind critics' designation of Contreras's prose style and personal life as "modern."

Contreras's partial upbringing in France is often used to explain her perceived departure from Dominican literary tendencies and social conventions. She lived in France with her Dominican family from 1914 to 1920 (from the age of four to ten) and from 1925 to 1933 (between fifteen and twenty-three).[6] References to her Parisian days frequently mention her friendship with the daughter of the French writer Colette, who is said to have secretly shared her mother's sexually explicit books with Contreras. Such biographical references are often accompanied by a famous picture of a pants-wearing Contreras in France and remarks about how scandalous and uncommon this was for women at the time. These "foreign" influences and "modern" (and implicitly "un-Dominican") gender mores are obliquely called upon to account for why Contreras was unconventional in both her personal life—she never married or had children—and her writing, where she showed a propensity for broaching, albeit with "modesty" (con pudor), "shocking sexual themes" (escabrosos temas sexuales).[7]

This implicit "othering" of Contreras's "modern" literary explorations, including her representations of same-sex desire, by attributing these to foreign (i.e., French) influence, however, is less convincing when one looks more closely at her literary path.[8] Contreras was initiated and deeply embedded in Dominican, not French, literary culture. In fact, her literary career was launched and prefaced by Juan Bosch, arguably the country's preeminent twentieth-century literary figure and the master of the Dominican short story (as well as, of course, a vitally important but less successful political presence for much of the twentieth century). In 1937 Hilma Contreras, using a pseudonym, sent Bosch a story penned by her, and he responded with a letter of encouragement, saying, "I have to tell you, with complete frankness, that you are a writer," and "You have all the likelihood of coming to command the short story form."[9] His main literary advice to her was: "Allow me to advise you one thing: near you there should be, as there are near all of us, many humble people: cooks, maids, poor elderly women, forsaken children.... Delve into these lives, extract that which common people don't see, but that you can see because you are gifted with a writer's faculties.... Don't turn to strange scenarios."[10]

The story that Contreras wrote in response and sent to Bosch, as he had urged her to do, found his approval, and he helped to arrange for its publication. It appeared, accompanied by a note of his, in the Dominican newspaper *Listín Dominical* on July 4, 1937. Contreras's public literary life in the Dominican Republic was hence initiated during the Trujillato in the late 1930s. She published stories in Dominican newspapers and later also in the government-sponsored *Cuadernos Dominicanos*. In the 1940s she studied at the University of Santo Domingo, receiving a degree in philosophy in 1949. From this period on she was close to an important group of Dominican writers and artists. The collection of photos in *Hilma Contreras: Una vida en imágenes, 1913–1993*, assembled by Ylonka Nacidit-Perdomo, attests to Contreras being friendly with the renowned Dominican writers Virgilio Díaz Grullón and Aída Cartagena Portalatín, among others, as well as with the pianist and important cultural figure Aida Bonnelly. These photos also show Contreras actively participating in larger cultural events next to such renowned Dominican writers as Manuel Rueda, Manuel Llanes, and Franklín Mieses Burgos. As Nacidit-Perdomo describes, "around this period Contreras was closely related to Dominican writers and poets and would frequent the Dominican Bookstore's literary gatherings ... the Music Club ... the gatherings at the Dominican Cultural Association, the discussions and interesting parties that take place in the studio of the exquisite pianist Aida Bonnelly."[11] Contreras thus partook in the many activities that developed around the new cultural institutions and events sponsored by the Trujillo regime; indeed, one photograph shows her receiving an award along with other writers during the Trujillo period. However, though she is thought to have written most of her oeuvre during the Trujillato, Contreras published relatively little of her work during this period. Indeed, the literary works for which she would receive national acclaim and eventually the national literary prize would not be published until much later, in the 1980s.[12]

Contreras's first stories, published in various newspapers, reflect her earnest endeavor to follow Bosch's advice. As Sheila Barrios Rosario, in the introduction to the posthumous collection of Contreras's early stories in *La carnada* (The Bait), notes, "the stories in this collection fall within the literary current of Social Realism with a *criollista* tone like many of Juan Bosch's stories, father and precursor of this literary tendency" (in the Dominican Republic).[13] Read together, these early stories give a clinical-report-like account of the ills affecting Dominican society at the time. They also often contain a thinly veiled critique of the Trujillato's damaging impact on the country and on the Dominican people.

The most obvious critique is levied in these stories at rural poverty and class and gender inequities. The stories' characters, all gravely afflicted by poverty, find themselves immobilized in a rigidly stratified social system where there is hardly any hope for change and upward mobility. Notably, this contrasts strongly with the ubiquitous discourse of progress and modernity that the Trujillato was propagating at the time.[14] Set almost entirely in a rural environment (unlike Contreras's later work), conditions of scarcity and the resulting hopelessness create a profoundly suffocating atmosphere that is literalized through the deaths of many of the stories' protagonists in ten of the nineteen stories. For example, in the story "Puñados de dolor" (Loads of Pain), the village is described by the narrator in the following words: "In my village life stagnated, it became covered in mold, and like a yawning swamp it sickened humans who had been born to fight and deploy their energies. Everything good was asleep there."[15] This festering atmosphere, where everything good is "asleep," and the total lack of any form of personal agency are symbolically represented through a character's literal inability to move. In the story the narrator encounters a poor peasant from her village who tells her in colloquial Dominican Spanish that he feels "almost dead. . . . All my bones ache, and the worst of all is that without my ID I cannot go to the town."[16] The peasant cannot leave to get medical help in town because without his social "identity card" he is not allowed to travel. This reference to the unaffordable social identity card is a certain jab at the Trujillo regime, which had established the mandatory identity card (cédula) for all citizens in 1932. Indeed, the narrator's acerbic comment on the situation—"These cruel modern times!"—leaves little doubt that the critique here is not directed simply at rural "backwardness," but rather at the conditions obscured by the facade of progress and the rhetoric of modernity that the Trujillato was wielding at the time.[17] These grim atmospheres and personal fates in Contreras's early stories thereby follow almost to the letter Bosch's direction to portray humble people's lives and avoid turning to "strange scenarios."[18] However soon Contreras would begin to turn precisely to such "strange scenarios," which would come to define her short stories and the said "modern" style for which she is most renowned.

Gender and "Traditional" Notions of Honor

Hilma Contreras's "strange scenes" are in fact often explorations of ingrained Dominican cultural logics and the constraints these place on women's lives in particular. This driving concern is obvious in one of her earliest and perhaps most peculiar published works. The essay *Doña Endrina de Catalayud*, published in 1955, elucidates an episode of the medieval Spanish writer Juan Ruiz's eminent book *Libro de buen amor* (The Book of Good Love). The essay retells the story of the recently widowed doña Endrina de Catalayud, who is being courted by her neighbor don Melón. Intercalated in this retelling of the episode are comments by Contreras that foreground the regulatory effects of notions of honor on women in the Spanish-speaking world.

Doña Endrina is described as greatly afraid of compromising her public reputation, and thus her honor, if she were to speak to or give in to don Melón's pursuit; "she was most worried, above all, about her honor."[19] Contreras describes how "Spanish honor is an extroverted sentiment, meaning that more than anything it tries to preserve the good name. It does not reside so much in the intimate satisfaction of having a clean, impeccable conscience as in retaining public respect."[20] The essay points to the incongruity between doña Endrina's own desires and interest in meeting her suitor and the constraints that the public sphere imposes on such an encounter. After all, as the text emphasizes, "she is not afraid of being alone with her beloved, but of how much of this could emerge in public, generating gossip that would tarnish her good reputation."[21] These constraints of "el qué dirán" (what would others say, or gossip) and the public surveillance of women's private behavior and how these regulate gender relations are the main concern of Contreras's essay.

The text suggests that this notion of honor "was brought by Spain to our American lands," and it meant, "'Keep quiet, preserve your reputation; nothing should leave your house.' For God's sake, nobody shall find out!"[22] The important role of honor as a key cultural logic in Latin American societies since the colonial period has been amply attested to in many scholarly works. For example, Lyman L. Johnson and Sonya Rivera-Lipsett, in *The Faces of Honor: Sex, Shame, and Violence in Colonial Latin America* (1998), describe how "the men and women of colonial Latin America referred to honor constantly in the documents they produced. The culture of honor provided a bedrock set of values that organized their society and their individual lives."[23] Similarly, Caulfield, Chambers, and Putnam affirm, in *Honor, Status, and Law in Modern Latin America* (2005), that "colonial Latin Americans had been all but obsessed with honor and status."[24] Later, in modern Latin America, "although the parameters of patriarchal authority were gradually narrowed, male control over women and women's sexual propriety remained at the core of modern definitions of honor."[25] The particular gendered effects of the working of honor remain, as Pablo Piccato asserts in *The Tyranny of Opinion: Honor in the Construction of the Mexican Public Sphere* (2010), a crucial but understudied terrain: "An entire dimension of life, domesticity, was a terrain for the negotiation of honor between actors.... Those negotiations, I propose, happened at the outer margins of the public sphere, where intimacy revealed itself not as an inherent attribute of family life but as the product of public opinion's judgment."[26] Piccato suggests here, then, how private life—domesticity and intimacy—as a principal domain of women's lives, was strongly determined and shaped by public opinion, gossip, and the forms of surveillance produced by them.

Importantly, this regulatory force of public opinion, of what some scholars call the fear of "el qué dirán," is embedded in a power matrix that does not function primarily as a top-down hierarchical mechanism of control. Rather, as scholarship on the function of "honor" in Latin America points out, it is a mechanism that is laterally reinforced by equals and peers, rather than primarily from powers above. In modern Latin America, "as was true in colonial times, individual struggles to restore injured honor or maintain status were most often between equals or almost-equals."[27] Teresita Martínez-Vergne, in *Nation and Citizen in the Dominican Republic, 1880–1916* (2005), similarly suggests how maintaining an honorable reputation was a laterally, rather than hierarchically, enforced cultural logic in the Dominican Republic in the late nineteenth century. She describes how in a "context of scarcity" much depended on "a constant reaffirmation of personal standing ... for example, credit at the local store, a neighbor's help in times of illness, a little cash for an emergency purchase, and other small, material advantages."[28] In fact, "notions of appropriate behavior, then, when invoking honor/respect/decency, did not emanate from the upper classes or from public officials and impose themselves violently on the popular classes but rather were shaped by a 'language of argument' between equals at the top and at the bottom and between the self-proclaimed models of bourgeois values and their 'inferiors.'"[29] Contreras's essay echoes this finding and suggests how it is primarily "la gente" (the people) who enforce social norms; it is what "la gente" might think and say and the effects this would have on her reputation in the community that doña Endrina fears most. Women's lives, the essay suggests, are caught up in ongoing concerns about their public standing that hinges in large part on the scrutiny of their private behavior. It is such continuities between the public and private spheres, rather than primarily their presumable separation, that determine and constrain women's experiences, according to Contreras.

The Trujillato's Reinventions of "Tradition"

Contreras's essay *Doña Endrina* addresses the gendered constraints produced by notions of honor with roots in the colonial past. In turn, Contreras's writings about the present moment, during the time of the Trujillato, suggest how the dictatorship reconfigured these regulatory mechanisms, and the impact that the dictatorship had on Dominican cultural logics, forms of relations, and notions of gender. The story "Viernes Santo sangriento" (Bloody Holy Friday) is one of four stories in Contreras's first published short-story collection, *4 Cuentos* (Four Stories) (1953), the only other monograph published by Contreras during the Trujillato.[30] In this story, the female narrator befriends a young woman, María Luisa, during her Easter vacation in a rural town. María Luisa is strongly at odds with her father, called "the jackal," who is also an "official" occupying "a good position" in the government.[31] The father is a terribly oppressive figure said to be at least indirectly responsible for the deaths of María Luisa's brother and mother, who died "content with breaking their ties" with him.[32] Familial relations, rather than providing close bonds and protection, are suffused here with terror and detachment.

Importantly, the story suggests that the terror of the father at home is contiguous with his oppressive role in the public sphere as a high-level official. María Luisa literally lives with the tyrant in her own house. She describes living with her father as being locked "in an ivory tower, with two windows that symbolized her life."³³ The tower literalizes the hierarchical and constraining social structure in which María Luisa is caught up and also speaks to her profound sense of isolation. The tower's two windows in turn symbolize her two "outlooks" in life: "Here I live—she explained to me—painfully distended between the two horizons. Here, a bit of sky, grey, hazy, or furiously blue, who spies on me through the anemic eye of the church.... In contrast, from the other window, look what mountains! Distant, blue, like a promise of true life on the other side of their crests. It's wonderful! Here my life as it is imposed on me; over there, my inextinguishable desire to transcend."³⁴ The window represents both the opening through which the watchful eye of the church penetrates into the protagonist's life, but it also signals the possibility and promise of a different perspective and a freer life.³⁵ Indeed, Contreras's stories, as I will show, consistently explore what spaces and dissenting perspectives can survive on the margins of a strongly oppressive reality and escape the grasp of its hegemonic logics.

The story unfolds during Holy Friday and presents the church and the oppressive paternal figure as coconspirators. The two new female friends watch the Holy Friday procession, and María Luisa notes with perturbation the participation of her father: "Look!—María Luisa pointed out—. He even deceives the Virgin!... Turned into a bearer of the saint being carried, her father, the jackal, the man of short-cuts, was marching with the procession."³⁶ The complicity of the patriarchal political figure and the Catholic Church tellingly echoes the reality of the Trujillato at the time. This context is only thinly veiled in Contreras's story under a distancing move: unlike the other stories, this one is said to be taking place in Europe. "Bloody Holy Friday. Women and children cannoned down, burnt cities, homes destroyed by bombs, and the men who kill each other, persecute and destroy each other like wild animals.... Holy Friday, and they kill each other in Europe."³⁷ This is the only geographical reference through which suddenly this story becomes a denunciation of war-ravaged Europe. The story continues with the following outcry: "Attacks, insults, abuses, injustices, crimes.... And while the few are horrified, the majority applaud and bet as if it were a cockfight. How many admirers of brute force accompany the Holy Burial? How many liars? How many slanderers? How many thieves?"³⁸ The hypocrisy of the majority and the applauding and betting on what is happening are hardly apt descriptions of Europeans' reactions to war-torn times. Rather, the reference to the cockfight, a popular practice in the Caribbean and Latin America, reveals how the story alludes to another violent and oppressive "local" force: the Trujillo regime and its diligent administrators, including those of the Dominican Catholic Church.[39]

This geographic displacement allows Contreras to articulate an unusually sharp critique of political oppression and paternalist power while living and writing under the Trujillato. Moreover, this permits the narrative to imagine an effective act of resistance to this oppressive power. The same night of the procession, the narrator dines with her new friend María Luisa and her tyrannical father. During the dinner the father argues "with an exasperating stubbornness.—May the weak one perish! May the just one be stoned, dragged, crucified if he disturbs! What the hell, this is the century of force . . ."[40] Vis-à-vis this violent strongman creed, "his daughter is overcome with a quiet indignation"; however, the narrator herself reacts much more virulently: "I yell at don Milo right in his face."[41] He wants to respond in kind, but "from his too-full mouth food falls out of the tense corners. The grey eyes bulge out of their sockets, he hurls a snort, and goes quiet."[42] He appears to have fallen asleep at the table, but later the two women realize that he in fact had died. The narrator's bold vocal protest here is able to bring down successfully the oppressive patriarchal tyrant. Contreras's story thus literalizes Torres-Saillant's epigraph: "In a phallocracy nothing offends as much as the insubordination of women given that it threatens some of the power structure's essential strata." The very literal effectiveness of this act appears both as a form of wishful thinking (someone just had to confront Trujillo loudly and directly) and as prescient, given that the Trujillato was fundamentally constructed around a hyperbolic discourse of masculinity that structured Dominican political and social relations in fundamental ways. In this sense the story rightfully suggests that countering the regime with a language based on very different, that is, antipatriarchal, terms constitutes a key antihegemonic strategy. Yet this challenge and act of resistance in "Viernes Santo sangriento" has to rely on a strategic displacement of the plot to Europe. Given that this story was written and published during the Trujillato, all else would have certainly posed a grave risk for the writer.

In contrast, Contreras's story "La ventana" (The Window), another of the four stories of the collection *4 cuentos*, published during the Trujillato, is clearly set in the Dominican Republic. "La ventana" is one of author's most renowned and anthologized stories, later re-published in her celebrated collection *Entre dos silencios* (1987). "La ventana" also offers a meditation on how to resist under oppressive circumstances, but here the female protagonists who live under the terror of the Trujillo regime have to seek out other, less directly confrontational strategies. The story takes place at night in an urban setting; as the first-person narrator describes, it was "a night as clear as a child's gaze, on a small, silent, floating terrace, with the breath of the ocean on us. We were four women in four towers of air."[43] Each woman inhabits a "tower," again alluding to individuals' insulation during the Trujillato; however, rather than ivory towers, as in the previous story, these "towers" are made of air and evoke thereby a less constrictive space. The women on this "floating terrace," largely unmoored from their social surroundings, commune with each other not through words but silently through music: "We were listening to music: the music of Liszt and our own; the one that each of us has in her blood, audible only to our own pulse."[44] In this instance the absence of speech is not a moment of repressive muting but a productive moment of silence that enables other, highly intimate forms of communication and linkage between these women.

As they are peacefully immersed together in these layers of silence and music, suddenly "a sharp ray of light cuts the air," emerging from "a window slit opened in the thick colonial wall, a hybrid hollow somewhere between being a window and an inverted skylight."[45] In the window appears an "implausibly naked torso," and on the outside "someone asks with a manly voice—Ready?"[46] The person inside answers, "—Yes—. . . but wait a moment; it's my hour to love"; it was, the story proceeds, "his hour, like all the hours of his tonsured life. As if a circle of tonsured hair would be sufficient to pigeonhole a life; an entire long life of a hairy man!"[47] The scene reveals here the illicit nocturnal encounter of a religious ("tonsured") man with another man. The female narrator notably refrains from making this private scene of same-sex desire a public concern or scandal, as she says, "I did not want to penetrate his sin or his death so much. . . . The emotion made me withdraw the eyes from that white wound."[48] Rather than being scandalized, the protagonist shares a distant but knowing understanding of this scene as she states, "Without looking I knew that in the window suspended in the luminous silent atmosphere, a robe whose time had come was turning red."[49] As in many other stories, the emotional tenor is reflected in the physical atmosphere accompanying the scene (rather than through characters' explicit statements). Here in this "luminous silent atmosphere," suddenly "there was a tremor in the sky. In slow steps the stars began to descend; little by little they stretched into a vertiginous fall, a long, unending rain fell on the earth."[50] While the trembling gestures to the significance of what is happening, the sky is not hostile or aggressive; instead, the "rain of stars" suggests that something extraordinary rather than sinful is taking place.

A sudden nearby light of one of the women lighting a cigarette on the terrace draws the narrator away from this scene of male same-sex desire. The window disappears and the lights have gone out, and one woman remarks, "—Better—... Now we are really alone."[51] The story hence presents two separate but related realms: the floating terrace with the four women, and the window revealing the priest's homoerotic desires. These two scenes share the silent night and these characters' need to withdraw from the surrounding reality. The relation between the two is neither antithetical nor tense; rather, the women are in a position to observe and even foretell what will happen. The story thereby speaks to a shared experience underlying these two scenes, including the need to escape the ever-present gaze of the dictatorship and its verbose discourse of hypermasculinity.[52]

Contreras's writing explores how silence and withdrawal from speech may persist as the only space of resistance under the all-encompassing discursive web of the Trujillo regime. Notably, Contreras's father, Darío Contreras, played a key role in cementing the Trujillato's gender discourse during the dictatorship. A well-known Dominican physician (from whom Hilma Contreras was estranged after he divorced her mother), he published one of the Trujillato's most important treatises about gender in 1942, the "Mensaje a la mujer dominicana" (Message to the Dominican Woman).[53] As Melissa Madera describes, "like his French counterparts, [Darío] Contreras promoted a conservative rhetoric of pronatalism, which promoted procreation as a national obligation and heralded patriarchal authority, maternal virtue, fecundity and traditionalism. He also followed other pronatalists in criticizing feminism and liberalism for producing 'modern' women who abandoned their prescribed domestic roles as wives and mothers."[54] Interestingly, it is this highly conservative doctrine that has become equated with "traditional" Dominican gender roles but that in fact emerged under the influence of outside, French models rather than Hilma Contreras's writings and explorations of Dominican gender and sexuality.

In fact, Contreras addresses Dominican gender and sexual formations in highly context-specific ways. While she hardly suggests that constraining gender and sexual logics were invented by the Trujillato and did not exist beforehand in the Dominican Republic, her writing nonetheless attests to a notable shift occasioned by the Trujillato in how gender (and other) logics were prescribed and regulated. In *Doña Endrina* Contreras shows how in colonial and modern Latin America gendered and sexual constraints were produced by how women's private and intimate lives were regulated through notions of honor that were policed by public opinion, gossip, and other practices of surveillance among equals. These communally regulated relations among equals were, however, reconfigured by the starkly hierarchical power structure of the Trujillato. This results, in these stories, in a sense of individual isolation that, tellingly, leaves the protagonists feeling as if they were secluded in a tower, a strong symbolic evocation of the phallic structure of power in which they are caught up. Under these conditions of constraint and repression, the story "La ventana" suggests how forms of knowledge and communication that have not been completely absorbed and appropriated by the dictatorial discursive system offer a much-needed escape from its hegemonic logics.

Resistant Remainders of Dominican Cultural Traditions

Contreras's only novel, *La tierra está bramando* (1986), further explores the question of what strategies of resistance can emerge from the margins of the dictatorship's hegemonic political and cultural logics and outside its masculinist and hypersexualized imaginary. In fact, the novel can be read as an extended meditation on Dominican letrados' possible and impossible forms of response and resistance to the Trujillo regime. *La tierra está bramando* unfolds in an urban, middle-class setting in Santo Domingo, and its protagonists are a group of educated young women and men of letters with close ties to the university. The novel takes place during the later years of the Trujillo dictatorship when state violence and surveillance reached levels that had not been seen before.[55] At that time, as Lauren Derby describes, "the culture of fear was strikingly asphyxiating for all, although the middle-class residents of Santo Domingo suffered perhaps more than most due to the fact that the capital city was the central hub of police and SIM intelligence gathering."[56] The following scene speaks to the toxic effects of this particularly asphyxiating climate in the capital.

> Doña Eugenia answered the entrance's ringing doorbell. Times had changed. Before, the door of the houses' living rooms remained open. The visitor entered freely. If there was no one in the living room, he would let out a loud "Greetings!" or a "Good Day" or "Good Afternoon," depending on the time, so that someone would come to greet him. Now, for fear of thieves milling around or to have time to find a safe haven from the Secret Police, the doors were barred with security locks, chains and bolts.[57]

This passage indicates how the deep distrust and suspicion produced by the Trujillato had profound effects on Dominican community relations, leading to their deterioration and to individual isolation behind closed doors.

The protagonist, Eugenia, is a middle-aged, educated woman, who works as a translator and lives with her mother and her young niece, a university student. Their suffocating and isolating reality makes Eugenia especially cherish her regular get-togethers with a group of (mostly male) confidants with whom she shares an interest in literature and music. Her mother, however, is gravely concerned about Eugenia speaking "imprudently" at "one of those literary get-togethers."[58] She informs her daughter that "there are rumors," and that she should know that "meetings behind closed doors raise suspicions."[59] The once relatively harmless practice of gossip, "chisme," has become a powerful social weapon under the Trujillato with possibly devastating consequences. Indeed, at their next get-together the protagonist and her friends note that a regime informer is shadowing them. When Eugenia leaves the meeting, the informant follows her and calls her by her name. When she turns around he reminds her that she knows him; he is "Toño, the messenger from the Diego María Motors Company." He then tells her, "with all due respect," to not continue meeting with the group, because "it is not advisable for you, I am telling you, those guys have a record."[60] This scene reflects how the regime relied on local networks of espionage and drew from people within the community to report on neighbors, friends, and even family members. However, the narrative also suggests, by having Toño the regime spy respectfully warn and protect the protagonist, that communal ties can also still work for opposite ends and interfere with regime-loyalty. As discussed in my first chapter, historians such as Richard Lee Turits and Lauren Derby describe how the Trujillato's iron grip on Dominican society was intimately linked to its appropriation and politicization of Dominican cultural logics to control and elicit the consent of the population. While Contreras's novel attests to this appropriation of Dominican cultural logics by the dictatorship, and its destructive effects on them, it also reveals how these cultural logics can still be mobilized for acts of resistance to the regime.

In fact, *La tierra está bramando* insistently argues that any opposition to the Trujillato needs to rely on autochthonous political strategies derived from the local cultural context rather than from political models imported from abroad. At first Eugenia considers that the only form of resistance to the dictatorship's oppression can be silence and remaining on the margins of its grasp, similar to what we saw in "La ventana." The protagonist thus recoils in her own silence: "I live aside from disputes because already a long time ago I sewed my mouth shut. I don't sing or talk."[61] Again, in the context of the Trujillato, where any discourse has become dangerous and overdetermined by the regime's propaganda, silence and music take on a particular relevance for the protagonist. The novel describes, for example, how Eugenia and other group members silently listen together to music: "Each was a vibrating silence, isolated and united at the same time with the emotion of the others. Eugenia felt like a sponge that expanded immensely when becoming saturated with music. . . . *If music is the heart of life*, then that night the group entered it reaching for *an infinite moment* the plenitude of their own lives."[62] Similar to the scene in "La ventana," silence and music enable an affective communion and intimate linkage that are no longer possible through words in a society where all discursive spaces are zealously patrolled by a virulently repressive regime.

The protagonist passionately wants to protect this space on the margins of the regime's reach. She defends it from her mother's concerns and protests the changes that the group wants to make. The abduction (and later death) of another friend, Pablo, at the hands of the regime leads her friends to create a new political organization, which they ask Eugenia to join: " . . . join us, enroll in PACOIN . . . the Independent Communist Party."[63] Eugenia reacts with disdain and scoffs at the name PACOIN, exclaiming, "Abbreviations, what an obsession with abbreviations!" and she laughs at the idea of it being an "independent" party: "An independent communist party. Of what or whom? Nonsense."[64] She in turn affirms, "I am truly *independent*," and exits the meeting.[65] Eugenia's disdainful response reveals a deep-seated skepticism of the usefulness of political ideology perceived as foreign to the local context. Those who are involved in forming PACOIN, including her young niece Genita, are described as inexperienced and imprudent: "They are very young, they are a bit aimless."⁶⁶ The novel's account of these young students' organizing appears to allude to the brief period of time when the Trujillato allowed a few new political groups to form, shortly after the end of World War II, among them the Partido Socialista Popular (Popular Socialist Party) and the Juventud Democrática (Democratic Youth), in which many university students participated.⁶⁷

This formal politicization of her group of friends is mourned by Eugenia as a devastating loss of the space they had created away from the regime's grasp: "With this PACOIN business they have fatally wounded our get-togethers. Someone had come up with the disastrous, perhaps *redeeming*, idea to spiritually decapitate us. Now begins the insecurity, the fear of treason, that they bust us before we flourish."⁶⁸ She sadly notes, "I will feel mutilated without these beautiful hours during which I forgot the sinister shudders of the world, and I consoled myself thinking that in life there were still pure emotions without the smell of gunpowder or with an aftertaste of blood."⁶⁹ Eugenia mourns the loss of this shared space in which close and trusting relations with others were still possible, even if often clothed in silence or mediated by music.

Thus, at first the protagonist considers any form of speaking out and open political protest under this regime as always already futile. Later on, however, when the well-being of group members and those close to them is threatened, a more direct engagement with the political situation becomes unavoidable even for her. The narrator becomes in fact much more responsive when a different political strategy is put forward by two friends, who decide to separate from PACOIN to form "a responsible party, with a *realist vision* of the country's problems."⁷⁰ While Eugenia previously recoiled from an ideological program that she considered incommensurate with their lived reality, she is willing to partake in a political group that responds more directly to the specificities of the Dominican context. The program of this new group advocates, more simply, a "respect for human rights, freedom of assembly, freedom to dissent, of movement, the right of the masses for a better standard of living."⁷¹ This political vision thus approximates more a liberal and social democratic (but not communist or socialist) political program that the new group wants to convey to the Dominican people.

Though Eugenia supports this approach, she asks how they would put these ideas forth to the Dominican people. The organizer responds, "Well, making it public."[72] Eugenia answers to this with irony, "—Oh, yes?—... Shouting it in the public squares?"[73] She knows, as they do, that such a direct public expression of dissent would be an effective death sentence. Ultimately, they come up with a much more ingenious strategy. One morning the entire city wakes up with thousands of fliers stuck everywhere with gum; "they had stuck them with chewing gum on park benches, on tree trunks, on the doors of homes, of churches, on the traffic signs, on the gates of public buildings."[74] The general public can hardly contain its glee, "after the first moment of astonishment passed, many almost drowned in the effort of having to contain their laughter."[75] This act of defiance is so successful precisely because it works within and against the constraints of the regime. The action is not tied by name to a particular author or group that could easily be persecuted, but rather it is an anonymous act that defies publicly and vociferously a regime whose vigilant discursive control was so essential for its effective functioning. The novel thereby endorses a political strategy that is thought to respond better to the local political reality over and above the activities of PACOIN, whom the protagonist dismisses as "crazies" (unos descabellados).[76]

Though the anonymous political counterstrategy of the "gummed fliers" (los papeles achiclados) is a resounding success, the response from the regime is immediate, and it begins to round up "all those suspected of nonconformity."[77] The military arrests many young men, including the boyfriend of the protagonist's young niece, in the hope that one of them will eventually lead them to the fliers' authors. This mass arrest of many young people leads to another protest, this time organized by religious women, "pious women [who] . . . traversed different sectors of the city" to mobilize other women under the guise of collecting donations for the repair of a chapel.[78] On the indicated day, about two hundred women gather and begin to march through the city toward the government palace to ask for the release of their imprisoned sons, brothers, and other relatives.[79] Eventually, they are stopped by a military truck with soldiers, and, given the defiance of the women, the sergeant orders the soldiers to shoot. However, among the soldiers there is "a shadow of annoyance in the face of many. They did not shoot to kill. The bullets, nonetheless, in ricocheting off the walls had wounded the legs of a dozen young women."[80] The injuries are superficial, and the women continue toward the government palace, where they successfully hand over their petition to a government official. The president in response decides to initially fulfill the demands of the women. He orders, "Let some of them go tomorrow to calm those feminists," but adds that the political prisoners will be granted "a short night with the family"; thereafter, "these idiots disappear from circulation and good-bye subversive fliers."[81] This political protest and its conditional success strategically build on the cultural logic of women as inherently apolitical subjects. It is this predominant view of women as defenseless and politically harmless that enables their act of public disobedience that would have been deadly for any male subject at the time.[82]

These women's resistance strategy notably echoes similar strategic uses of femininity for political ends in Latin America. The women's public protest in front of the government palace, and their demand to have their children and relatives released from prison share many facets with the public protests of the Argentine mothers of the disappeared during Argentina's Dirty War (1976–1983). As Diana Taylor describes, "the Madres attempted to manipulate the maternal image that was already overdetermined by the State" and claimed "that it was precisely their maternal responsibilities that took them to the plaza in search of their children."[83] Contreras's novel similarly suggests how Dominican cultural logics can work both ways: as tools of oppression at the hands of the Trujillo regime, but also as practices of resistance to it.

The novel speaks also to the resistance potential of another key social mechanism and cultural logic in the novel, the so-called *compadrazgo/comadrazgo* system. The regime's sinister plan, to first set free and then capture again all male political dissenters, is uncovered beforehand through the alliances produced by the *compadragzo/comadrazgo* system. The son of a gardener of an important general overhears a discussion of this plan and informs his *madrina* (godmother), the mother of one of the prisoners, of it. This is not the only instance in which social relations and allegiances produced by the *compadrazgo* system prove to be stronger than allegiances to the regime and mitigate some of its brutal force. Eugenia turns twice for help to her own mother's *compadre*, a high-level military captain, and each time he averts a fatal outcome. For example, the first time they call upon Captain Mirano (Capitán Mirano) when Eugenia's niece, along with other student protesters, is corralled by police on the university campus. Eugenia urges her mother to call her *compadre* to ask him to intervene. Shortly after, as the police already begin to shoot at the students, Captain Mirano is able to defuse the situation and stop the imminent bloodshed. This and other scenes suggest how the social system of co-parenthood creates strong ties of loyalty and kinship that can still work to thwart the oppressive grasp of the dictatorship.[84] While the Trujillato extensively used prevalent practices of *compadrazgo* to ensure loyalty for itself, including by the dictator becoming a godparent to an endless number of Dominican children, this cultural practice can also, as Contreras's novel suggests, be employed for opposite ends.

Ultimately, however, these strategies of resistance are not sufficient to counter, much less topple, the dictatorship. At the end of the novel, the released political prisoners gather and barricade themselves in the colonial zone. Eugenia in turn finds herself walking alone near the ocean, until a weapon-brandishing soldier demands to know what she is doing. She provocatively answers, "I was looking at . . . a UFO," alluding to the stark unreality of the country's situation; the soldier furiously responds, "A UFO! This crazy woman, make her move. Move."[85] The protagonist heads home but then suddenly decides otherwise: "At the first corner I turned to the right and began to run with all my strength, propelled by desperation toward the rebel zone."[86] In the last instance—since the novel ends with this scene—she decides to head toward the political rebels to what is an almost certain death. If the ending suggests in some ways that the ethically correct answer for Dominican letrados under these conditions would have been to choose resistance, it also clearly reveals how deadly this choice would have been.

Contreras's Challenges to the Canon of Dominican Dictatorship Novels

This novel's meditation on the stance of Dominican intellectuals and on possible strategies of resistance during the Trujillato notably sets it apart from most other Dominican dictatorship novels. As López-Calvo notes, this body of work "does not usually provide ways to combat dictatorship; instead, it tends to concentrate on the recreation of the last days of the Era, the events that brought it to an end, and the sociopolitical consequences that followed."[87] Though Contreras's novel also unfolds toward the end of the Trujillato, unlike many other narratives it does not present the actual events that occurred, that is, Trujillo's assassination. In contrast to the many salacious accounts of the dictator's death, this novel forgoes the famous final episode of the dictator's life and explores instead what political possibilities of resistance were or could have been available to urban middle-class intellectuals and writers such as Hilma Contreras herself. Other authors who lived and wrote during the dictatorship have rarely reflected critically in their works on their own position during the regime. In turn, the writers who have produced the bulk of literary works about the Trujillato tend to be younger authors, who are saved, by virtue of their age, from having to face such difficult questions themselves (as we see in Veloz Maggiolo's *De abril en adelante*). The works of these writers who came of age at the end of or after the Trujillato tend to represent Dominican intellectuals and letrados during the dictatorship simply as sycophants without much moral complexity. Of this tendency, Efraim Castillo's novel *El personero* (1999) is perhaps the most conspicuous example.

Such canonical representations of letrados' complete submission tend to go hand in hand, as discussed earlier, with the fixation on the figure of the dictator himself. The dictator emerges in these literary accounts as an incarnation of irrational evil on which the (primarily male) authors focus their literary gaze with repulsion and at times with a thinly veiled fascination. Contreras's dictatorship novel, in contrast, desists not only from fixating on the dictator himself but also turns away from the hypersexualized language of masculinity of the dictatorship echoed in many Dominican post-dictatorship works about the Trujillato. Indeed, in comparison to her sexually charged short stories in *Entre dos silencios*, published just a year apart from *La tierra está bramando*, the novel is remarkably chaste, and overt sexuality is notably absent. The novel mainly offers the memory of a mostly platonic romance between the female protagonist and a former professor who had to leave the country. Their relationship is carried out in the novel largely through an epistolary exchange that remains ancillary to the principal plotline. Moreover, the protagonist's memories of the professor and the letters they write to each other, intercalated in the narrative, are tinged with sexually detached romanticism, and the only moments of physical proximity are described with an utterly restrained *pudor* (modesty): "So in the twilight hour, a beautiful afternoon in April, they looked into each other's eyes in a different way. He came a bit closer. He kissed a virgin mouth whose sweetly craving lips did not know how to answer the eager kiss that fluttered over them."[88] The narrator's ethereal and intellectually driven love contrasts with the more fleshly observations she herself makes throughout the narrative, albeit about other women. Eugenia more than once observes her newly arrived niece with physical candor, describing Genita as a "pretty girl ... with her flexible thighs, her well-rounded little breasts under the polo shirt and her warm skin of the extraordinary color of Christmas hazelnut."[89] And, curiously, Eugenia's romantic reminiscences about the absent Agustín tend to be interrupted by her niece barging in.[90] Her niece is not the only woman who incites a fleshly appreciation in the protagonist. She also remarks about a friend's mother, how she "appreciated her still young body of tight, harmonious flesh."[91] This language of female sensuality and general circumvention of a heterosexual imaginary and language (beyond chaste romanticism) is a significant evasion, not only of the Trujillato's discourse of heterosexual virility, but also of the excessive heterosexual and often homophobic sexual detailing in many canonical Dominican dictatorship novels.[92]

These notable divergences I believe help to explain why Contreras's novel is so noticeably absent from existing critical studies of Dominican dictatorship novels. Nonetheless, this omission remains perplexing to me, given that Contreras figures as one of only two women writers included in the anthology *El fantasma de Trujillo: Antología de cuentos sobre el tirano y su Era* (2006), which clearly signals how she is thought to pertain to this body of work in the Dominican literary sphere. Against such critical omissions, I insist on the importance of including Contreras's novel in the corpus of Dominican dictatorship novels and on the lasting urgency of the issues that it foregrounds. In fact, the question of to what degree Dominican cultural practices and forms of relation that were appropriated, politicized, and reconfigured by the Trujillo regime escaped its hegemonic grasp and can be recuperated for anti-hegemonic ends remains a pressing question. Importantly, the novel does not present the cultural practices underwriting the various acts of resistance it describes as "traditional" throwbacks frozen in time or forever "spoiled" by the Trujillato. Rather, *La tierra está bramando* represents these as malleable cultural practices, open for redeployment in ways that can never be entirely preordained. This nuanced exploration of cultural logics and their political potential remains highly relevant today, long past the end of the dictatorship.

Indeed, Hilma Contreras's exploration of the anti-hegemonic political potential of Dominican cultural logics resonates in surprising ways with political developments that were unfolding in the country just before she published this novel, in 1986. In the early 1980s massive popular protests began to erupt in response to worsening living conditions (partially the result of IMF policies) that constituted the strongest challenge by the Dominican people to the political status quo since the 1965 revolution.[93] The popular movement that emerged was shaped around strategies of resistance similar to those explored in Contreras's novel: it built on communal linkages that were horizontally rather than hierarchically structured, it drew from cultural logics that allowed women to emerge as strong agents, and it articulated shared demands that were oriented not by preformulated political ideologies, but rather by pressing real-life needs that brought people together. Yet this popular movement and its alternative logics soon came to a violent clash with the hegemonic forces of the political sphere; this resulted in a number of deaths, and ultimately the protests and the popular movement, just like Contreras's protagonists, would run up in vain against the powers that be, especially once Balaguer returned to the presidency in 1986.

The question of what cultural and social forces may challenge more successfully the hegemonic social order and the political status quo would be asked again with renewed urgency at the turn of the century in the Dominican literary sphere. The remainder of this book thus turns to this new generation of writers that came of age during the second Balaguer government (1986–1996) and resisted the proscriptions of its hegemonic political, social, and literary formations in part by drawing from new global repertoires.

Dedication

This chapter is dedicated to Ylonka Nacidit-Perdomo.

Still Loving *Papi*

Globalized Dominican Subjectivities in the Novels of Rita Indiana Hernández

In 1996 a new president took office in the Dominican Republic and seemed to promise a significant break with the previous government (1986–1996) of the now very old, feeble, and almost blind Balaguer. In contrast, Leonel Fernández was relatively young, educated, New York–raised, and thus also part of the Dominican diaspora. Fernández's political discourse avidly reinforced this sense of a new beginning in Dominican politics; he stylized himself emphatically as a "modern" president and vociferously embraced neoliberal economic policies and modern technology as ways to fast-track the country's *progreso*, all encapsulated in his government's ubiquitous forward-looking slogan "E' pa'lante que vamos"—"We Are Moving Forward."

Past political patterns, however, asserted themselves quickly under the "modern" Fernández presidency. This continuity became evident early on when the new president decided not to investigate the blatant corruption cases from the Balaguer years, and when his government got caught up in the same clientelist and corrupt patterns that had long predominated in Dominican politics. As Michiel Baud asserts, the government remained "anchored in a political culture in which clientelism and authoritarianism played an important role. Fernández could not break with these cultural ties."[1] The important role of such "cultural ties" indicates how paying attention to formal political processes alone misses how cultural forces contribute to shaping the political landscape in the Dominican Republic (as they do elsewhere).

Specifically, what is overlooked thereby is how understandings and expectations that have become "common sense" among Dominicans continuously reinforce prevailing relations between the populace and the political realm. These relations, I argue, help contribute to reproduce the practices of clientelism and corruption that are generally considered responsible for the country's often perplexing political stagnancy vis-à-vis its dramatic economic, social, and cultural transformations over the past decades.[2] Scholars frequently remark upon this apparent paradox: while developments closely associated with rapid modernization and globalization—including urbanization, migration, tourism, and free trade zones—are seen to have led to a profound transformation of the country's society, culture, and economy, the political sphere has remained notably stagnant.

This chapter considers this paradox of persisting political patterns, reinforced by certain "common sense" conceptions, existing alongside processes of rapid modernization and globalization through the lens of the literary work of Rita Indiana Hernández, a key figure of the generation of writers that emerged at the turn of the century in the Dominican Republic.

Gender in the Global Age

Among one of the most notable Dominican cultural transformations is the "great explosion of media and consumer culture" during the twentieth century.[3] As Jesse Hoffnung-Garskof describes, in *A Tale of Two Cities: Santo Domingo and New York after 1950* (2008), "after midcentury, Dominican middle and lower classes learned of the practical allure of automobiles, household products, electronics, and leisure goods. They grew attentive to the symbolic value of brand names, hairstyles, clothing, and commercial media. What Dominicans, even those of modest means, owned, wore, watched, or heard became progressively more important in defining their everyday lives."[4] This eruption of consumer culture reshaped Dominican society in ways that would have important political implications as well. For example, Dominican sociologist Laura Faxas describes with great concern, in *El mito roto: Sistema político y movimiento popular en la República Dominicana, 1961–1990* (2007), how "the predominance of behaviors oriented toward the private sphere" resulted in individuals "moving from a feeling of communal belonging to one of exclusion, of nonintegration, and the criteria for what is social success changed."[5] The individualization of survival strategies in an increasingly consumption-oriented society further encumbered the possibility of citizens successfully making collective demands on the state and fed directly into the individualizing mechanisms (or, in Laclau's terms, the differential relations) that help to sustain clientelism. The radical opening of the country to outside forces and the dramatic transformations this has resulted in have thus ultimately helped to further compound existing political patterns rather than proffering a decisive challenge to them.

New globalizing impulses, without doubt, profoundly impacted and transformed Dominican society and culture, including predominant notions of gender and sexuality. However, these reconfigurations have been uneven and at times paradoxical-seeming; they do not simply follow a straightforward path toward greater gender equality. For example, developments that are often associated with decreasing gender inequality, including women's participation in the labor market, have not unequivocally led to a significant overall reconfiguration of gender norms. The strong embrace of neoliberal policies has prompted "the incorporation of women in the labor market, especially in the free trade zones industries. In 1992 between 60 percent and 64 percent of the workers in the free trade zones were women."[6] Yet the feminization of the Dominican workforce has had at best an ambivalent impact on gender relations. Faxas suggests that "with . . . the incorporation of women into the workforce . . . we can see the questioning of male authority in the household and a certain restructuring of male–female relations."[7] However, she concludes that, ultimately, "even if an economically independent woman has achieved a greater autonomy and a new self-reappraisal and respect from others, she has not been able to erase the force of the machista tradition. Therefore, in the barrios, the masculine figure continues to dominate women."[8] Women's employment and their greater economic independence have reconfigured women's lives, but they have not brought about a significant change in larger gender patterns, nor have they unsettled hegemonic notions of femininity and masculinity. For example, Ramonina Brea and Isis Duarte conclude in their study *Entre la calle y la casa: La mujeres dominicanas y la cultura política a finales del siglo XX* (1999) that despite the many important changes since the 1980s with regard to women's education, work, antidiscrimination laws, and political representation, what remains the same is that "as much in the family as in the political sphere the legitimacy of male predominance in positions of power and decision-making prevails."[9]

Indeed, the notable push since the 1980s to increase women's political participation, eventually resulting in the establishment of a quota of 33 percent women for all political parties' electoral candidates lists, also has had ambiguous results. Margarita Cordero, in her 1991 study *Mujer: Participación política y procesos electorales (1986–1990)* describes how while the importance of women's participation in the political sphere was increasingly recognized and paid lip service to, political discourse continued to reflect a "dissociation between the modern pretensions of the theoretical proposals and underlying visions that reproduced the patriarchal order."[10] Notably, over a decade later, the study *Poder y representación femenina* (2002) reveals how such dissociations persist and how the women's quota has not significantly changed women's political participation and political practices more broadly.

Importantly, this study makes clear that it is not solely men's attitudes but also women's views that contribute to reproducing conventional gender norms and constraining women's political roles; this is reflected, for example, in the suggestion of various women in this study's focus groups that women should run for municipal offices because "women like cleanliness more," and in a possible political slogan that they proposed for this: "For cleaning and trash collection, a woman for municipal office" (La mujer con la limipieza y la recogida de basura para la Sindicatura).[11]

The work of various anthropologists similarly attests to how certain gender patterns endure in a rapidly changing and globalized context. Denise Brennan, in *What's Love Got to Do with It? Transnational Desires and Sex Tourism in the Dominican Republic* (2004), studies the "transnational social field" created by tourism, specifically sex tourism, and its interaction with gender norms in the Dominican Republic. In her research on the Dominican northern coast, she "did not find among the sex workers in Sosúa challenges to gender relations that grew out of a feminist consciousness. Rather, even as sex workers become their families' main breadwinners—and out earn male migrants there—they still cling to traditional understandings of gender relations. Traditional gender ideologies are most clear, for example, in women's pursuit of marriage to men—either Dominican or foreign—as a solution to their financial problems."[12] Brennan further notes that "the central image sex workers overwhelmingly use in their self-descriptions and in gossip is that of the 'good mother.'"[13] Brennan's findings thus attest to how the globalizing impulses of tourism and of women's greater economic earning power do not neatly translate into significant change in prevalent gender discourses and beliefs. Developments that fall under the broad category of modernization and that are driven by globalizing forces, in fact, can further consolidate or even increase gender inequalities at times. Indeed, the anthropologist Stephen Gregory, in *The Devil behind the Mirror: Globalization and Politics in the Dominican* Republic (2007), also finds that presumably modernizing forces associated with tourism can just as well contribute to producing unequal power structures and gender relations.[14] Interactions between global and modernizing impulses and local Dominican gender formations are thus not easily predictable and often seem paradoxical.

Nowadays, there are without doubt multiple discourses about gender and sexuality circulating in the Dominican Republic. As Baud describes, "among the middle-class youth of the Dominican cities there exists a gender discourse that is much more articulated, in which the liberation of women and the equality of men and women appears as a basic characteristic of modernity."[15] Yet, at the same time, "strongly unequal gender relations continue to be a basic element of contemporary society."[16] This chapter explores closely the role of new discourses of gender and sexuality of younger generations and considers how they interact with hegemonic Dominican formations.

New Dominican Subjectivities

The impact of globalizing and consumer forces has produced, as described above, a new set of behaviors and orientations, and hence new forms of subjectivity in the country. As Miguel D. Mena describes, "we can see an outlining of a new subjectivity emerging under the heat of the migrations and the weight of the communication media."[17] Thus, "while this country of title holders and of spectacles unfolds, there is another underground [subjectivity], more active and ample than the first, with more punch because it is the most tactile, from the street, from around the corner. Despite being neglected and even underestimated by officialist wisdom, it is there where the weaving of the soul that we are occurs."[18] Rather than considering this new subjectivity primarily as a deformation of authentic *dominicanidad* brought on by corrupting outside impulses (as many others do), Mena identifies this new subjectivity with the actual Dominican "soul." He thereby implicitly addresses the distortion of Dominican identity by the homogenizing officialist discourses that became ingrained during the Trujillato. It is these new globalized subjectivities that may evolve, according to Mena, into an effective challenge to these hegemonic notions.

This new subjectivity, however, has yet to become "a new notion of dominicanidad" and until now has found itself articulated mainly in the Dominican cultural realm.[19] Indeed, "only in art and literature has this new dominicanidad come to be represented. Thinking it, opening oneself to the street, to its mobility, to the necessity of breaking with the constrained world of the island, is part of the next agenda."[20] Mena, as well as Néstor E. Rodríguez, points to a new group of Dominican writers that began to challenge in their writing hegemonic Dominican national discourses that previous writers and intellectuals, even those associated with the political Left, had failed to offer.[21] As Rodríguez describes, "literary production from the eighties onward began to break out of the canons that had been designed to establish a specific cultural identity. This is a literature written in the outskirts of the Trujillista city and that found its capacity to resist in its close proximity to the order against which it rebels."[22]

This revisionary impulse has been shared by many Dominican writers since the 1980s, as well as by many Dominican artists; however, Mena, Rodríguez, and Rita de Maeseneer as well all point to the same writer as a particularly poignant rupture with past tendencies: Rita Indiana Hernández. Hernández, born in 1977, is part of the generation that came of age during the politically disenchanted and newly consumerist years of the second Joaquín Balaguer administration (1986–1996). Hernández's debut novel, *La estrategia de Chochueca* (1999), gives voice to the new Dominican subjectivities that are deeply skeptical and critical of dominant notions of Dominican national identity and the cultural, gendered, and racialized conceptions that underlie these.

De Maeseneer defines the new subjectivities portrayed by the novel as "youth without direction that look for precarious escapes through drugs, friendship, music, and dreams," and who until then had "little presence in Dominican narrative."[23] Rodríguez further describes how

the characters in *La estrategia* (including the narrator) may be characterized as possessing nomadic subjectivities that accentuate the prevalence of hybridity and fragmentation in the novel's dynamic plot. This is arguably *La estrategia*'s strongest feature, especially when the text is read as a counter-narrative to the traditional Dominican knowledge system. The parody of cultural icons, the language of the streets, and the inclusion of popular culture bear witness to the emergence of new popular imaginaries.[24]

Indeed, these new voices and popular imaginaries challenge the dominant discourses of national identity and its cultural, gendered, and racialized conceptions, and offer, as Celiany Rivera-Velázquez cogently notes, "an alternative idea of the Dominican gendered and national self."[25]

I fully share these critics' evaluation of *La estrategia de Chochueca* as an important counternarrative to hegemonic conceptions of *dominicanidad*; however, both Rodríguez's description of these characters as "nomadic subjects" and de Maeseneer's suggestion that they are "directionless" inadvertently obscure what I consider to be the novel's most important critical move: its rewriting of the country's hegemonic forms of relations. It is not in individuals' stances, for example, that of Silvia, the seventeen-year-old narrator, where I detect the novel's principal critical challenge. Rather, I find that it is the relations that she is embedded in with her group of friends and acquaintances that present the strongest affront to the status quo.

Silvia and her amorphous group of friends hang out together in the streets of Santo Domingo, heading "up and down, making a racket, sharing one cigarette among us ten, getting annoyed when we could."[26] Their friendships and the relations they form among themselves largely appear to sidestep established hierarchies of class, race, gender, sexuality, or even national identity. Most of them are not particularly well off (though neither are they very poor), and while many appear to belong to a struggling Dominican middle class, some do have access to more economic resources. For example, one of Silvia's friends is Lorena, "a very cool chick," whose parties bring together people from very different social backgrounds: "Lorena lived in Naco in a huge apartment, a few blocks from the Galleries, there we celebrated some tremendous parties that always ended in disaster, an intoxicated rich girl vomiting through the nose over a fifteen-year-old rapist who gropes his male friend who is asleep from the Lorazepam and Brugal rum."[27] This scene speaks casually of heterosexual as well as homoerotic encounters without the accompanying denigration of masculine identity that we saw in

Veloz Maggiolo's work, but also without ascribing a greater significance to these.

One of the key figures in the novel is Franco, whose sexual preference for young male hustlers is repeatedly and offhandedly described.[28] Silvia, the protagonist, is attracted to both a woman, her Norwegian friend Amanda, and a Dominican man named Eduardo. Sexual desires, however, remain largely marginal to the bonds and relations that this group of friends shares. In fact, the only stable romantic relationship of Silvia's friend Tony is ridiculed and described in highly negative terms. In contrast, the shared bonds among this loosely configured group, in which gender differences appear to recede in significance, take on much more positive connotations.

Some of the male members of the group, for example, Octaviano or Silvia's close friend Salim, have emotionally and financially abusive relations with other women. Yet their relations with the women in the group are described in different, more equal terms.[29] Even though Silvia notes to Salim that "knowing how you told one of your women that she was the only one and pursued another one with a barrage of arrows and little hearts seemed disgusting to me," she still considers the two of them as "above all, accomplices of the absurd."[30] In fact, gender is not the only difference that recedes in significance in their friendship. While Silvia is white and even considered at first sight a foreigner by some, Salim is black. Silvia imagines how "people, always being so stupid and not very subtle, probably thought, 'look at the poor little gringa who fell into the hands of a gigolo.'"[31] Beyond gender and racial differences, Silvia foregrounds the affirmative force of their shared bond. When she and Salim were together, "the day shook off its dust and became an enormous firefly on which you and I traversed the city in perfect and useless circles, delving into this fuzzy maze that is Santo Domingo."[32] The two would laugh at everything, "as if trying to gain advantage over the sadness, that damn witch who is always poking her head out."[33]

Silvia, Salim, and the other members of the group, including Amanda, a foreign-exchange student, are joined by a deeply skeptical and critical view of Dominican reality and the rules that govern everyday life, which they consider absurd, even laughable. They constantly overstep these rules, often resulting in a conflictive relation with their environment. Silvia almost boasts,

> we always ended up being kicked out from everywhere, not that we were that obstinate, it was our way of smiling, as if with our going into

bathrooms three by three, our kissing men and women on the mouth, our way of laughing with a full mouth, we spattered those who were looking at us with an intolerable substance, making them feel even more as mortals, because in our irritating guild there was only room for us, because we had married each other without knowing it, thanks to Brugal rum . . . [34]

The strength of this group's links, despite their apparent informality, is conveyed here in Sylvia's claim that they are "wedded" to each other and belong to an exclusive "guild" that clearly sets them apart from mainstream Dominican society.

Not surprisingly, their irreverence often generates consternation in others. For example, Silvia describes how she and her group are thrown out of a nightclub by the owner angered by their "damn noise and that we were not consuming anything and disrespect, delinquents where are your parents and amen, as always."[35] Their distance and disconnection from their social context is also reflected in the general absence of adults, parental figures, and any form of strong familial relations, which makes this group of youth appear almost orphaned. Silvia lives with her grandmother, her mother is barely mentioned, her father died in an accident together with her grandfather, and the only adult male in the household is an uncle who has withdrawn from work and life. This absence of any significant authority figures in the household is evident, for example, when Silvia returns to her grandmother's house after being out all night: "They had already gotten up when I arrived, my uncle looked at me with little interest and again gave his body and soul over to the television, grandma, who would never get used to me, to my speaking little, eating little, laughing little. She did not make much effort to sermonize me either and remained quiet with her eyes on the coffee with milk."[36] Silvia generally avoids spending time at home: "I am never at home, at most I sleep there, though my dreams get populated by unpleasant stuff in this bed where my grandfather and grandmother created their eight children."[37] Her home, equated with the familial past and heterosexual procreation, represents a bewildering and oppressive reality to her.

It is not only parental and familial relationships but any other kind of hierarchical relation that is sidestepped as much as possible in the narrative. None of the group members appear to follow a regular schedule or go to school or work. At one point Salim says to Silvia, "Have you thought about how millions of children get up each day, brush their teeth and go to school? Even I went."[38] The past tense indicates how utterly implausible this appears to him now. Other institutional and hierarchically ordered settings are also rejected in the novel. For example, the only friend with a steady job (at a Wendy's restaurant) is mocked mercilessly by the other characters, who find his diligence nonsensical.

Social relations and spaces that are hierarchically organized and imbued with any form of authority are generally avoided by this "guild." Instead, the principal spaces where these characters encounter one another are in the city's streets and public spaces, in nightlife venues, and in the private apartments of people who also snub social customs. In fact, the apartment of the aforementioned Franco is one of the principal settings for this group's get-togethers. As Silvia describes, "more overheated people would arrive and the cave would grow like a balloon, a happy rubber purgatory where we slept one on top of the other."[39] Besides such private parties and get-togethers, Silvia mentions "los *raves*," and "a decidedly nocturnal world" that her group inhabits.[40] This centrality of the nocturnal world in the novel accurately reflects the profound transformation that Dominican nightlife underwent after the end of the first Balaguer regime in 1978. As Hoffnung-Garskof describes, "for the first time in decades, young people began to venture out into the city at night," and "by the beginning of the 1980s, new commercial venues for leisure activities, dance clubs, and beer halls began to appear downtown."[41] Dominican nightlife became a key space for the emergence of new subjectivities; as Mena notes, "the nocturnal revolution" in the Dominican Republic, expanded "the night . . . as a space for consumption but also for the constitution of new subjectivities."[42]

The bonds that Silvia shares with her group are closely tied to these nocturnal spaces, where they assemble as "a wall of cokeheads, megalomaniacs, a brotherhood in the most delicious hysteria."[43] Importantly, their "familial" relations, even if placed in such commercial venues, cannot simply be identified along consumerist lines. This is evident in the novel's principal plotline that unfolds in the aftermath of a large nightlife event, a rave, at which a set of oversized speakers was stolen by one of Silvia's friends, Octaviano. The novel's plot follows Silvia's effort to return these speakers as the police are already closing in on her friends. Notably, Octaviano did not steal the speakers for financial benefit, but rather as a form of personal revenge, because the organizer, a friend of his, did not want to let him into the rave. It is precisely the friend's betrayal of their bond and the prioritizing of commercial interests that lead to Octaviano's robbery as an act of protest. The relations formed by these characters, though intertwined with these nocturnal spaces, are not reducible to these spaces' commercial logics and their individualizing tendencies.

What joins these new subjectivities in Hernández's novel is their shared resistance to everything that is encompassed by what the Dominican "people" (la gente) are, say, and do. Silvia repeatedly remarks on her dislike of and distance from "la gente," saying that "it bothers me that people talk to me, touch me, say things to me as if they knew me, . . . because I want to talk to people as little as possible."[44] In their eyes, "la gente" are everyone who enforces or is complicit with the status quo, including the police, tourists, and anyone else who does not question what is presented as common sense in the Dominican Republic. Silvia acerbically describes such people as inhabiting "a showy and terribly arid world. A space installed on the movement, the loathsome trotting of the people, lonely people who go nowhere at all, who at the same time shake their heads to a great symphony of disillusionment and scandal."[45] The novel suggests at least implicitly here, then, that it is in part the passivity of "la gente" that helps to uphold this disappointing world.

At first this may appear primarily as a social rather than a politically oriented critique. Indeed, critics have pointed to the presumable absence of "politics" in Hernández's novel, as well as in the writings of her generation more broadly. However, the novel does not take place in a political vacuum; rather, it denounces clearly its time period's loss of meaning of differentiated political positions that are diffused and overridden by clientelist compulsions. Silvia alludes to this present political reality when she describes "this absurd gelatinous world that our parents have left out, after so much what do we want, so much 'we want the world and we want it,' so much histrionic guffaw, so much Marx and comrade for this, this hopping around of small beasts without any ideas . . ."[46] The father of Sylvia's good friend Salim, Don xxxxx, epitomizes this loss of political ideals. Salim describes how during Balaguer's first "doce años" (twelve years) his parents' "parties were to elaborate strategies; the posters go there, here the pamphlets, here the bombs, and they put their little bombs."[47] He refers to his father, "who got shot in the knee in the hills, and with all that he survived," as "a real big shot . . . , a hero."[48] However, in the present "Don xxxxx works for the government and has this strange look of those who were tortured during the 'twelve years' and now work with the torturers."⁴⁹ Salim's father exemplifies how former leftist political forces have been bought up through clientelist positions that tie them to the Dominican state apparatus that they once had fervently resisted. Just as in Marcio Veloz Maggiolo's *Uña y carne: Memorias de la virilidad* (published at the same time), political concerns and forms of collective identification have been displaced by concerns with personal and financial gains. Thus, when Silvia sees Don xxxxx, she realizes that "nothing matters, that in the end everything is a lie, we all want a little Japanese car and a pool."⁵⁰

Silvia recognizes that everyone, including herself, desires consumer goods and cultural products, "cool clothes, always new and just-released CDs."⁵¹ The novel critiques on one hand how such material desires reinforce the emptying out of political positions, but, on the other hand, it demonstrates how having access to these outside cultural repertoires and products is essential to how Sylvia's group differentiates itself from "la gente." For example, Silvia recalls how she and her friends "talked about Cobain and Meat Puppets and blah blah blah," or how she and Octaviano discussed "Madonna and Darwin and the giraffes. . . . And Plato and Plotinus and the Count of St. Germain and Henry Miller and Pollock."⁵² These varied cultural references reveal that the outside repertoires that they draw from not only are from an easily accessible mass and popular culture but also include "high" culture materials. The eruption of consumer forces, including of mass media, in the Dominican Republic leads to a selective appropriation of these materials rather than a straightforward adoption of the most ubiquitous global cultural trends. These shared globalized references and cultural repertoires help bring this group together, and it is with the help of these new symbols and vocabularies that they mark their difference from mainstream Dominican society.

Among the various group members, it is Octaviano, whose theft of the loudspeakers sets the plot in motion, who embodies the strategy of resistance the novel considers most apt. Silvia exclaims that "it is not easy being the Octano, one needs balls, one needs an absurd and consistent amnesia, one needs to have a certain way to be with him in this world of his, in his hell of latex and reinforced concrete, his shoes . . . one would have to be Chochueca to beg for a little time from his life."⁵³ The evocation of Chochueca, who titles the novel, refers to a Dominican urban legend of "a crazy old guy who hounded the terminally ill and their families for a donation of rags, so they would give him the clothes of the dead after the funeral. Thus, he would walk around dressed in dead people's clothes."[54] The protagonist greatly admires Chochueca's strategy of survival in this "city full of snakes and nylon cadavers," exclaiming, "What balls you have Chochueca. Everyone cries, bites their lips in pain, pulls their hair, but you are calm Chochueca, you do your thing, no one matters, damn, the world will end and the dead just need a bit of gravel, your magic Chochueca, making the shoes of a dead man walk."[55] "La estrategia de Chochueca"—Chochueca's strategy—involves an overstepping of social customs and notions of propriety, and turning, from the margins, seemingly abject subjects and materials into a new kind of life. Through a form of material reappropriation that does not follow standard avenues of capitalist accumulation and circulation, this material can be put to use in new, subversive ways that rupture prevalent notions of what is possible, as the phrase "making the shoes of a dead man walk" suggests.

In summary, I argue that one of the novel's principal critical strategies lies in the estrangement of what is thought of as Dominican common sense. Another key strategy, that other critics also remark on, is the narrative's giving voice to new Dominican subjects who reject this hegemonic common sense and define themselves in opposition to it. Their strategy in fact may be described best by the concept of "savage hybridity" put forth by Latin American cultural theorists Alberto Moreiras and Gareth Williams (following Homi Bhabha). Williams, in *The Other Side of the Popular: Neoliberalism and Subalternity in Latin America* (2002), defines this as a conception of the subaltern that no longer relies on "a given subaltern cultural identity" and instead constitutes "a disruptive site that 'fractures from within' the unitary signs underlying national and global narratives of capitalist development and/or emergence."[56] Similarly, Moreiras, in *The Exhaustion of Difference: The Politics of Latin American Cultural Studies* (2001), insists that "savage hybridity is *not*, to be sure, the subaltern. But, as the 'other side' of the hegemonic relationship, savage hybridity preserves, or holds in reserve, the site of the subaltern, just as it preserves the site of subalternist politics."[57] Indeed, the characters in Hernández's novel cannot be identified with any stable or definite subaltern position, since they diverge greatly in terms of race, class, gender, sexual orientation, and even nationality. While they mostly belong to the same generation, there are also significant age differences between, for example, Silvia and Franco. None of these standard identity markers determine the links that they have formed; rather, they are tied together by a shared sense of distance from Dominican "reality" and the hegemonic logics that underlie it. It is from this anti-hegemonic stance, and from what Moreiras and Williams term a position of "savage hybridity," that they challenge the unitary signs that sustain Dominican hegemonic formations.

Just as the figure Chochueca brings together the worlds of the dead and the living, so do these youths assert their presence within the deadened spheres of Dominican official culture and against the common sense it propounds. The text thereby offers its critical challenge to the homogenizing force of Dominican officialist national discourse, as several critics also note. However, I find this novel's critical impulse not principally embodied in any one character, but rather in the relations formed between them. These relations renounce dominant forms of affiliation based on ingrained notions of gender, family, race, class, and the hierarchical structures of educational, religious, and political institutions. Yet, while these relations in many ways ignore social hierarchies and conventions, we may ask what kind of subjects can afford to inhabit this position of "savage hybridity." After all, it is only those without binding familial and communal ties and the responsibilities that come with them, and those who do not have to work daily for their economic survival or need to partake in other more formal structures (e.g., education), who can follow the irreverent path of Sylvia and her friends. The apparent absence of any such demands put on them reveals that these characters are ultimately not as unmoored from certain social and class privileges as the narrative would like to suggest.

Furthermore, the question we may put to Moreiras's and Williams's conception of "savage hybridity" as well as to Hernández's "savage subjects," is how such a position can evolve to reconfigure hegemonic formations, including the political realm in its more conventional sense. Drawing from Laclau's formulations, we may ask how these heterogeneous forces could come together to form a strong collective will that can come to challenge the political status quo. Beyond the fracturing of signs that Williams evokes, this would have to involve, according to Laclau, new forms of unity through the coming together of demands with the help of a shared signifier. Hernández's novel, by foregrounding the relations that form among her characters, gestures toward the latent possibility of such a unity, but these "new subjectivities," as Mena and Rodríguez term them, have yet to find a shared signifier that could give them an effective collective voice in the Dominican public sphere. While they are without doubt joined by generational affinities as well as by their access to outside, global repertoires of culture, neither can fully encompass these characters' affinities or bind them together sufficiently to form a new collective will.

The absence of a strong shared signifier for this group's dissatisfactions gestures more broadly to the absence of potent political and social signifiers that Dominicans can identify with strongly and rally around—whether in the name of democracy, equality, justice, antiracism, class struggle, etc. The weakness of such crucial "empty signifiers," as Laclau terms them, reflects also the insidious and long-lasting effects of the Trujillo dictatorship's appropriation and resignification of this emancipatory vocabulary for its ends, as discussed in the first chapter. Indeed, tellingly, the shared signifier of resistance of the two principal anti-hegemonic figures, Octaviano and Chochueca, is their "tener cojones" (having balls). This speaks to how, even among those who appear to forgo all conventions of Dominican society, forms of resistance continue to be phrased and imagined through prevalent notions of virile masculinity. While at times these hegemonic notions of masculinity can perhaps be employed for subversive ends, the question remains if they can become a truly destabilizing force and help bring about the much-desired social and political reconfiguration. In fact, this question is at the very forefront of Rita Indiana Hernández's second novel, *Papi* (2004), where Dominican hegemonic masculinity takes center stage.

Loving *Papi*: Lasting Desires for Hegemonic Masculinity

The heterogeneous and marginal elements of Dominican society foregrounded in *La estrategia de Chochueca* give way in Hernández's second novel to a portrayal of precisely the opposite, namely, Dominican hegemonic formations and the notions of masculinity central in them. While the repressive force of masculinity is implicit throughout the text, the novel's explicit focus is on its seductive force, and how it strongly interpellates Dominicans, regardless of gender, race, class, or age. The novel's critique of this hegemonic masculinity emerges ultimately out of its constant hyperbole and fantastical elements that make up the entire narrative and the often comical exaggeration and, thereby, estrangement of the "normal" Dominican masculinity of "Papi." Again, albeit through a very different literary strategy, Hernández insists on rendering strange and even utterly absurd what often is thought of as common sense in the Dominican Republic.

Papi is told from the presumably innocent and nonjudgmental perspective of a young Dominican girl, about eight years old, who lives with her mother but is always waiting for her Dominican father, "Papi," to return from the United States. The novel tells of the child's continuous disappointments caused by her unreliable father, who often does not show up or arrives very late to pick her up. As she declares, "Papi is just around any corner. But one cannot sit down to wait for him because that would be like the longest and most painful death."[58] In a similarly nonchalant way, Papi's unreliability and many betrayals and mistreatments of women are conveyed. For example, he convinces the narrator's mother, his first wife, that he wants to remarry her but then instead weds another woman. Papi in fact is described as having married so many times that when the protagonist and her mother receive another wedding picture, the little girl says, "I put a number to organize the photos along with Papi's other weddings that accumulate like baseball collector cards held together by a green rubber band."[59]

Alongside his current wife, Papi always has several *novias* (girlfriends). As his daughter notes, "he almost always ends up in the house of one of his girlfriends who is always more curvaceous than the previous one and has more gold chains."[60] These *novias* are in a desperate pursuit of "Papi" and try everything to get into his good graces, even by contacting his daughter, much to her mother's dismay: "Papi's girlfriends are quite a damn thing. They call me, they send me letters, Mami burns them, Mami pulls at her hair."[61] In fact, in the novel the *novias* are the principal enemy, a furious female mass in pursuit of Papi. They "come like madwomen, screeching," and "have started meeting up in the parking lot and they call and call him and walk in circles with signs and photos of Papi and they call me and then they form a human tower sinking their pointy heels into shoulders to get to the last floor of the tower where Papi and I are."[62] In one scene the young girl and her father are in a car being pursued by the *novias*, and she says, "They are catching up with us . . . Papi . . . takes out a gun . . . and gives it to me saying 'shoot.'"[63] This scene tellingly brings forth how the daughter's loyalty to her father comes at a damaging cost to other women, as well as how women are divided against one another in their competitive pursuit of Papi.

Women are desirable but disposable and are just one of the many things owned by Papi, whom his daughter describes as having limitless riches. She exults, "My Papi has so many clothes and so many closets for them that sometimes when he wants to put on a shirt he has to buy it again because he doesn't remember in which closet it is. . . . My Papi has more cars than even the devil has. My Papi has so many cars, so many pianos, so many boats, machine guns, boots, coats, jackets, heliports, my Papi has so many boots, he has more boots, he has so many girlfriends."[64] While the legendary riches of Papi are described in hyperbolic terms throughout the novel, the personal betrayals and hurt he causes, principally to women, emerge only implicitly, through the nonchalant observations of the child narrator. For example, she describes how, "when Papi went for the first time to the United States with a Cuban woman who did not want him to send money to anyone, my grandmother Cilí said: He is dead to me. And when Papi told Mami that he was going to get married again, but not with her, Mami said: to me, you are dead."[65] The fact that Papi, despite their death wishes, remains alive and well is taken by his daughter—to humorous effect—as a sign of his immortality and invincibility.

Importantly, Papi forms part of the Dominican diaspora; he is a car dealer who, like many migrants, frequently returns to the island, eager to show off his new riches. He arrives with "the caravan of self-driving Pontiac Trans-Am replicas that Papi brings to sell. Dozens of $5,000 suits that Papi brings for himself. Thousands of watches, chains, rings and white gold jewelry."[66] In the Dominican Republic he is met with the eager expectations of everyone surrounding him.

> Everyone already knows that you are coming back, that you will return, that you are coming back triumphant with more gold chains and more cars than the devil himself. Everyone already knows. . . . And they dream of you filling your suitcase with gifts for them, you only live for them, they dream that you owe them everything in life, in their dreams. They imagine your reunion with them. You, with your silver suit, your jet black shoes, running from the airport, no, paying for a plane from the airport to their houses, to first and foremost, knock on their door and wake them up with a shower of green bills that taste like sugar from the pastry shop.[67]

Papi is at the center of everyone's hopes and expectations on the island, and he is strongly beholden to these. His own mother insists, "Remember your people."[68] As he makes a list of everyone who will receive something, "Cili checks over Papi's shoulder if everyone's names are there. Money, refrigerators, cars, even houses for some in the name of the good old times."[69] Indeed, his handouts are seen not as favors but as an expected reimbursement for friendships or mere acquaintance: "Some have made a list in their minds of each thing that you owe them and for each thing they also write in their mind what you will bring them, the way in which they think you should repay them. . . . It is a very long list (because they even included the times they spoke to you)."[70] However powerful, Papi is also caught up in a social web of expectations that extends far beyond his immediate family and represents the social equivalent of the clientelist relations of the Dominican political realm.

At the very crest of this hierarchy, "Papi is enthroned," as a "mountain-castle-tower of a thousand floors" that is "the source of all suffering and happiness here on earth and in neighboring worlds."[71] Papi is the pinnacle of this universe's social hierarchy, and his masculinity is its principal ruling signifier. Surrounding him is, in a privileged position, what the narrator calls "the Royal Family, which is me, my grandmother, my aunts, the twins Puchy and Milly, and my mother, whom Papi's royal family acknowledges as Papi's only woman because she was the first and they got married in the church as is God's will."[72] Next to the immediate biological family and the first "official," church-blessed wife are, albeit of lesser importance, all his other women and children, who remain undifferentiated. Thus, similar to the adulation of Trujillo's official family, here such elite notions of masculinity and of official family constellations remain alive and desirable alongside other more underclass styles of masculinity embodied by Papi.

The practice of patronage and *compadrazgo* and the social relations they produce are also in evidence in all of Papi's business dealings in the novel. The narrator describes her father's relation with his business "partners" (socios) as follows: "I think this [being a *socio*] is like saying Godfather, meaning that Papi baptizes his partners' babies and that is why his partners' children come and, as a way of greeting, stick their hand in Papi's pocket and take out two, three bills."[73] People's materialist desires are said to override everything, including any familial bonds, and these desires continuously strengthen the position and power of Papi: "Papi becomes more powerful thanks to the energy emitted by all those who crave a new car in the world. Papi's powers flourish when the spirit of those desiring vibrates to the maximum, making them rent their women to the security guards and sell their children in parts to buy themselves a car in Papi's dealership, where they receive the magic key that helps you to take off, get women, and possibly, more keys."⁷⁴ The novel hence suggests how this society's materialist desires and consumerism further ingrain existing patterns of distribution and the forms of social and political relation these rely on.

The political connotations and implications of these relations are hard to miss. The child narrator describes, for example, how "Papi is already growing and his partners with him, going forward so fast that you lose sight of him."⁷⁵ Not only is Leonel Fernández's political sloganeering of progress, of "E' pa'lante que vamos" echoed here, but Papi also evokes both Trujillo and Balaguer in his actions. His daughter's suggestion that "The Confraternity and United World Fair" was a "name . . . given to it by Papi and when Papi gives a name to something nobody can change it," replaces Trujillo with Papi and evokes the dictator's penchant for naming and renaming national sites (often after himself).⁷⁶ Papi is also described, like Balaguer, as constantly inaugurating new works, "and in front of each new project [is] a sign that reads: 'THIS WAS MADE BY PAPI.'"⁷⁷ Indeed, the ubiquitous propaganda for Dominican politicians that litters the urban landscape, especially during elections, is also evoked in the novel: "Everywhere on billboards, on street banners, on electronic signs, on murals on the saltpeter walls of the Malecón the face of Papi, with all the colors of the flag, under a motto that states: WE ARE ALL FAMILY."⁷⁸ Dominican politics, it is suggested, is headed by a patriarchal leader and driven by paternalist handouts: "The houses are distributed following a urine test that proves one's relation to Papi, the result of this test can be falsified by drinking Papi's blood or vinegar and thereafter filling out a thirty-page form in which the applicant needs to explain all kinds of anecdotes experienced with Papi with exact dates and places."⁷⁹ Papi's hyperbolic masculinity, material riches, and power all go hand in hand, one appearing to reinforce the other, and place him at the apex of the country's power structure.

Importantly, the power of this masculinity survives even after his death. Papi is killed over a car dispute, but he does not simply disappear, nor does his power vanish. People continue to see apparitions of him and treat him as if he were a religious phenomenon. His daughter fans people's obsession by talking of "the great power that Papi is"; the people follow her blindly.⁸⁰ Papi, in fact, zombielike returns and "very soon [is] part of all the rituals" that had formed around him with the help of his daughter and nephews.⁸¹ Tellingly, even with his death, Papi's power does not disband, and his followers' desires and expectations for clientelist favors remain undiminished. It is his daughter who steps up and begins to promise future posts to them: "What people liked the most, though, was to be appointed to a post and I . . . distributed titles en masse: delegate of Papi's telepathic circumcision, viceroy of the state's siege that Papi represents, commander in chief for all of Papi's messes . . ."[82] People's expectations and notions of justice help revive the cult of Papi and ensure his long afterlife. The power of Papi is therefore not simply dependent on his actual persona but is reproduced by the people who clamor for and demand his paternalist presence and count on his clientelist handouts.

This system continues to function and easily perpetuates itself after Papi's death. What the novel powerfully conveys is precisely the seductiveness of this mechanism, and why it continues to reproduce itself in the Dominican Republic with no signs of waning. Tellingly, the young daughter herself wants to be just like her father (never like her mother) and desires the power that his masculinity grants him.[83] More than once she imagines usurping her father's position, declaring, "I was just like Papi, I was Papi, I am Papi." She also has romantic fantasies of seducing her stepmother: "María Cristina and I took off from the ground and from Papi very quickly and while we kiss each other with our eyes closed, and I am so strong that my eight-year-old arm holds us both."[84] This is not the only instance that a female character desires and usurps a masculine position. The narrator's cousin Milly, after she is discovered pursuing women, has a private conversation with the narrator's father, and thereafter she and her twin brother "look alike, with their suits, their rings, their chains, their cassettes strewn under the car seats."[85] The position of hegemonic masculinity is here not necessarily tied to a biological essence in the novel; however, neither does the narrative suggest that these transgressive-seeming female appropriations in any way modify the hegemonic masculine script or temper its virulent effects.

However desirable this hegemonic masculinity is acknowledged to be in the novel, the text's opening line "Papi is like Jason, the one from the movie *Friday the 13th*" (Papi es como Jason, el de *Viernes trece*), declares it from the very beginning to be the ultimate horror story.[86] The father is ultimately a fearsome figure with too many bodies on his conscience. This Dominican horror story is critiqued not through the viewpoint of the victims, but through the extreme hyperbole with which it is portrayed and the absurdities produced by it. By rendering this masculinity farcical in many ways, the novel estranges familiar and commonsense notions of Dominican masculinity.

This critical strategy is notably opposite to that of *La estrategia de Chochueca*, which foregrounds a group of youth that willfully remains on the margins of mainstream Dominican society. However, ultimately *Papi* similarly seeks to destabilize hegemonic notions that have become common sense, which it provocatively suggests is reinforced rather than denatured by the returns of the Dominican diaspora—an issue that the next chapter addresses at length. Notably, despite the vast stylistic and thematic differences of Rita Indiana Hernández's two novels, their similar endings speak to their shared critical concerns.

The last scene in each novel takes place in a hospital and speaks to some of the costs and the primary victims of this Dominican hegemonic formation. In *La estrategia de Chochueca* it is Franco, the gay man and popular host of the group of youngsters, who is almost beaten to death by another man. In *Papi*, in turn, it is "Mami," the narrator's mother, who is in the hospital after undergoing surgery for two tumors. She is not the only one; in fact, the narrator declares, "My friends were almost all children of other sick mothers."[87] Clearly, Dominican hegemonic formations and the social order they sustain, as described by Hernández, are shown to have damaging gendered and sexual effects that are naturalized through the language of masculinity and the power of "Papi." The reciprocal and mutually reinforcing relations between notions of masculinity and Dominican hegemonic formations suggest that, perhaps, the transformation of this masculinity may occur more easily once it enters other cultural contexts in more prolonged ways, a question that I consider in my final chapter about masculinity in the Dominican diaspora.

5

How Not to Read Junot Díaz

Diasporic Dominican Masculinity and Its Returns

The difficult economic circumstances that constrain many Dominicans' lives on the island continuously drive large numbers toward emigration. Once abroad, they become essential sources of support for their families and kin back at home. Indeed, nowadays the Dominican Republic receives one of the highest amounts of financial remittances in the region, and the diaspora has become a key national economic pillar.[1] The diaspora not only supports the livelihood of many Dominicans on the island but has also introduced new social and cultural repertoires in the country. Yet, as Jesse Hoffnung-Garskof notes, in contrast to the valued economic contributions of the Dominican diaspora, what has been "much more complicated and controversial were the cultural changes migrants in New York began to transmit to the homeland."[2] Dominicans on the island tended to view the diaspora either in a positive vein, as bringing "the benefits of modernization to the homeland," or negatively, as the epithet *dominicanyork* suggests, as "infecting the Republic with modern social ills like materialism, perverse sexuality, crime and, drug use."[3] Hoffnung-Garskof cogently critiques how both views "share a basic, unfounded presupposition that New York steeped Dominicans in modern notions, for good or for ill, while Dominicans who stayed on Dominican territory remained blissfully isolated from contemporary affairs."[4] Indeed, interactions between what are thought of (problematically) as "modern" and "traditional" impulses but also between global and local formations, as this book argues throughout, are rarely as straightforward as they appear at first sight. This also holds true when it comes to the Dominican diaspora and the "modern" and "outside" mores that for better or for worse are brought back home to the island, including those related to notions of gender.

With regard to gender formations, several scholars suggest how the Dominican diaspora has contributed to amplifying existing gender repertoires in the Dominican Republic. For example, Michiel Baud describes how "the 'absent Dominicans' brought new life and dress styles and different perceptions of gender relations."[5] Peggy Levitt, in *The Transnational Villagers*, coined the term "social remittances"—an elaboration of the diasporic practice of sending back "financial remittances"—for the new behaviors and beliefs brought back by migrants. As Levitt describes, "migrants send or bring back the values and practices they have been exposed to and add these social remittances to the repertoire, both expanding and transforming it."[6] Levitt's ethnographic research in the Dominican village Miraflores suggests that new gender behaviors are an important part of the "social remittances" brought back by the diaspora.

> In Miraflores, there have been particularly strong challenges to gender identity. Migrant women's ideas about what women should do and how they should behave changed in response to their more active participation in the workforce and to their contacts with school, health clinics, and social welfare agencies. They transmitted these new ideas about identity back to Miraflores. . . . While their [nonmigrant women's] ideas were often romanticized, they still represented a marked change in thinking about gender relations.[7]

Despite these changes, Levitt also sounds a note of caution, remarking how "we might expect women to be transformed by the immigrant experience and to introduce social remittances that would strongly challenge existing gender relations," but, ultimately, "the truth, of course, is far more nuanced."[8]

This chapter gauges these much more nuanced truths through the lens of two recent literary works by Junot Díaz, arguably the most renowned Dominican American writer since he received the Pulitzer Prize for his novel *The Brief Wondrous Life of Oscar Wao* (2007). The impressive success of Díaz's novel has put Dominican American literature—and by extension Dominican themes—on the American literary map in unprecedented ways;

yet *The Brief Wondrous Life* not only impacted the U.S. literary scene but also received widespread attention in the Dominican Republic, the country that Junot Díaz had left with his family when he was a young child. Indeed, it would be hard to find any Dominican with some interest in literature who is not aware of Díaz's novel and its themes in some detail. In this sense, Díaz's novel may be considered one of the most potent "cultural remittances" that the Domnican diaspora has sent back to the island in recent years. Juan Flores's concept of "cultural remittances," developed in *The Diaspora Strikes Back: Caribeño Tales of Learning and Turning* (2008), expands on Levitt's concept of "social remittance" to address the diaspora's influence on cultural practices and repertoires in their country of origin. It is in this sense that I ask what Díaz's novel, as an influential Dominican American cultural remittance, sends back from the diaspora to the Dominican Republic. Specifically, I ask how, according to Díaz's novel and his recently published short-story collection *This Is How You Lose Her* (2012), Dominican gender relations and hegemonic notions of masculinity are articulated in the Dominican diaspora and what new gender models might emerge there.

Who Killed Oscar Wao?

The Brief Wondrous Life of Oscar Wao foregrounds the themes of Dominican masculinity, male sexuality, and the diaspora, similar to Rita Indiana Hernández's novel *Papi*. However, Díaz's novel offers a multigenerational story of the Dominican diaspora and gestures to the generational changes that take place within the diaspora, thereby complicating the purposefully unidimensional portrayal of the diaspora in "Papi." The protagonists in Díaz's *The Brief Wondrous Life of Oscar* Wao, Belicia Cabral, a Dominican single mother and her two children—daughter Lola and son Oscar—along with Yunior, a friend of Oscar's and the onetime boyfriend of Lola, live in the greater New York metropolitan area, where Oscar, Lola, and Yunior go to school and eventually to college at Rutgers University.

The novel offers an account of Oscar's "brief wondrous life," as the title declares, but it also ventures extensively into the Dominican Republic's past to describe his mother's and grandfather's life under the Trujillo dictatorship. While the author himself and other critics, such as Silvio Torres-Saillant, rightfully have noted that his novel cannot be read as a straightforward history of the Dominican Republic, the book certainly conveys a serious and sincere desire to understand and address extensively certain aspects of the country's history. This investment in pondering the Dominican past, in particular the Trujillo dictatorship, is what sets this work apart from Rita Indiana Hernández's writing and that of her generation of writers back on the island. These writers, like Díaz, first began publishing in the late nineties and may be considered roughly of the same generation as Díaz. However, Dominican writers such as Hernández, Juan Dicent, and Frank Báez distance themselves from representing the country's political past, especially the Trujillo dictatorship, and foreground instead the immediate present and its vicissitudes.

In contrast, *The Brief Wondrous Life of Oscar Wao* reveals its sweeping historical view beginning with its opening lines.

> They say it came first from Africa, carried in the screams of the enslaved; that it was the death bane of the Tainos, uttered just as one world perished and another began; that it was a demon drawn into Creation through the nightmare door that was cracked open in the Antilles. *Fukú americanus,* or more colloquially fukú—generally a curse or doom of some kind; specifically the Curse and the Doom of the New World.[9]

The fukú of the "New World" poetically ties together the region's history, including the extinction of the indigenous peoples and the practice of slavery as part of a doomed trajectory that began with Columbus's arrival. In fact, the main characters' misfortunes in the Dominican Republic are described as just another "fukú" story. This fukú, or curse, of the New World is thus not simply a matter of the past—"the fukú ain't just ancient history"—given that it found its "high priest" in the twentieth century dictator Rafael Leónidas Trujillo Molina.[10] As the narrator proclaims, "no one knows if Trujillo was the Curse's servant or its master, its agent or its principal, but it was clear he and it had an understanding, that them two was *tight.*"[11] Almost half of the novel is dedicated to the Trujillo Era and the stories of Oscar's mother, Belicia Cabral, and of her father, Abelard Cabral. In these parts, similar to the tendency of other Dominican dictatorship novels, the text fixates primarily on the dictator's violent and sexual excesses.

While this is a literary commonplace in the Dominican Republic, in the United States mainstream literary critics and the literary establishment embraced these excesses in Díaz's novel with particular glee. Critics' blurbs reprinted on the back and in the front matter of the novel describe it as "giddily glorious and hauntingly horrific" (*San Francisco Chronicle*).[12] The story is found to be "enchanting" even as it is "set against the extraordinarily cruel history of the Dominican Republic in the 20th century" (Edward P. Jones).[13] Indeed, the Dominican Republic emerges in the book, according to the *Washington Post*, as "wild, beautiful, dangerous, and contradictory . . . both hopelessly impoverished and impossibly rich."[14] The novel is described as so vibrant and volatile that *USA Today* finds that it should require "a highly flammable warning" because of how it is "drenched in the heated rhythms of the real world as much as it is laced with magical realism and classic fantasy stories."[15] It is perhaps not too surprising that with the novel's effort to recount parts of Dominican history to an English-speaking audience, the language of magical realism slips in.

Of course, Díaz's novel is hardly the only or the most culpable of feeding into an appetite for stories that feature a quintessential Latin American dictator, an irrational, passion-driven strongman and his violent and sexual excesses. In fact, this appetite is not limited to the United States either. The renowned Peruvian writer Mario Vargas Llosa found the Trujillo dictatorship sufficiently titillating to spend months gathering materials in the country for his novel *La fiesta del chivo*, published in 2000, which was turned into a movie in 2005 (starring Isabella Rossellini).[16] In many ways Díaz's novel earnestly tries to dispel any such "magical" misapprehensions or exoticizing views of Dominican history and reality by North American audiences. For example, the book features extensive footnotes explaining Dominican history and social and cultural life in a highly colloquial but nonetheless earnest tone. As Ignacio López-Calvo describes, "these footnotes reflect Díaz's totalizing attempt to grasp the entire reality of the period by considering, albeit in a succinct way, most of the historical landmarks and highlights of the Trujillato."[17] These footnotes, together with long parts of the novel dedicated to life under the Trujillato in the Dominican Republic, give the novel a historical dimension that is largely absent in Díaz's first published work *Drown* (1996), which reaches generally no further back than its young protagonists' early childhood.

While in *The Brief Wondrous Life of Oscar Wao* the insistent evocation of the "fukú" functions as a compelling literary device and shorthand for much of what is wrong with the Dominican Republic, from the conquest up until today, it also obfuscates rather than illuminates these wrongs. For example, the presentation of Oscar's ill-fated life and subsequent death as another Dominican "fukú" story ultimately distracts from the powerful logics that quite rationally explain his death. Oscar's death was neither wondrous nor mysterious—no fukú here—but rather he is killed as a result of his overstepping the scripts of hegemonic masculinity in the Dominican Republic.

His death is not sudden or unexpected but deemed almost inevitable once Oscar, during a stay in the Dominican Republic, insists on pursuing a woman, Ybón, despite a memorable warning by her jealous lover. The lover, a military policeman, has his henchmen first administer as a warning a round of beatings that leaves Oscar with a "broken nose, shattered zygomatic arch, crushed seventh cranial nerve, three of his teeth snapped off at the gum, [and a] concussion."[18] When despite this severe warning Oscar returns again to the Dominican Republic to be with Ybón, defying the "capitán," his death seems inevitable to everyone around him as much as to himself.

Getting mixed up in the love affair of a military policeman turns Oscar's life in the end into a chronicle of a death foretold, given his dangerous overstepping of masculine prerogatives that are particularly robust in Dominican military culture.[19] Also, while the preeminent role that the military played during the Trujillo dictatorship has greatly receded in the post-dictatorship period, military officials continue to have a special and safeguarded status in Dominican society with many "rights," protections, and impunities afforded to them that other citizens do not enjoy. The protected status of the military is reflected in the notable absence of any consequences for the perpetrators of Oscar's assassination: "Four times the family hired lawyers but no charges were ever filed. The embassy didn't help and neither did the government."[20] The military policeman's murderous violence is not simply a case of individual pathology. Rather, as the narrative clearly suggests, it responds to the social logic that "taking" a woman from another man profoundly challenges his masculinity and its prerogatives. Notably, this logic applies not only to wives or formal partners but also to informal relations between men and women, as is the case with Ybón, a prostitute who is claimed by the *capitán* as his "girlfriend." The overstepping of the claims that a man believes to have to a woman, or even to several women, justifies strong and even murderous measures if his claim is challenged. While in Díaz's novel this leads to Oscar's death, in the Dominican Republic more often this results in the murder of the woman involved; such femicides by jealous partners in fact constitute a widely recognized and ongoing crisis in the country.

The novel is clearly troubled by this hegemonic logic of masculinity and its murderous consequences. Moreover, it points to the strong links that connect the Dominican present to the past, especially to the Trujillato. Yet I find that a better understanding of these continuities and the logics that underwrite these is ultimately not aided but obscured by the "magical" language of the fukú that the novel repeatedly takes recourse to. The "fukú," as a literary device, helps the novel gesture towards the interconnectedness of a series of wrongs, from Oscar's death, to Trujillo's reign, all the way back to Columbus's arrival, but their conflation through the language of the magical, the cursed, the spellbound, the fukú, also encourages the kind of reader responses found in the book's blurbs. Namely, mainstream American readers are easily compelled to perceive this "New World" doom as being at a far remove from North American reality, an exotic and opaque "Other" world vastly different from their own, rather than one with long-standing close relations with the United States and that was shaped by U.S. imperial, economic, and cultural politics.

In fact, the treatment of the theme of the Trujillato in *The Brief Wondrous Life of Oscar Wao* echoes some of the problematic commonplaces of other canonical Dominican dictatorship novels that, however, have not found their way into the U.S. literary sphere. As I suggest in my second chapter, these tend to foreground and ultimately exoticize the dictator and his regime by fixating on its violent and sexual excesses and forgo paying closer attention to its more mundane forms of power. A similar fixation on these excesses emerges in Díaz's novel. In fact, López-Calvo finds that Díaz's novel does not help in any way "to de-mythify his [Trujillo's] image," and that "in many ways Díaz's novel involuntarily perpetuates Trujillo's myth as much as, if not more so than, *The Feast of the Goat*" by Vargas Llosa.[21]

Moreover, similar to other Dominican dictatorship novels, certain aspects of the hegemonic notions of masculinity nationalized during the dictatorship remain intact in *The Brief Wondrous Life of Oscar Wao*. Without doubt, Junot Díaz's writing is strongly critical of Dominican hegemonic notions of gender and sexuality; nonetheless, I suggest that his novel, in less self-conscious ways than Hernández's writing, remains caught up in the lasting desirability and lures of hegemonic Dominican masculinity. While the novel clearly denounces the destructive effects of this masculinity, some of its ramifications remain uninterrogated, including the tendency to divide women into "good" and "bad" women.

Dominican Diasporic Masculinity

In contrast to Hernández's all-powerful character "Papi," the main character in Díaz's novel, Oscar Wao, is nerdy and overweight and struggles mightily to approximate the hegemonic masculine ideal embodied by "Papi." In fact, the novel's entire plot could be summarized as Oscar's quest to have sex with a woman for the first time. When at the end of the novel, during one of his visits to the Dominican Republic, he falls in love with Ybón, whom he hopes to bed, he himself feels that this might be "the Higher Power's last-ditch attempt to put him back on the proper path of Dominican male-itude."[22] The novel presents his path toward "Dominican male-itude" with a healthy dose of irony that reveals its critical view of these notions of masculinity. Moreover, not only does Oscar himself never quite match up to this model, but also Yunior, his friend and his sister's on-and-off boyfriend, who comes closest to this ideal model of Dominican masculinity, ultimately recoils from it. Yunior declares himself toward the end of the novel a "new man" and renounces his previous ways: "I have a wife I adore and who adores me..... I don't run around after girls anymore. Not much, anyway.... These days I write a lot ... I'm a new man, you see, a new man, a new man."[23]

Yet the narrative's stance toward Dominican masculinity remains conflicted. Though it explicitly critiques this masculinity, implicitly it cannot entirely renounce its desirability and evaluates the male characters' success or failure through some of its standards. Nowhere is this conflicted stance more obvious than in the ending of the novel, when after Oscar's death a letter arrives that he had written previously and that reveals that he did not die a virgin after all. As Yunior exclaims, "Ybón actually *kissed* him. Guess what else? Ybón actually *fucked* him. Praise be to Jesus!"[24] While it is not necessarily the sexual encounter but the intimacy that he discovers with Ybón that Oscar is awed by, the novel nonetheless posits this revelation as tempering in important ways the tragic ending. In fact, the critic Elena Machado Sáez is similarly wary of this final turn, when the reader is encouraged "to accept the romance of sex" and its implications "as a realistic ending for Oscar."[25]

The arrival of this final news is accompanied by the revelation that Oscar also sent an extensive manuscript from the Dominican Republic that was lost in the mail. However, this loss is ultimately much less noteworthy in the narrative than the "gain" made by this final revelation that emerges as the "happy ending" tempering the tragedy of Oscar's death. It is in such instances that the novel does not entirely escape the desirability of certain hegemonic notions of masculinity—presented as typically Dominican throughout the narrative. In fact, it is more the lasting desirability, and not necessarily the waning, of this masculinity in its transnational displacement in the Dominican diaspora that the novel also points to. Importantly, rather than this speaking to how diasporic subjects fail to "modernize" and follow presumably more commendable and egalitarian U.S. gender models, I argue that this outcome rather speaks to how Dominican male scripts interact with dominant American scripts of masculinity and to how processes of racialization shape this interaction in the United States. Indeed, as Díaz himself has ascertained in several public presentations and interviews, he does not consider U.S. masculinity any less problematic or noxious than the Dominican forms of masculinity that he addresses in his writings.

The Brief Wondrous Life of Oscar Wao thus raises important questions about how immigration impacts diasporic subjects and their gender norms and beliefs. New waves of immigration to the United States, many with origins in Latin America and the Caribbean, have reinvigorated the field of migration studies in the United States since the late twentieth century. This has also led to revisions of earlier assumptions about processes of migration and their impact on gender formations. In her introduction to a special issue of *American Behavioral Scientist*, "Gender and Contemporary U.S. Immigration," Pierrette Hondagneu-Sotelo describes how "early proclamations of immigrant women's emancipation have been reassessed, and the consequences of immigrant women's employment on gender equality in the family no longer seem as straightforward as they once did."[26] More recently, scholarly studies have begun to compare and contrast transnational communities and how gender is variously impacted by migration. In their study "International Migration and Gender in Latin America: A Comparative Analysis," Douglas S. Massey and colleagues compare how the gender formations of five Latin American countries—Costa Rica, Mexico, Nicaragua, Puerto Rico, and the Dominican Republic—impact their migration patterns. The Dominican Republic is described notably as the most "matrifocal" and least "patriarchal" society among these countries:[27] "Mexico and the Dominican Republic anchor the ends of a continuum of family and gender relations. In Mexico a relatively large share of those aged 15 and older are married, few are in consensual unions, and there is little divorce or separation.... Within the Dominican Republic, in contrast, consensual unions outnumber legal marriages and divorce and separation are far more prevalent than in Mexico."²⁸ This evaluation of the Dominican Republic as the least "patriarchal" society hinges here on the instability and informality of Dominican male–female unions. Recent scholarly work on gender in the Dominican diaspora suggests that this conclusion is simplistic at best. There are clear limitations in measuring the "patriarchal" or "matrifocal" orientation of the Dominican diaspora solely through the lens of the presence or absence of male–female stable unions. Such an approach entirely misses, for example, the investments in normative masculinity that Carlos U. Decena detects among Dominican immigrant men who have sex with other men, as well as the ways in which women and other female (and male) family members help to sustain and enforce normative scripts of masculinity.²⁹

This more complex reality is attested to amply in Díaz's *Brief Wondrous Life of Oscar Wao*. The protagonists form a matrifocal family, with Belicia Cabral as the head of the household, while the father of her two children is entirely absent in the narrative; Belicia had migrated alone and unmarried to the United States. This novel dispels the simplistic suggestion that an absence of marriage and stable unions implies necessarily a waning of ingrained gender beliefs and translates into a positive experience of greater autonomy and independence for women. Belicia Cabral's life experience greatly complicates this story line. In the first place, it is precisely her subordinated position as the lover of someone with ties to the Trujillo regime that results in a savage attack on her and forces her to flee the country (rather than her laying claim to autonomy and independence through migration). Belicia's "informal" unions, including with the father of her children, hardly offer an escape from a patriarchal gender system, but rather increase her vulnerability and leave her without any social guarantees that a formal marriage may have proffered more readily. The novel itself presents the lack of stable unions as a troublesome facet of Dominican social relations rather than a gain for women and triumph over "patriarchal" predominance.

The ending of the novel suggests for both Yunior and Lola, Belicia's daughter, that entering a stable union is a key way for overcoming ingrained Dominican gender patterns and the inequalities that are reinforced through these. Lola's marriage to a Cuban man, and the fact that they "travel everywhere together," is presented as a happy outcome for her and not at all as a curtailing of her autonomy and independence.³⁰ Similarly, as described above, Yunior declares himself to have becomes a "new" and implicitly "better" man only once he stops incessantly cheating and chasing other women.

The novel thereby gestures to a shift in gender norms from one generation to another in the Dominican diaspora. It is not Belicia Cabral who breaks with ingrained patterns, but the next generation, represented by Oscar, Lola, and Yunior. However, this break is not a smooth one and contributes to riddling Belicia and Lola's mother–daughter relation with great tension. It is ultimately Belicia who aims to maintain conventional gender roles within her home and reinforces notions of hegemonic masculinity and subordinated femininity in the household, even in the absence of any male authority figure. Thus, neither her "freedom" from matrimonial union nor her many years of work and economic independence in the United States reconfigure the gender beliefs that Belicia holds onto and tries to enforce with her daughter but also, albeit in different ways, with her son, Oscar.

What is underlined thereby is how these gender ideologies cut across the biological divide of males and females. They are not solely reproduced by men but are shared and also enforced by women. Díaz's novel ends with the promise of a different set of gender ideals, fantasies, and desires taking hold among the sons and daughters of Dominican immigrants in the United States, even if, as argued above, hegemonic notions of masculinity remain desirable in ways that the novel does not fully account for. Neither of these two tendencies corresponds simply to Dominicans either adjusting to presumably more "modern" egalitarian gender mores in the United States or stubbornly holding on to "backward" patterns; rather, I would suggest that these tendencies respond closely to how in the United States monogamous relations and marriage are widely proffered as ideal arrangements; yet this language of coupled intimacy in many ways renders lasting gender inequalities and male privilege in the United States simply more opaque and harder to address. It is this gendered context and how racializing dynamics in the United States interact with it and act on these diasporic subjects that help explain why certain notions of Dominican masculinity can also thrive rather than recede in the United States.

Díaz's Reinscriptions of Dominican Masculinity and Femininity

The lasting desirability of certain notions of Dominican masculinity is addressed with much more forthrightness in Díaz's most recent work, the short-story collection *This Is How You Lose Her* (2012). This collection has been described in several reviews as a continuation of Díaz's previous short-story collection, *Drown*. For example, Nicholas Wroe from the *Guardian* describes how "*This Is How You Lose Her* . . . returns to the characters and settings from *Drown*."[31] I want to emphasize instead how the reappearing character of Yunior also offers a continuation of the life story and path of Yunior in *The Brief Wondrous Life of Oscar Wao*. In fact, the collection itself suggests that these texts should be read together. After all, if at the end of the novel Yunior appears as a "new" man, dedicated to maintaining a stable relationship with a "negrita from Salcedo whom I do not deserve," then in this collection we encounter a Yunior who mourns the loss of his fiancée, who is described now as a "a bad-ass salcedeña."[32] His "negrita from Salcedo" has ended their relation after finding out that he had cheated on her over fifty times during their relationship. In other words, the shift that the *Brief Wondrous Life of Oscar Wao* gestured to in Dominican gender beliefs among a younger generation of Dominican Americans is complicated in this recent collection of stories; certain aspects of Dominican male behavior that the novel had appeared to step away from continue to persist here, albeit to greatly damaging effects.

In *This Is How You Lose Her* the ongoing power of hegemonic notions of Dominican masculinity, including in the second generation of the diaspora, ultimately spells personal misery for the main narrative voice, Yunior. This is powerfully described in the story "The Cheater's Guide to Love," first published in the *New Yorker* magazine in July 2012. The story chronicles the five years after Yunior's relationship with his fiancée ended and concludes with his beginning to write an account of his cheating days. What differentiates this short-story collection from Díaz's previous two published works is that it offers a more sustained and intimate engagement with adult male–female relations in the Dominican diaspora. In *Drown* these adult relations were mostly described through the voices and views of children, adolescents, and young adults who observe them. A few of the stories in *This Is How You Lose Her* also take on this perspective, including the stories "Nilda," "The Pura Principle," and, especially, "Invierno." In turn, the stories "The Sun, the Moon, the Stars," "Alma," "Flaca," "Miss Lora," and the "Cheater's Guide to Love" address (young) adult relations in a more sustained way and from a first-person perspective.

The latter story is the diary-like chronicle of an adult male protagonist who is deeply afflicted and pained by the end of his relationship with his former fiancée. Despite his best efforts and various strategies—abstaining from dating, having sexual relations with many women, withdrawing from life, or going out to exercise, run, and do yoga—he cannot overcome his pain and the feelings he harbors for her. The depth of his feelings of loss appears to contradict strongly his actions during the relationship, documented in detail in the "The Doomsday Book," which contains "copies of all the e-mails and photos from the cheating days, the one the ex found and compiled and mailed."[33] In many ways the main character seems to be caught in two incommensurate scripts of masculine behavior, wanting at once his relation with his fiancée, whom he describes as a "good Dominican girl," and his many more informal sexual encounters with women whom he calls his "sucias" (dirty ones). Indeed, the rigid division of women in the story into "good girls" on the one hand and, on the other, "sucias" for those women who are willing to have more casual sexual encounters with the narrator, reflects a gender system where women are constrained in ways that men are not, especially when it comes to sexuality. The narrator, for example, is notorious for his many sexual trysts and is called a "puto" (a male whore) by one of his former lovers, but this does not seem to damage his belief that he is also an appropriate partner for a Dominican "good girl." In contrast, the reverse does not appear to hold true for women, who cannot as easily lay claim to being both a "good" and a "bad" woman in this narrative universe.

The greater male flexibility when it comes to the roles they can access without doubt carries a great psychological cost for the narrator. If this story reads as a strong indictment of hegemonic notions of Dominican masculinity, I find it, however, more difficult to also read it as a similarly powerful indictment of the notions of femininity that it produces. In this sense I disagree with some Euro-American mainstream interpretations that have circulated in the press, for example, in the *Guardian*, where these short stories are described as "more obviously informed by feminist ideas."[34] Díaz himself is highly critical of what he describes as the "strongly segregated masculine world" he grew up in; he denounces the demands that are put on men's public personas as having to embody constantly a stance of being "tough and constantly aggressive" and finds that "the entire culture leads us toward dehumanizing women in our imaginations."[35] This stance is echoed in other interviews with the author as well; for example, Díaz answers the *New York Times Magazine*'s first question, "What was your plan for this new collection?" by stating, "I wanted to capture this sort of cheater's progress, where this guy eventually discovers for the first time the beginning of an ethical imagination. Which of course involves the ability to imagine women as human."[36] However, in "The Cheater's Guide to Love" women have yet to emerge as fully human as the main male characters are. The story offers a detailed portrayal not only of Yunior but also of his best male friend, Elvis. In turn, the only female character who appears to escape the neat division of women into good girls and *sucias* in the story is Yunior's friend Arlenny. Yet, despite her playing an important role in Yunior's life, she remains notably disembodied in the story, especially in comparison to the ever-present Elvis. The reader never receives a description of what she looks like (unlike the manifold physical details of the other women), and she never appears in the narrative in person.

Similar to Díaz's novel, this story at times falls short at fully grasping the ramifications of its critique of hegemonic notions of Dominican masculinity. There is a clear critical intent to show that Yunior's behavior follows problematic Dominican male codes, for which his friend Elvis calls him "a D.R. original."[37] The problematizing of this masculinity, which is indubitably the principal concern in this and other stories, nonetheless does not extend to a more complete narrative awareness of how it circumscribes and delimits female roles. For example, during the chronicling of Yunior's suffering, Elvis, who is married and has a young daughter, has at least two affairs outside his marriage. Despite Yunior's own experience with infidelity and the lessons he is trying to draw from it, he remains a passive onlooker and even an enabler of these affairs. Yunior allows Elvis to bring another woman to his apartment and accompanies Elvis to visit a lover in the Dominican Republic who claims that Elvis is the father of her young child. Elvis's wife in turn, while she makes several appearances, is never fleshed out fully and remains a schematic figure with no psychological complexity in her role as "wife" and "mother" of Elvis's daughter.

Thus, even in this diary-like and highly self-conscious narrative, the gender awareness does not extend much past the narrator's own afflicted self or beyond the male world. As a consequence, the two male main characters appear caught up in lasting patterns with little hope for significant change. Children, or the next generation, at times seem to offer hope for a break with these old patterns, especially when Elvis and Yunior both briefly believe that they fathered a child with a lover, which turns out to be false in both cases. During the brief time periods that they each grapple with this news, both consider it as a possible sign of something new and positive emerging in their lives. Nonetheless, there are few signs that these are more than just fleeting idealizations, given that the very real child that is in the story's midst, Elvis's young daughter, does not bring forth similar forms of hopefulness, nor does she inspire any notable changes in their patterns of behavior.[38]

Ultimately, women appear to have mainly two choices in Díaz's writing: to turn a blind eye to their boyfriend's or husband's philandering or to stay away from Dominican men, as Lola chooses to do in *The Brief Wondrous Life*. Similarly, in this story the main character himself also comes to the conclusion that leaving him was the only option for his ex-fiancée. "You did the right thing, negra. You did the right thing," he exclaims.[39] There is little hopefulness expressed here when it comes to imagining a happier resolution for male–female relations in the Dominican diaspora in *This Is How You Lose Her*. In this context Yunior turns again to writing, just as at the end of *The Brief Wondrous Life of Oscar Wao*. But, if in the novel Yunior does so while being in a relation he cherishes with a Dominican woman, at the end of this short story, the possibility of such relations seems much more remote.

Dominican male scripts, this story strongly suggests, are largely responsible for Yunior's long, drawn-out personal misery. Díaz's writing speaks of the personal conflicts and suffering that arise from characters' enactment of Dominican male patterns of behavior and suggest that these do not recede as straightforwardly in the diaspora as Díaz's own earlier novel had presaged. While in these stories this mainly leads to Yunior's personal misery, in *The Brief Wondrous Life of Oscar Wao* the overstepping of these scripts leads straightforwardly to Oscar's death in the Dominican Republic. This difference speaks to the harmful, in fact deadly, implications that these notions of masculinity can carry in the Dominican Republic. Yet equally, if not in some ways more, noxious is how Díaz's narrative is read by mainstream media, as a progress narrative leading toward greater "feminism." Critics' willful reading and detection of a progressive gender politics especially in Díaz's most recent book ultimately has more to do with ethnic/racial dynamics that remain largely unspoken in such comments. Inevitably, what resonates in critics' comments is how they applaud Díaz's writing appearing to move beyond a "bad" and "backward" Dominican gender politics to embracing a more "modern," equal, and implicitly U.S.-style gender politics. This progress narrative is deeply problematic in several ways; for one, Dominican masculinity is evoked to bolster implicitly a presumably less problematic American masculinity. In fact, this encounter of backward "Dominican" and implicitly modern "American" gender patterns disavows both how gender inequalities remain alive and well in the United States and how historically these formations have never been as separate as they now appear to U.S. mainstream critics and readers.

As I show in my first chapter, U.S. imperialism has contributed in key ways to the emergence of what are thought of as "typical" (or "traditional") notions of Dominican masculinity today. Rather than understanding Dominican gender notions as caught up in a crux of "traditional" and "modern" impulses, we might do better to ask how historically these notions emerged and how they evolved, often in close interaction with other nonlocal gender models. In closing I thus want to return to the scene of the first U.S. military occupation of the Dominican Republic (1916–1924) by the U.S. Marines. At that time, the U.S. Marines' culture of masculinity was, as the historian Mary A. Renda describes, suffused with an "ethos of male rivalry based on competitive claims to toughness and physical prowess—whether enacted on the battlefield or in a brothel. . . . Marines' fast talk about women and yarns about brave deeds in battle echoed the barroom boasts of immigrants and migrant workers in Brooklyn, Philadelphia, and Norfolk."[40] These U.S. repertoires of masculinity—in fact, U.S. diasporic repertoires (of "immigrants and migrant workers")—resonate strongly with the hegemonic notions of Dominican masculinity discussed in this book. Interactions of Dominican and American masculinities long precede the mass migration of Dominicans to the United States in the 1960s, and they cannot be separated as neatly as U.S. accounts tend to do. Recent scholarship on Dominican migration, such as Danny Méndez's *Narratives of Migration and Displacement in Dominican Literature* (2012), similarly insists on the importance of historically expanding our view and understanding of the Dominican diaspora and its relation with the United States, and on looking further back to the "roots of transnational culture."[41] Indeed, what I hope that the above-cited example and this book in general offer is a reminder of how we cannot afford to lose sight of the specific historical and cultural contexts that inform today's globalized encounters. Moreover, we must remain attentive to how marginal groups, ethnic minorities, and diasporas often get marshaled, even by well-meaning critics, not to unsettle an exclusionary U.S. American identity but rather to consolidate and bolster it.

Conclusion

I argue throughout this book how discourses of gender and sexuality, rather than being merely "personal" expressions, have important broader political ramifications and effects in the Dominican Republic. Specifically I show how they continue to structure officialist Dominican political culture and society in ways that were lastingly shaped by the Trujillato and enabled by U.S. imperialism. Indeed, *Masculinity after Trujillo*, as its title suggests, concurs with Ramonina Brea and Isis Duartes's insistence in *Entre la calle y la casa* that "any attempt to study the processes of the hierarchizing of the sexes and of female subordination ... cannot ignore the extraordinary function of ideology, of state mechanisms, and the educational system during the thirty years of Trujillo's authoritarian regime."[1] Without understanding better the lasting force of these gendered notions, I argue, one cannot in fact account for the country's notable political paradox, namely, its "dramatic political stagnation in spite of ... socioeconomic transformations."[2] Ultimately, answering to this political stagnation will have to include a critical confrontation with the notions of masculinity that naturalize predominant forms of relation in the political sphere that feed into prevalent practices of clientelism and corruption.

The patterns of political and social relations that became ingrained and discursively encoded in particular ways during the Trujillato are still evident in rhetorical ploys that remain alive and well in the country. Among these are key facets of the Trujillato's national-populist discourse that erased racial and class difference to create a homogenizing conception of the Dominican national community. Within this national-popular imaginary, social and political differences were primarily phrased and rationalized through the language of masculinity. In fact, political opinion surveys in the Dominican Republic attest to the lasting impact of this national-popular discourse in shaping Dominicans' political perspectives. For example, a large percentage of Dominicans continue to assert that they prefer more "order" and "less democracy," an answer that resonates strongly with both Trujillo's and Balaguer's authoritarian mantras of "order." It is such preferences that ensure that at a time when political scientists speak of a recent shift to the left in Latin America, in surveys from 2006 and 2008, the Dominican Republic continues to rank "in first place on the right end of the ideological scale."[3] Other survey results that seem contradictory at first also reveal ultimately the paradigmatic influence of the Trujillato and of its national-populist discourse.

For example, the Dominican Republic emerges paradoxically in these surveys as the country with the most populist inclinations without there having been recently a political leader that political scientists consider actually "populist." It is the specific questions responsible for ranking the Dominican Republic as the most populist country that offer some telling insight. Among the nine questions that were used by the survey to determine populist tendencies, four were key for placing the Dominican Republic at the top: (1) the belief that there is a fight between good and evil, and that people have to choose between them (80.4 percent agree), (2) the belief that the president should follow the will of the people (78.1 percent), (3) the belief that the dominant class exploits the people (66 percent), and (4) the belief that minorities should not oppose the people (58.9 percent).[4] This Manichaean view of society is, as Rosario Espinal points out, part and parcel of the "hegemonic political discourse" of the Trujillato, which "for three decades had been structured around two antagonistic poles, one divine (of order, peace, and progress) and another malicious (of disorder, war, and misery)."[5] These findings also echo other key rhetorical strategies of the Trujillato, such as appealing to "the people" (whom Trujillo claimed to embody) and the vanishing of racial difference (and other minoritarian identities) in a homogenizing vision of *dominicanidad*. Vis-à-vis this homogenizing view of "el pueblo dominicano," Haiti and its people continue to be seen as radically other and incommensurate with Dominican national identity. For example, the biennial Americas Barometer survey shows that a high percentage of Dominicans are against granting Dominican citizenship to the children of Haitian immigrants born in the Dominican Republic. Indeed, there are widespread reports of Dominican citizens of Haitian ancestry who were deported and taken to Haiti, actions that spring from the often latent but lasting sense that the Haitian presence in the country poses a threat to Dominican national sovereignty. These much-critiqued homogenizing and deracializing notions of *dominicanidad* persist even as important challenges have been and continue to be mounted by different Dominican-Haitian and Dominican organizations, as well as in Dominican cultural expressions, including literature, visual and performance art, and music.

This homogenization of the Dominican national imaginary and the flattening out and emptying of meaning of racial difference, but also of class and other forms of difference, I insist, is enabled greatly by notions of masculinity that became hegemonic under the Trujillato and that continue to play a pivotal role in spelling out differences and hierarchies within the national community. Being more or less of a "man" remains closely tied up with conceptions of "virility" (such as "having balls" [tener cojones]) and continues to naturalize existing political and social hierarchies. As Brea and Duarte describe, political power remains organized around "the principle of masculine preeminence," and authority itself is imagined and expressed through notions of masculinity.[6]

Not surprisingly, then, the Dominican Republic emerges in the Americas Barometer surveys as the Latin American country where those surveyed least believe that women make good political leaders. Indeed, the attempted presidential campaign by the wife of the (now ex-) president Leonel Fernández, Margarita Cedeño de Fernández—in a political move hoping to imitate the success of the Kirchners in Argentina—under the slogan "Llegó Mamá" did not succeed in the incumbent party (PLD). In contrast, the slogan of the opposition candidate of the PRD, Hipólito Mejía, "Llegó Papá," as described in the introduction, was ubiquitous throughout the election year, though ultimately Mejía lost the election to the incumbent party's candidate, Danilo Medina. Medina, long a mainstay of the PLD, won the presidency with Margarita Cedeño de Fernández as his vice president. Yet this hardly spells a "feminist" victory or speaks to the receding of the political patterns that I have outlined. Medina's win has not offered a clear rupture with the eight preceding years of the Fernández presidency and of the vast clientelist network attached to it. While his campaign's principal promise has been "to do what never has been done" (hacer lo que nunca se ha hecho), early accounts of his presidency, inaugurated on August 16, 2012, suggest that whatever will be done, it will be difficult to do so outside of clientelist demands and forms of relations, despite Medina's own best intentions.

Importantly, how gender discourses structure political relations, as well as Dominican social and cultural formations, cannot be understood if one approaches gender primarily through the lens of individual identity. Instead, this context (as well as any other) calls for what Michael Kimmel terms a relational approach or what is termed by some an intersectional approach. In fact, thinking about the kinds of relations that are enabled or forestalled through certain notions of gender, I argue, is part and parcel of understanding how potent challenges to hegemonic configurations and the political status quo can arise, as Ernesto Laclau outlines. Thus, I argue for the usefulness of bringing gender studies together more closely with Laclau's political theories about hegemony to help think about how gender works as a structural force and about the role of "culture" in the political realm more broadly.

Neither problematic gender nor political patterns are usefully explained through still prevalent evocations of an ingrained and seemingly stable cultural "tradition" and, in the case of Latin America, a presumably authoritarian-inclined political culture. Laclau's framework helps to think how cultural and political processes interact and work together without freezing either of these into everlasting "traditions." Indeed, this allows one to address in a more sustained fashion the underexamined question of how cultural effects and positive mechanisms of power remain in place in Latin American post-dictatorship societies after the dismantling of formal dictatorial structures, institutions, and repressive mechanisms.

Masculinity after Trujillo argues thus throughout for the importance of Caribbean studies engaging with questions about the possibility of reformulating hegemonic formations and of reconfiguring the postcolonial political status quo. Moreover, I insist that in the case of the Dominican Republic—and in other contexts as well—this will have to involve also a reconfiguration of hegemonic notions of masculinity and the social and political relations naturalized by them; yet neither the critical work on decoloniality nor the current debates surrounding hegemony/posthegemony in Latin American cultural studies sufficiently consider the gendered aspects of power in their visions of anti-hegemonic strategies and struggles.

Importantly, if we want to critically foreground such struggles and strategies, we must remain mindful of David Scott's injunction that how "one defines an alternative *depends* on the way one has conceived the problem."[7] Scott thus draws critical attention to the conceptual issues that underlie the definition of any problem and the answers that can be found for it, as well as to the importance of understanding the historical context out of which a given problem arose in the first place. For the purposes of this study of Dominican gender politics, this means moving beyond conceptualizing Dominican gender inequities as problems of a "traditional" culture to be solved by increasing modernization and redirecting the focus to how local gender formations historically have continuously interacted with outside repertoires and impulses in a starkly unequal context shaped by colonialism, imperialism, and globalization.

Notes

Introduction

1. Scott, *Conscripts of Modernity*, 2.
2. Torres-Saillant, *Intellectual History*, 28.
3. Edmondson, *Caribbean Romances*, 2.
4. Ibid.
5. Ibid.
6. Goldman, *Out of Bounds*, 28. According to Goldman, "island" and "nation" tend to be equated in the Caribbean, and the ongoing "importance of insularity in the region is undeniable" (14). Thus, even if, "during the second half of the twentieth century . . . the presumed alignment between the space of the island and the place of the nation is disrupted by the large-scale emigration of Caribbean peoples," consequently, "insularity" was not displaced as a central mode of self-definition. . . . [and] it continues to be cited as a defining characteristic of identity" (15).
7. Ibid., *Out of Bounds*, 209.
8. Puri, *Caribbean Postcolonial*, 6.
9. For example, at the height of the financial crisis in 2008, the Dominican Republic had the highest growth rate of all Latin American countries, with a 3.5 percent GDP increase, while many of its regional neighbors posted negative numbers.
10. Lozano, "Development Opportunities," 118.
11. Table, "Vulnerable Employment, Total," *Worldbank*.
12. Lozano, "Development Opportunities," 114, 113, 127.
13. In fact, the 2013 Latin American Studies Association chose this decrease in inequality in the region as its congress's theme. As the description states, "in the first decade of the 21st century, income inequality has gone down in a substantial number

of Latin American countries. This is the first time that inequality has declined on such a broad scale since we have had reasonably reliable data on income distribution" (http://www.lasa.internatonal.pitt.edu/eng/congress/).

14. Beverley, *Latin Americanism after 9/11*, 115. Beverley acknowledges how "globalization has undoubtedly weakened in some ways the sovereignty of individual nation-states, and neoliberal policies have weakened in turn the bond between populations and states; but it is also now generally understood that the state continues to serve a necessary if (in some people's minds) transitional function within globalization" (114).

15. Ibid., 115–16, author's emphasis.

16. Laclau, *On Populist Reason*, 73.

17. Tinsley, *Thiefing Sugar*, 24.

18. Ibid., 24, 25.

19. Benítez-Rojo, *Repeating Island*, 5.

20. Ibid., 10.

21. Kutzinski, *Sugar's Secrets*, 175.

22. Ibid., 175–76.

23. Laclau, *On Populist Reason*, 74.

24. Notably, the persuasiveness of this slogan was thought to be sufficient to override the fact that this was not the first time that "Papá" had "arrived" in the Dominican Republic. Hipólito Mejía already served as the country's elected leader from 2000 to 2004. During this period, he presided over one of the country's worst bank frauds and financial debacles.

25. The two main Dominican presidential candidates—former president Hipólito Mejía and the incumbent party's candidate, Danilo Medina from the PLD (Partido de la Liberación Dominicana), with the past president Leonel Fernández's wife as his vice-presidential candidate—are both closely tied to clientelist governments that have deeply disappointed the Dominican people's hopes of improving their difficult living conditions. Thus, as a student member of the Grupo Quisqueyano at Columbia University aptly put it on the February 27, 2012 independence day celebration, as the presidential elections in May 2012 approached, Dominicans found themselves "between a rock and a hard place."

26. Krohn-Hansen, *Political Authoritarianism*, 125.

27. Ibid., 134.

28. Báez and Paiewonsky, *Género y ciudadanía*, 19. The Ministerio de la Mujer was until 2010 called the Secretaría de Estado de la Mujer.

29. Morgan, Espinal, and Hartlyn, "Gender Politics," 56. As they describe,

> the period prior to 2004 was one in which Dominican political elites, led by coalitions of female civic leaders and then legislators, encouraged women's

rights and women's access to elected office. Significant legislation to combat domestic violence was approved, state policy machineries to promote women's interests were introduced and strengthened, and gender quotas for local and legislative elections were passed. (51)

30. Ibid., 60–61.
31. Rodriguez, "Construction of Gender Identities," 54.
32. Ibid., 60, 62.
33. Ibid., 63.
34. Ibid., 62, 64.
35. Ibid., 64.
36. Ibid.
37. Ibid., 65.
38. Ibid.
39. Ibid., 67.
40. De Moya, "Power Games and Totalitarian Masculinity," 116.
41. Decena, *Tacit Subjects*, 6; and Padilla, *Caribbean Pleasure Industry*, 26.
42. De Moya, "Power Games and Totalitarian Masculinity," 139.
43. Ibid.
44. Connell and Messerschmidt, "Hegemonic Masculinity," 838, my emphasis.
45. Kimmel, *Gendered Society*, 97, author's emphasis.
46. Alexander, *Pedagogies of Crossing*, 193.
47. Ibid., 185.
48. Segal, "Gender Equality," 60.
49. Jackson and Balaji, *Global Masculinities and Manhood*, 28–29.
50. Gutmann, *Changing Men and Masculinities*, 18.
51. Scott, *Conscripts of Modernity*, 6.
52. This dearth of scholarly work is especially marked in contrast to the sizable amount written on the broad and sustained effects that U.S. imperialist intervention have had on national imaginaries elsewhere in the Caribbean and in Central America. See, for example, Michel Gobat's *Confronting the American Dream: Nicaragua under U.S. Imperial Rule* (2005); Laura Briggs' *Reproducing Empire: Race, Sex, Science and U.S. Imperialism in Puerto Rico* (2002); Eileen J. Suárez Findlay's *Imposing Decency: The Politics of Sexuality and Race in Puerto Rico, 1870–1920* (1999); and Marial Iglesias Utset's *A Cultural History of Cuba during the U.S. Occupation, 1898–1902* (2011).
53. See Ginetta Candelario's *Black behind the Ears: Dominican Racial Identity from Museums to Beauty Shops* (2007); Néstor E. Rodríguez, *Divergent Dictions: Contemporary Dominican Literature* (2010); Ernesto Sagás, *Race and Politics in the Dominican Republic* (2000); Silvio Torres-Saillant's "Tribulations of Blackness: Stages in Dominican Racial Identity" (2000).

54. Mena, *Poética de Santo Domingo II*, 33, my emphasis. "El Generalísimo fue ajusticiado, pero todo su otro cuerpo—*más cuerpo que el suyo físico*—, la burocracia, la educación, los saberes, las prácticas, los usos, las disciplinas, los estilos de la vida social y política se mantuvieron" (33).

55. Oviedo, "Los intelectuales y la dictadura de Trujillo," 151. "pautas y valores provenientes del trujillismo... aún operan como límites a nuestro imaginario colectivo, aún diciéndonos cómo ser y hacer, qué somos y qué no somos... [y] perviven en el sentido común de muchas y muchos dominicanos, en sus modos de vivir e interpretar 'lo dominicano' y de percibir el Estado y la política" (151).

Chapter 1. De-tropicalizing the Trujillo Dictatorship and Dominican Masculinity

1. Turits, *Foundations of Despotism*, 64.

2. This view of the two countries locked in an inevitable seeming struggle has been increasingly critiqued and modified in important ways by scholars such as Silvio Torres-Saillant, Samuel Martínez, Sibylle Fischer, and Sara E. Johnson.

3. Maingot and Lozano, *United States and the Caribbean*, 1.

4. As a result, various Dominican scholars insist on how Dominican racial and nationalist formations cannot be understood outside the impact of U.S. imperialist ideologies. Silvio Torres-Saillant, for example, argues that "it is not inconceivable ... that the texture of negrophobic and anti-Haitian nationalist discourse sponsored by official spokespersons in the Dominican state may have drawn significantly from North American sources dating back to the first years of the republic" ("Tribulations," 1088). This is further fleshed out by Ginetta Candelario's *Black behind the Ears: Dominican Racial Identity from Museums to Beauty Shops* (2007), where she notes how "the representation of Dominicans and the Dominican Republic as a nation with a minimal degree of 'pure blackness' ... should be understood as part of a geopolitically framed racial project of U.S. imperialism that intersected unevenly but importantly with Dominican nation-building projects through anti-Haitianist discourses and ideologies" (14).

5. Roorda, *Dictator Next Door*, 15.

6. Rosenberg, *Financial Missionaries to the World*, 41.

7. Ibid.

8. Ibid., 60.

9. As Gail Bederman, in *Manliness and Civilization: A Cultural History of Gender and Race in the United States, 1880–1917* (1996), puts it even more bluntly, U.S. international involvement at the time was driven by the "ideology of manly, civilized stewardship of the savage and barbarous races" (196).

10. Rosenberg, *Financial Missionaries to the World*, 73.

11. Madera, "'Zones of Scandal,'" 22, 229.

12. Madera, "'Zones of Scandal,'" 77. This finding is echoed by Teresita Martínez-

Vergne, in *Nation and Citizen in the Dominican Republic, 1880–1916*, where she insists that "the public discourse against prostitution . . . was neither well developed nor widespread" at that time in the Dominican Republic (140).

13. Ibid., 69.

14. Mayes, "Why Dominican Feminism Moved," 357.

15. Ibid., 357. Lauren Derby, in *The Dictator's Seduction*, similarly points to the resurgence of Dominican nationalist mythologies, including the embrace of Catholicism and *hispanismo*, as "counter-identities" to those associated with U.S. imperialism. She notes that prior "hispanismo was far from a primordial, never-changing, or generalized aspect of national identity in the Dominican Republic" (57).

16. Madera, "'Zones of Scandal,'" 81, 17.

17. Zeller, "Appearance of All," 50.

18. Derby, *Dictator's Seduction*, 62.

19. Ibid., 62.

20. Zeller, "Appearance of All," 52–53.

21. Ibid., 53.

22. Madera, "'Zones of Scandal,'" 99.

23. Martínez-Vergne, *Nation and Citizen*, 24. Indeed, such gendered effects of imperial geo-politics also marked Nicaragua, another Latin American country with heavy U.S. involvement. As Michel Gobat describes in *Confronting the American Dream: Nicaragua under U.S. Imperial Rule*, when the U.S. invaded the country in 1912, some thought this resulted in the "'emasculating' (*desvirilizando*) of Nicaraguan men, and it triggered a crisis of elite masculinity" (135).

24. Crassweller, *Trujillo*, 3.

25. Ibid.

26. "Tropicalism," according to Frances R. Aparicio and Susana Chávez-Silverman, in *Tropicalizations: Transcultural Representations of Latinidad* (1997), is the Latin(o) American correlative to Edward Said's "orientalism," "the system of ideological fictions" (Said 321) with which the dominant (Anglo and European) cultures trope Latin American and U.S. Latino/a identities and cultures" and is part of "a long history of Western representations of the exotic, primitive Other" (1, 8).

27. Crassweller, *Trujillo*, ix.

28. Ibid., 92.

29. Ibid., 118.

30. Ibid., 4.

31. My critique is prefigured in Howard J. Wiarda's *Dictatorship and Development*. Wiarda describes how

> two of the more comprehensive studies of the Trujillo era, that by Ornes and that by Galíndez, conclude that the dictator had no political philosophy and that his sole motivating principle was power of its own sake. Even

Crassweller, who has written perhaps the best and most comprehensive biography of Trujillo, gives insufficient consideration to this aspect of his regime and concludes that Trujillo most closely resembled the oriental despots of ancient times. (103)

32. Crassweller, *Trujillo*, 78.

33. Ibid., 195.

34. Ibid., 118, 426.

35. Wiarda, *Dictatorship and Development*, 13.

36. Peña, "Reportaje Robert D. Crassweller." "En 1967, Crassweller comenzó a ser conocido entre la generalidad de los dominicanos con la primera edición de la obra en inglés. . . . El libro fue traducido al español en 1968 y en muchos hogares se convirtió en referencia obligada sobre la llamada 'Era de Trujillo.' . . . Las ediciones piratas se sucedieron al extremo de que . . . no se conoce una segunda edición 'legal'" (Areíto sec.).

37. Trujillo, *Era de Trujillo*, lxxvii. "No es posible determinar hasta que punto se halla ese hombre genial y predestinado inmerso en el alma dominicana ni hasta que grado, asimismo, se halla nuestro pueblo encerrado amorosamente en . . . el alma de Trujillo."

38. Balaguer, "Principio," 5. "Las multitudes . . . seducidas por la arrogancia del hombre de armas o conquistadas por el prestigio que ya empezaba a irradiar aquella personalidad cesárea."

39. Ibid., 5–6. "La sola presencia de Trujillo en el escenario nacional, mueve desde el primer instante a la admiración, y estimula la sorpresa, y enciende en sus propios adversarios prevenidos asombros, desconcertándolos a todos con su incandescente frialdad y con su helada violencia. ¡Qué sorprendente fisonomía humana y que inaudito perfil histórico el de este caudillo huracanado . . . !"

40. Peguero, *Militarization of Culture*, 71.

41. Ibid., 23.

42. Qtd. in Roorda, *Dictator Next Door*, 60.

43. Betances, *State and Society*, 6.

44. Roorda, *Dictator Next Door*, 2.

45. Ibid., 22.

46. Peguero, *Militarization of Culture*, 46, 51.

47. Ibid., 75.

48. Ibid., 59.

49. Ibid., 38, 39.

50. Ibid., 131.

51. Ibid., 133, 132.

52. Trujillo, *Era de Trujillo*, xlvi. "La Patria era solamente una mendiga haraposa

que incitaba a la compasión ofensiva y al desprecio ultrajante. Trujillo restauró su posición y su prestigio, devolviéndole su fisonomía de nación respetable y honesta."

53. Stephens, *Black Empire*, 23.

54. Ibid., 20.

55. Ibid., 15.

56. Balaguer, "Principio," 17. "El principio de la alternabilidad ... sólo ha tenido, pues, vigencia para los presidentes que no supieron vestirse en el solio la toga de la virilidad.... Para un titán como Trujillo, superior en genio político y en capacidad de mando a todos sus antecesores, el principio de la alternabilidad se tenía por fuerza que reducir a una abstracción inoperante."

57. Trujillo, *Era de Trujillo*, 54. "Lo repetimos: jamás hemos tenido el problema de la discriminación racial."

58. Balaguer, "Principio," 11. "Trujillo ha eliminado de la vida dominicana el viejo y secular principio de que los cargos públicos de representación deben trasmitirse, por una especie de privilegio hereditario, a ciertas familias de abolengo distinguido."

59. Ibid., 12. "Ni los Estados Unidos, con sus discriminaciones raciales, aún preponderantes en numerosos estados de la Unión, ni Cuba, país donde todavía la sociedad se halla organizada, como en los días de la colonia, sobre el antagonismo entre blancos y negros y entre blancos y cuarterones, han logrado dar a su democracia, en este terreno eminentemente humano, la perfección que ha adquirido la nuestra bajo la rectoría sin prejuicios y sin pujos aristocráticos del Generalísimo Trujillo."

60. Manley, "Poner un grano de arena," 14.

61. Zeller, "Appearance of All," 10.

62. Ibid., 100.

63. Ibid., 15. Zeller insists that this established a lasting pattern, namely, that "forms of participation that allowed Dominican women's political insertion into the polity were intrinsically shaped by authoritarianism and continue to be fundamentally undemocratic to this day" (16).

64. Ibid., 207.

65. Madera, "'Zones of Scandal,'" 122. As Madera further elucidates,

> poor women who did not follow the state's mothering dictates were demonized, especially women who were accused of abortion or infanticide. ... The state continually depicted them, and other women in their situations, as sexually promiscuous, jealous and hopeless deviants who threatened Dominican society. Moreover, honorable women and wives were defined against their deviant sisters. (163)

66. Ibid., 161.

67. Ibid., 162.

68. Baud, "Patriarchy and Changing Family Strategies," 365.

69. Walker, "Power Structure and Patronage," 495.
70. Ibid.
71. Crassweller, *Trujillo*, 51.
72. Ibid.
73. Derby, *Dictator's Seduction*, 174.
74. Ibid., 133.
75. Turits, *Foundations of Despotism*, 206.
76. Baud, "Patriarchy and Changing Family Strategies," 358. Malcolm T. Walker points to the prevalence of the same phenomenon (for the pre-Trujillo era): "in agricultural activities, there is a good deal of cooperation and mutual help, the most institutionalized form of which is the *junta* system—loosely organized mutual help groups which are recruited by an individual from among his personal kindred" (486).
77. Baud, "Patriarchy and Changing Family Structures," 361.
78. Ibid., 363. For example, in the case of tobacco farming, merchants "had a moral obligation that even in years of bad harvests they would continue to buy the crop for reasonable prices" (363).
79. According to Walker, "it is customary to form *compadrazgo* (godparent) ties with local men of influence, and this places the individual in a better position to extract favors whether they be in the form of credit in the store, or the occasional day of paid work, or the loan of some item of equipment. Influential campesinos also frequently act as intermediaries on behalf of their clients in dealings with the police and the court and other government functionaries located within the pueblo" (487).
80. Christian Krohn-Hansen strongly emphasizes that "what we must realize is the extent to which the Trujillo regime managed to link this society to the national state-system, or the nation-state, and hence to the dictator's patronage after 1937" (*Political Authoritarianism*, 68).
81. Hartlyn, *Struggle for Democratic Politics*, 50. Regarding the expansion of the military force by Trujillo, Hartlyn states that "when he assumed power, the country's security force numbered just slightly over 2,000," but towards the end of his regime "the number had grown to around 31,000" (46). At the same time, as Betances describes, government employment "of middle-level technical workers and professional administrators went from 5,579 in 1935 . . . to 23,190 in 1960" (*State and Society*, 100).
82. Peguero, *Militarization of Culture*, 125–26.
83. Ibid., 91.
84. Ibid., 92.
85. Trujillo, *Discursos, mensajes y proclamas*, 240. "Todo campesino que se sienta perjudicado por las autoridades locales en su persona o en sus intereses, puede dirigirse a mi directamente en la seguridad de que será atendido."

86. Ibid., 232, 234. "desgracias"; "desorden"; "el orden es la condición más necesaria para la Nación, y el Gobierno es el encargado de mantenerlo."

87. Ibid., 238. "Si por tu casa pasa un hombre que quiere alterar el orden, hazlo preso: es el peor de los malhechores. El criminal está en la cárcel, ha matado a un hombre o se ha robado una cosa. El revolucionario quiere matar todos los que pueda y cogerse todo lo que encuentre: lo tuyo y lo de tus vecinos: ése es tu peor enemigo. Por eso a un soldado lo verás como a un hermano que te defiende lo tuyo. Ayúdalo. Guíalo. Señálale el camino y acompáñalo para establecer el orden, que es tu garantía."

88. Turits, *Foundations of Despotism*, 19.

89. As Baud affirms, peasants' "continuous commentaries about the behavior of patrons in peasant discourse were an indication of the peasantry's attentive scrutiny of patron-client relations in which they were involved" ("Patriarchy and Changing Family Structures," 364).

90. The Trujillato thereby transformed "peasants into unpaid soldier-spies (as denunciation became more and more pervasive and institutionalized)" (Peguero, *Militarization of Culture*, 107).

91. Turits, *Foundations of Despotism*, 229.

92. For example, Jesús de Galíndez recounts how it was "natural among Dominicans to think that the maid or a visitor could be a regime spy; the fact is that not even in the intimacy of the home would they dare to speak freely" (natural entre los dominicanos pensar que la criada o un visitante puede ser espía del régimen; el hecho es que ni siquiera en la intimidad del hogar se suelen atrever a hablar libremente) (*Era de Trujillo*, 246).

93. Turits, *Foundations of Despotism*, 228, 230.

94. Walker, "Power Structure and Patronage," 497. Walker describes this change and how it coincides with the Trujillato, but he cautiously adds that "the extent to which Trujillo was responsible for the brittleness and suspicion that today is characteristic of interpersonal relationships among pueblo dwellers and campesinos can probably never be known" (ibid.).

95. Krohn-Hansen, *Political Authoritarianism*, 185.

96. Ibid., 183, 185.

97. Peguero, *Militarization of Culture*, 179.

98. Collado, *Tíguere dominicano*, 27. "El tíguere original, [es] el que en los años cuarentas y cincuentas logró colocarse sobre las crestas del liderazgo juvenil dominicano de los contados barrios tradicionales en el reducido espacio urbano de la capital."

99. Ibid., 156–58. "Simulador social," "el héroe de todas sus batallas . . . aparece como el centro del drama y maneja la situación hacia sí favorablemente," "salirse con la suya," "es un oportunista," "amigo de las mentiras."

100. Ibid., 157. "Protector de amigo, allegados y familiares."

101. Krohn-Hansen, *Political Authoritarianism*, 153.

102. Derby, *Dictator's Seduction*, 175.

103. Ibid., 174. The tíguere offered a subject position for young lower-class (and generally mixed-race) men that let them come out on top in a tyrannical society where "only Dominican party hacks and military men could achieve political rank" and where all men had to accept total subservience to Trujillo, who "depleted the collective honor of all Dominican men except himself" (175, 174).

104. Ibid., 174.

105. Mena, *Poética de Santo Domingo II*: 61. "crisis del conocimiento, sino también del sujeto, de su autopercepción. . . . El decir tiránico no solo fundaba un saber, sino también una ética, una corporalidad, un gesto, un decir, una forma de expresarse."

106. Derby, *Dictator's Seduction*, 124.

107. Under the Trujillato, as Peguero describes,

> through a coded public discourse, every day, in many locations (mainly in the headquarters of the Partido Dominicano) across the country, the regime orchestrated many manifestations of public support. With sophisticated language or popular expressions, eloquent speakers with grandiloquent phrases delivered Trujillo's message to the multitudes. Thus, the people became more and more susceptible to demagoguery. (*Militarization of Culture*, 158)

108. Derby, *Dictator's Seduction*, 169.

109. Mateo, *Mito y cultura*, 13. "Los intelectuales desempeñaron un papel preponderante."

110. Galíndez, *Era de Trujillo*, 299. "En algunos aspectos la tiranía de Trujillo actúa de un modo similar a otras dictaduras latinoamericanas . . . pero difícilmente se dará en cualquier otro país una abyección tan absoluta de las fuerzas intelectuales."

111. Alcántara Almánzar, *Escritores dominicanos*, 189. "contó con una serie de poetas, narradores, críticos de arte y literatura, historiadores y juristas que, junto a profesionales liberales, le sirvieron como funcionarios, diplomáticos e ideólogos."

112. Vega, *Unos desafectos*, 9. "desafectos pasivos"—"aquellos que no conspiraban contra la dictadura pero que mantenían una postura pública contraria al régimen."

113. Ibid. "Si su rebeldía no era mortal porque eran considerados hasta cierto punto como inofensivos, su criticidad les costaba el peor de los exilios: El exilio social, el ostracismo en su propio patria. . . . Se mantenían a buen recaudo en sus casas, no eran invitados a actividades sociales, no estaban inscritos en el partido oficial y les resultaba muy difícil conseguir empleos, aún en el sector privado. Vivían, pero no existían como seres sociales."

114. Oviedo, "Los intelectuales y la dictadura," 148, 149. "Emergente aparato institucional," "una verdadera cadena de producción y circulación simbólica, . . . cadena

que ofreció el tejido institucional necesario para el exitoso despliegue de los mitos culturales."

115. Mateo, *Mito y cultura*, 93. "parte inseparable del esquema defensivo total."

116. Rodríguez, *Divergent Dictions*, 32.

117. Mateo, *Mito y cultura*, 14. "La simbología discursiva del régimen trujillista habitó mágicamente la totalidad de la vida ciudadana. No había una casa de dominicano en la que éstos símbolos no estuviesen colgados de la pared, como signos rituales de la prevención y el miedo. No había un solo acto de la vida de relación social que no estuviese mediado por la presencia intimidatoria del mito-sistema trujillista."

Chapter 2. One Phallus for Another

1. As Rosario Espinal recounts, "in July of 1963, the Dominican Episcopacy publicly protested against what it labeled a campaign against the Church coming from communist sectors. . . . In a very fragile political atmosphere the tensions between the Church and Bosch's government contributed to the debilitation of the government" (en julio de 1963 el Episcopado Dominicano protestó públicamente contra lo que calificó de campaña contra la Iglesia proveniente de sectores comunistas. . . . En un ambiente de mucha fragilidad política, las tensiones entre la Iglesia y el gobierno de Bosch contribuían a debilitar el gobierno") (*Autoritarismo*, 98). Bosch in fact had at that point never identified his political beliefs with communism, to the contrary.

2. Jiménez Polanco, *Partidos políticos*, 120. "La intervención militar de los Estados Unidos se convirtió nuevamente (como sucedió durante el preludio trujillista) en el vehículo 'perfecto' para un nuevo tránsito hacia el autoritarismo."

3. Scholars generally concur that it was U.S. interests that led to the reinstallment of Balaguer into power. As the Dominican historian Roberto Cassá declares, "the return of Balaguer to the presidency was mediated by a pact between fractions of power that were driven by the North Americans" (El retorno de Balaguer a la presidencia estuvo mediado por un pacto entre fracciones de poder impulsado por los norteamericanos) ("Algunos componentes," 119).

4. Emelio Betances describes how

> when Balaguer took power on 1 July 1966 the first item on his political agenda was to provide "order" and "social peace," in other words, to destroy the popular movement. The Dominican security forces terrorized those who had participated in or sympathized with the revolution, targeting organized labor, student organizations, and leftist political parties as enemies of the state. State-sponsored terrorist groups secretly killed hundreds and jailed thousands during Balaguer's twelve years in office. His campaign of terror crushed the left and deepened a crisis within the PRD, the most important opposition party. (*State and Society*, 119)

5. Jiménez Polanco, *Partidos políticos*, 122, author's emphasis. "Una garantía *ritual* de aquel derecho, sustentada en elecciones fraudulentas." As Hartlyn further elucidates, "Balaguer ruled in an authoritarian fashion. Human rights violations by state security agents were unacknowledged and unpunished, and civil and political liberties were curtailed. In both 1970 and 1974, in the face of open military harassment, most opposition forces opted to abstain from participation in elections" (*Struggle for Democratic Politics*, 101).

6. Hartlyn, *Struggle for Democratic Politics*, 100. Indeed, the Dominican sociologist Laura Faxas speaks of "an almost 'colonial' redefinition and strengthening of the dependency of the country on the United States" (una redefinición y un fortalecimiento casi "coloniales" de los nexos de dependencia del país frente a los Estados Unidos) (*Mito roto*, 153).

7. NACLA, "Feminismo balaguerista," 4.

8. Mena, *Poética de Santo Domingo II*, 133. "El prototipo de lo que debimos ser y tal vez nunca seamos."

9. Torres-Saillant, *Retorno*, 64. "Sólo Balaguer puede hacerlo."

10. Ibid., 342. "El Presidente Balaguer, encubrió el crimen y se mofó de la ley, en numerosas ocasiones. Rompió promesas y traicionó aliados. Ese comportamiento, sin embargo, le ayudó a sostener el mando absoluto por varias décadas y usufructurar de la prestidigitada admiración que el poder evoca en el alma de seres sin grandeza. . . . Sus veleidades subieron al rango de genialidad política. Así, una vida pública repleta de improbidad se tornó seductora como modelo viable de conducta política."

11. Ibid., 245. "La fuerza fálica del régimen balaguerista."

12. Krohn-Hansen, *Political Authoritarianism*, 126.

13. Based on his research in the Dominican southwest, Krohn-Hansen outlines the following five categories through which Dominicans evaluated leadership: "Ordinary men's categories for reflecting on, and judging, each other's and leaders' maleness may be discussed in terms of five sets of ideas: notions (1) of autonomy and courage; (2) of men's visibility in public spaces; (3) of the man as seducer and father; (4) of the power tied to a man's verbal skills; and (5) of a man's sincerity and seriousness" (138).

14. Ibid., 140.

15. Bosch attempted to institute what political scientists call a "programmatic" politics, "programmed" around stated policy goals (rather than clientelist practices). Laura Faxas describes some of Bosch's measures promised in the constitution, which included "the right to strike and workers' guaranteed participation in companies' profits, as well as their collaboration with their administration; an agrarian reform that went against the large estate holdings . . . [and] a minimum prize guarantee for the products of small farmers" (el derecho de huelga y garantizaba la participación de los trabajadores en las utilidades de las empresas, así como su colaboración en su gestión

. . . una reforma agraria que iba contra la gran propiedad latifundista . . . [y] la garantía de unos precios mínimos para la producción de los campesinos) (*Mito roto*, 107).

16. Álvarez, "Siglo de literatura dominicana," 418. "La revolución del 65 marcó con fuego a los escritores y los artistas del 60. En la ciudad intramuros sitiada por las tropas norteamericanas, poetas, escritores y artistas plásticos empuñaron en una mano el fusil y en la otra la palabra." Among these were Miguel Alfonseca, René del Risco, Juan José Ayuso, Miñín Soto, Iván García, Rafael Vásquez, who "junto a los pintores Silvano Lora, Ada Balcácer, Ramón Oviedo, José Cestero," "integraron el Frente Cultural y realizaron numerosas actividades en parques, plazas y comandos de guerra" (together with the painters . . . [who] formed the Cultural Front and undertook numerous activities in parks, plazas and war commando posts) (418–19).

17. Alcántara Almánzar, *Escritores dominicanos*, 145. "Varios escritores insurgentes en el '65 entraron en un largo silencio y no publicaron más; un buen grupo ingresó al campo de la publicidad, que lo absorbió parcial o totalmente; otros se dedicaron a la docencia universitaria."

18. Álvarez, "Siglo de literatura dominicana," 420–22.

19. Rosario Candelier, "Tendencias, ciclos y valores." "El ciclo de las revoluciones montoneras," "el ciclo de novelas de la caña," "el ciclo de novelas biblícas."

20. Bruni, "Trujillismo," 155. "La novela se desarrolla notoriamente en torno . . . [a] la dictadura de Rafael Leonidas Trujillo (1930–1961)."

21. De Maeseneer, *Encuentro con la narrativa*, 40. "Dar un recuento de todas las novelas relacionadas con el Trujillismo equivaldría a escribir una historia casi completa de la narrativa dominicana de la segunda mitad del siglo XX."

22. Valerio-Holguín, *Presencia de Trujillo*, 210. "'boom de la novela del trujillato,' sobre todo a partir de los 90."

23. Gallego Cuiñas, "Trujillo," 39–40. "El auge del tema dictatorial se sitúa en la década de los setenta. . . . En los ochenta se observa una notable disminución que se prolonga hasta la década de los noventa. Esto no ocurre en el panorama literario dominicano, que recorre el camino inverso, pues las publicaciones sobre la dictadura trujillista irán *in crescendo* y experimentarán una auténtica eclosión novelística en los noventa."

24. Avelar, *Untimely Present*, 75.

25. Ibid., 2. In his book he analyzes "five of the finest novelists writing in Latin America today: the Argentines Ricardo Piglia and Tununa Mercado, the Brazilians Silviano Santiago and João Gilberto Noll, and the Chilean Diamela Eltit" (16).

26. Ibid., 15, 77.

27. Ibid., 20.

28. Indeed, at the risk of reading Avelar too literally here, both in political and social terms, it is much more difficult to stake out which "ruins" produced by Trujillato are to be mourned, given how officialist and popular Dominican discourse continues

to view the regime as the very creator (and not destroyer) of the modern Dominican nation-state.

29. Avelar, *Untimely Present*, 69. Dominican writers did turn to allegory to address the Trujillato under another guise while the dictator was still in power (for example, Veloz Maggiolo employed biblical allegories). However, allegorical fictions were rare after the end of the dictatorship, as were works in the vein of magical realism. Though Veloz Maggiolo did experiment with magical realism, for example, in *La biografía difusa de Sombra Castañeda* (1981), there were no significant works comparable to Miguel Angel Asturias's *El Señor Presidente* (1946) or Gabriel García Márquez's *El otoño del patriarca* (1975).

30. Fernando Valerio-Holguín, in *Presencia de Trujillo*, argues, to the contrary, that "allegory constitutes one of the most used tropes to resolve the problem of the representations of history" (la alegoría constituye uno de los tropos más usados para resolver los problemas de representación de la historia) (36). However, he also attests to "the inclination toward realism among Dominican writers and readers... evident in the many works written about the Trujillato" (la afición por el realismo entre los escritores y lectores dominicanos . . . en evidencia en las multiples obras escritas sobre el trujillato) (132). While I do not dismiss that these texts also take recourse to allegory, I nonetheless maintain that these uses are not comparable to the pervasive forms of allegorization, for example, in the work of Diamela Eltit, that Avelar refers to, whose argument about allegory is also referenced by Valerio-Holguín.

31. Sommer, *One Master for Another*, 21.

32. López-Calvo, *God and Trujillo*, xvi.

33. For example, Freddy Prestol Castillo's *El masacre se pasa a pie* (1974), which describes the 1937 massacre of Haitians by the Trujillato, has been labeled a novel by the author, but, as López-Calvo notes, it also "has been argued that the text is closer to the testimonial subgenre" (*God and Trujillo*, 114).

34. Avelar, *Untimely Present*, 67.

35. Ayuso, "Generación del 60," 303. "La idea del arte social y comprometido y la idea de la libertad y justicia populares."

36. Álvarez, "Poesía de los sesenta," 311. "Pocas generaciones literarias tan estigmatizadas como la del sesenta."

37. Torres-Saillant, *Retorno de las yolas*, 106. "Otro temor sería que se le niegue valor a la obra debido a su naturaleza 'política,' lo cual, según el credo que legisla la estética oficial, se acepta en el patio como sinónimo de pobreza artística."

38. Álvarez, "Un siglo de literature dominicana," 422, my emphasis. "Los libros de la post-guerra fueron muchos. Ninguno ha quedado como título significativo, a excepción de *Los ángeles de hueso* (1966) de Marcio Veloz Maggiolo. . . . *Los ángeles de hueso* es un texto precursor a *la novelística moderna* en el país."

39. Ibid., 422. "Utiliza los recursos tipográficos, las superposición de planos tem-

porales, el monólogo interior, el desplazamiento espacial, la imbricación de distintos puntos de vista y de diversos narradores, y la dislocación verbal."

40. Unlike many other Dominican and non-Dominican literary critics, Torres-Saillant is troubled by this tendency. He critiques "the great liking of many of our most promising literary artists for trying out formal novelties, conceptual innovations and however many aesthetic variations are suggested to them through their readings of works validated in Western capitals. One can make out in their writing practice an unbridled interest in reaching the stage of modernity, a plane whose frame of reference is always outside of the country" (La gran afición de muchos de nuestros más prometedores artistas literarios por ensayar novedades formales, innovaciones conceptuales y cuantas variaciones estéticas les sean sugeridas por la lectura de las obras vigentes en la capitales occidentales. Se deja entrever en su práctica de la escritura un desenfrenado interés por alcanzar los estadios de la modernidad, plano cuyo marco de referencia se ubica siempre fuera del país) (*Retorno de las yolas*, 153). Torres-Saillant sees this stance taken by some of the most prominent literary critics working in the Dominican Republic, including José Alcántara Almánzar and Bruno Rosario Candelier.

41. Torres-Saillant describes him as "the most prolific contemporary Dominican writer and [who] is hailed as the most impressive of his country's intellectuals" ("Marcio," 322). Some of the national prizes he has been awarded include Premio Nacional de Poesía (1961); Premio Nacional de Novela (1962); Premio Nacional de Novela (1981); Premio Nacional de Cuento (1981); Premio Nacional de Novela (1990); Premio Nacional de Novela (1992); Premio Nacional de Literatura (1996); and Premio Feria Nacional del Libro (1997).

42. As Torres-Saillant describes, his novels *El buen ladrón* (1960) and *Judas* (1962), as well as his *Seis relatos* (1963) and his play *Creonte* (1963), treat "biblical themes," which "provided a safe venue at the time for the author to comment on the relationship between the individual and the state without offending the Trujillo regime" ("Marcio," 325).

43. For example, at the end of the novel it is suggested that the young main narrator, Paco, might be just another figment of the imagination of the "real" narrator, a wheelchair-bound older writer and professor.

44. This experimentalism has met with criticism both on and off the island. For example, Sharon Keefe Ugalde concludes, "so much ambiguity and negation of previously introduced patterns appear to relegate the work to that of an absurd game" (tanta ambigüedad y tanta negación de patrones introducidos parecen relegar la obra a la posición de un juego absurdo") ("Veloz Maggiolo," 217).

45. López-Calvo, *God and Trujillo*, 126.

46. Veloz Maggiolo, *De abril en adelante*, 63. "Cómo meterlo en una novela de manera verosímil, eso ya es otra cosa."

47. Sommer, *One Master for Another*, 203.

48. Veloz Maggiolo, *De abril en adelante*, 36. "No puedes vivir sin la opinión del otro; no puedes hacer nada sin que el otro te dé su asentimiento; ni siquiera te sientes seguro de ti mismo si el otro no te asegura."

49. Ibid., 34. "Miro a Samuel. Se ha dejado crecer las patillas; le gustan los pantalones apretados y las hebillas grandes. . . . No puedo explicarme cómo se predican ideas revolucionarias vestido como un señorito de la burguesía."

50. Ibid., 179. "Llegarán donde Juan y allí reunidos volverán al asunto, contra mí. Volverán a la crítica . . ."

51. Ibid., 177. "Le digo a Paco que deje esa vaina del comunismo, para ser culto no hay que ser comunista."

52. Ibid., 171. "tantas amistades ricas y tantos nexos con la pasada tiranía."

53. Ibid., 161. "Es un tema formidable." This disavowal of any strong personal ties contrasts tellingly with the fact that Paco's current livelihood is precisely dependent on his deceased father's powerful political connections during the Trujillato, which his mother uses to secure employment for Paco. Such disavowals and continuities speak amply to how relations between the past and the present are much more complex than the narrative makes explicit.

54. Neil Larsen similarly critiques this character's representation, noting that he "is cause of considerable difficulties in Veloz's narrative" (es causa de considerables dificultades en la obra narrativa de Veloz), not least because the narrative, "after creating with Colonel Aguirre one of the most tangible characters of greater historical interest, does not find an adequate form for his end" (después de crear en el coronel Aguirre el personaje más palpable y de mayor interés histórico, no encuentra la manera adecuada para darle fin) ("¿Cómo narrar el trujillato?," 97).

55. Gallego Cuiñas describes how the novels written in the sixties and seventies about the Trujillato "would recreate crude, horror-inducing scenes" (recrearán escenas crudas, patibularias) ("Venganza," 310).

56. As Gallego Cuiñas describes, "The novel about the Trujillato in the sixties and seventies wants to thematize the effects of the Trujillato and the different forms of abuse of power, that is, depicting the cruelty of the Trujillista assassins (members of the military, spies, etc.)" (La novela del Trujillato de las décadas sesenta y setenta pasa por tematizar los efectos del trujillato y las diferentes formas de abuso del poder; esto es: por la caracterización de la crueldad de los sicarios trujillistas [militares, espías, etc.]) (ibid.).

57. López-Calvo, *God and Trujillo*, 9–10. The tendency to approach Trujillo through the lens of the grotesque is noted also by H. J. Manzari in his discussion of Enriquillo Sánchez's *Musiquito: Anales de un déspota y de un bolerista* (1993) and by Gallego Cuiñas, who notes how the tyrant is "grotesquely characterized" (caricaturizado de modo grotesco) by Dominican writers ("Novela del Trujillato," 7).

58. Gallego Cuiñas, "Novela del Trujillato," 7.

59. Larsen, "¿Cómo narrar el trujillato?," 90. "en el mejor de los casos, como un sinnúmero de anécdotas sensacionales ensartadas en el hilo biográfico del propio dictador."

60. Ibid., 93–94. "Trujillo es presentado, por un lado, como un tipo de loco casi cómico. . . . Por otro lado, es un Satanás gigante y dantesco."

61. Veloz Maggiolo, *De abril en adelante*, 53. "el sexo y el desenfreno quebraban el sentido de la propiedad privada en aquellos que se decían sus mejores defensores. Aquel era un experimento del Generalísimo, al cual se incorporaba mes a mes la mejor sociedad de Santo Domingo."

62. Interestingly, the narrative seems to reveal here some unease with the partial destabilization of class and racial hierarchies occasioned by the Trujillato.

63. Ibid., 207. "Pienso en Matilda, anoche, ¡brutal! . . . tres veces. Y Melissa, anteanoche, sensacional."

64. Ibid., 15. "Comenzó la cosa por ver quién se la tiraba. . . . Total, que a la semana Alberto le puso cuernos al marido y desde entonces sus poemas salen domingo a domingo—con putísima insistencia—en las páginas de los suplementos."

65. As others have noted, "Zinia" is a thinly veiled reference to the Dominican writer Aida Cartagena Portalatín and her novel *Escalera para Electra* (1970), a finalist for the Seix Barral Prize in Spain. In fact, the characters and some of the plot of the novel are directly addressed in Veloz Maggiolo's *De abril en adelante*, making her identity unmistakable (Sommer, *One Master for Another*, fn. 16, 221).

66. Veloz Maggiolo, *De abril en adelante*, 11. "Anda mojón, escribe una novela. ¿No ves que Zinia dice que ha quedado finalista?"

67. The following passage is exemplary in this sense: "We publish a little story from Sunday to Sunday; we are in the newspaper announcing our next great unedited work. If a female approaches us, we write her an anti-aesthetic poem, only to go to bed with her the soonest possible" (Publicamos un cuentecito de domingo en domingo; salimos en el periódico y anunciamos nuestra gran producción inédita. Si alguna hembra se acerca a nosotros, le escribimos un poema antiestético, sólo para irnos a la cama con ella lo más pronto . . .) (ibid., 37).

68. Sommer, *One Master for Another*, 212, 213.

69. Ibid., 213, 214.

70. Ibid., 214, author's emphasis.

71. Ibid.

72. Ibid., 13.

73. Ibid., 27.

74. This behavior, as discussed previously, is in popular parlance associated with someone having "tigueraje," referring to the popular national male subject of the Dominican "tíguere" that emerged during the Trujillato.

75. This includes Efraim Castillo's novel *El personero* (1999), Diógenes Valdez's novel *Retrato de dinosaurios en la Era de Trujillo* (1997), and Francisco Nolasco Cordero's novel *Papaján* (1973), as well as short stories by Armando Almánzar Rodríguez, Pedro Peix, and many others.

76. Gallego Cuiñas, "Trujillo," 464. "El machismo ha reverberado en la novela del trujillato."

77. Valerio-Holguín, *Presencia de Trujillo*, 133. "La narración del trujillato," "un arte machista."

78. De Maeseneer, *Encuentro con la narrativa*, 64. "Se corroboran unas estructuras muy conservadoras en la relación hombre-mujer en toda la novela."

79. López-Calvo, *God and Trujillo*, 121.

80. Ibid.

81. López-Calvo describes how

> Trujillato narratives . . . concentrate—at times perhaps excessively—on the tyrant's eccentricities and on the numerous and outrageous anecdotes collected during the three decades. Eventually, the lack of subtlety and the tedious enumeration of commonplaces (the adulatory *merengue* songs, the theatricality of the regime, the sexual exploits or alleged homosexuality of some member of the Trujillo family, the tyrant's crimes) end up desensitizing the reader. (Ibid., 140)

82. Ibid., 105.

83. Ibid., 106. Undoubtedly, some of the dictator novels apprehend this virility with critical intentions; yet, as López-Calvo suspects of Latin American dictator novels more generally, "paradoxically, behind the denunciation, some of the novels hardly hide their authors' obvious fascination with these larger-than-life patriarchal figures" (ibid., 6). Similarly, Rita de Maeseneer, in her reading of Efraim Castillo's *El personero*, points to this same ambivalence and wonders "to what point the authors succeeded in capturing the complexity entailed by the sexual encounter with the authority and if it rather actually inspires a combination of contradictory feelings, of attraction and rejection" (hasta qué punto los autores llegaron a captar la complejidad que suscita el encuentro sexual con la autoridad y si no inspira más bien una mezcla de sentimientos contradictorios, de atracción y rechazo) (64).

84. The critic Nina Bruni perceptively points to the broader political implications of the virile imaginary that predominates in these texts when she notes how "from the myth of virility the ideological support of his regime is born" [and] "through the logic of osmosis, society is also virilized and is ferociously masculine" (del mito de la virilidad nacen los puntales ideológicos de su régimen . . . [y] por lógica osmosis, la sociedad también está virilizada y es ferozmente masculina) ("Trujillismo en *Uña y carne*, 172). However, despite recognizing the contiguity and interdependency of

political and social imaginaries, she stops short of critiquing Veloz Maggiolo directly for reproducing these hegemonic sex-gender patterns and politics.

85. Veloz Maggiolo, *Uña y carne*, 154. "Me alejé lentamente de las ideas políticas iniciales. No eran necesarias. . . . [M]e harté y encaminé mi mundo hacia una vida sosegada, por encima de los romanticismos."

86. Ibid., 155. "Yo no era ya un seguidor de ninguna izquierda, sino un diputado reformista, con un pasaporte diplomático, con un 'pent house,' tres automóviles Mercedes, y una vida placentera que quise odiar en principio, pero a la que me acomodé."

87. He thus represents what Torres-Saillant has called the "'repentent leftist' . . . a new species in the social fauna, together with the emergence of a militant individualism" ('izquierdista arrepentido' . . . una nueva especie en la fauna social, a la par con el surgimiento de un individualismo militante) (*Retorno de las yolas*, 315).

88. Veloz Maggiolo, *Uña y carne*, 94. "un país sin memoria."

89. Ibid., 12–13. "Durante los últimos gobiernos en los que tomé parte el olvido ha sido una de las políticas fundamentales de varios regímenes. La paz de estos tiempos se cimenta en el olvido. . . . La amnesia dirigida y manipulada produce resultados políticos y abona la riqueza y el bienestar."

90. Ibid., 39. "Algo que tiene mucho que ver con este relato es la virilidad."

91. Ibid., 20. "Lograba una erección como forzada de la que me reía en silencio."

92. Ibid., 40. "que el Jefe lo que tenía 'era una palomita de nada.'"

93. Ibid., 43. "la virilidad del Jefe era chiquita, poco duradera."

94. Ibid., 48, 96. "El Jefe amado tenía una pinga breve y débil, según cuentan"; "el mandamás de mayores poderes en el Caribe 'lo tenía como una palomita.'"

95. Ibid., 192. "Todo ese allante de que es muy potente sexualmente es un cuento."

96. Ibid., 46, 99. "Su virilidad . . . era la pincipal fuerza política y social del Jefe amado"; "la fórmula de la virilización era también una fórmula para perpetuarse en el poder."

97. Ibid., 67, 90, my emphasis. "Daguerre tenía su vena de maricón, lo ocultaba . . ." y "sus *fallas* . . . le venían de familia, pues su hermano Boni, médico, era también pajarillo."

98. Álvarez, "Oposición y similtudes," 29.

99. Ibid., 30. "Los personajes masculinos de la novela reproducen la ideología de la época."

100. Valerio-Holguín, "Bolero, historia e identidad," 240.

101. Veloz Maggiolo, *Uña y carne*, 178. "Se acabó el bongó, se acabaron los 'chances,' no tengo dónde trabajar. Se reirán de mí en las calles, cuando explote el chisme habrán de verme como un ridículo al que violaron con un mísero vegetal para transformarlo en caricatura. . . . Mi hermano Boni ha vuelto a decirme que no tengo escapatoria. Quiere que me largue cuanto antes hacia donde sea."

102. Ibid., 137–38. "Durante algunas horas él podía mantener un contacto

inagotable," "el miembro viril," "inmenso y caliente como un tizón que derramara parafina," "ese mazo de fuego reverberante."

103. Ibid., 205. "Habíamos apostado a que demostraría cómo hacer el amor durante una noche completa. No era la primera vez."

104. Ibid., 75. "Mi oferta fue una especie de bomba en mi vida emocional reciente. Dorila abrió los ojos como enloquecida. Se dejó caer en la mecedora de cana, y comenzó a llorar, a llorar. Yo sabía que el efecto sería parecido. Dos días después fue hospitalizada, abortó un feto morado y amarillo, se consumió en una cama de la clínica Altagracia . . . Decidí no verla más. Alguien pagó su tratamiento y hasta su entierro."

105. Ibid., 187, 210. "La muerte de Muriel no resultó nada novedosa. Fue un tajo solitario sobre el cuello y un mar de sangre sobre el colchón de forro plástico"; "los bomberos y policías . . . me encontraron navegando en un mar de sangre y con un cuerpo hermoso de mujer degollada."

106. Ibid., 211. "las muertes imaginarias de Muriel o de Sadia."

107. Torres-Saillant, *Retorno de las yolas*, 105. "El miedo a cerrarse puertas le impide al escritor incursionar genuinamente en el plano de la criticidad."

108. Torres-Saillant, *Tigueraje intelectual*, 45–46.

> [L]a comunidad letrada queda . . . mediada por la necesidad de armonía con los políticos, empresarios, generales y prelados del poder . . . para fines de un cargo en el funcionariado, una asesoría en las fuerzas armadas, un empleo como relacionador público en la banca o como director del Patronato de la Ciudad Colonial o otra de las instituciones públicas o privadas donde influye el clero.
>
> De la afabilidad con que interactúe la comunidad docta con las instancias del poder dependerá el que se le privilegie con un premio literario cuyo monto en efectivo baste para costear el remozamiento de su residencia. Añádase la obtención del financiamiento para la publicación del próximo libro, la entrada a los periódicos y los medios electrónicos para seguir vigente en la esfera pública y la recaudación de recursos económicos para apoyar sus proyectos culturales o sus programas de televisión.

109. The concern with this relation has since been taken up more widely, as seen, for example, in the 2002 debate that the short-lived Dominican journal *Xinesquema* convened in its pages with a group of Dominican sociologists, philosophers, and literary and art critics, including Roberto Cassá, Silvio Torres-Saillant, Fernando Valerio Holguín, Delia Blanco, Emilia Pereyra, Avelino Stanley, and Odalís G. Pérez.

110. Franco Pichardo, *Tigueraje intelectual*, 11–12. "En abril de 2002 ocurrió en nuestro país un hecho insólito y sin precedentes en la historia de la intelectualidad dominicana. Un libro editado en 1990, *El ocaso de la nación dominicana* de la autoría

de Manuel Núñez, fue galardonado con el Premio Nacional Feria del Libro, que patrocina la firma E. León Jimenes, y en tal virtud, declarado 'Libro del Año.' . . . La noticia del otorgamiento de ese premio cayó como una bomba en los círculos intelectuales nacionales. . . . Tanto Torres-Saillant como Avelino Stanley y quien suscribe criticaron el otorgamiento de ese premio al libro de Núñez . . . fundamentalmente, porque estimaron que el ensayo en cuestión es profundamente racista con una sobrecarga de prejuicios antihaitianos."

111. Torres-Saillant, *Tigueraje intelectual*, 21. "Una obra burdamente consagrada a reivindicar los esquemas ideológicos promulgados por la historiografía trujillista."

112. Ibid. "Sirvieron de jurado como parte del personal de la Secretaría de Estado de Cultura."

113. Ibid., 22. "Si de hecho participaron en la decisión que apareció validada con sus firmas, hay que intepretar su juicio como una retractación pública. Al galardonar el grueso tomo *El ocaso de la nación dominicana* (1990, 2001) de Manuel Núñez, un autor conocido por su fogosidad antihaitiana, hispanófila y conservadora, los citados colegas nos están diciendo que se arrepienten de haberse suscrito a las causas que otrora defendieron."

114. Rodríguez, *Divergent Dictions*, 68.

115. Ibid.

116. Torres-Saillant, "Tribulations of Blackness," 1106.

117. This is despite the fact that, as Torres-Saillant notes, "the post-Trujillista academic world has exhaustively studied that distortion of our racial composition" (ya la academia post trujillista ha estudiado exhaustivamente esa distorsión de nuestra composición racial) (*Retorno de las yolas*, 82).

118. Rodríguez, *Divergent Dictions*, 33, 63.

Chapter 3. Engendering Resistance

1. Other critics detect this change as early as the 1970s. Gallego Cuiñas suggests that "in the mid-seventies, a group of poets and story writers is forged who would solidify their career especially in the eighties . . . some formed the Writers Collective ' . . . and Period,' all of them linked to the realm of advertising: Raúl Bartolomé, René Rodríguez Soriano and Pedro Pablo Fernández, among others." (A mediados de los setenta, se fragua un grupo de poetas y cuentistas que consolidarán su carrera sobre todo en los ochenta . . . algunos conformaron el Colectivo de Escritores " . . . Y Punto," todos relacionados con el ámbito de la publicidad: Raúl Bartolomé, René Rodríguez Soriano y Pedro Pablo Fernández, entre otros) (Gallego Cuiñas, "Novela del Trujillato," 3).

2. The poet and critic Ylonka Nacidit-Perdomo is now in charge of the late writer's archives. She describes her dogged endeavor to bring Contreras back from silence

and solitude to the public eye in the biography accompanying the photographic chronicle of the writer's life, *Una vida en imágenes, 1913–1993*.

3. Writers loosely associated with the Generación del 60 had been for decades the predominant recipients of the national literary award for a writer's lifetime oeuvre, beginning with Marcio Veloz Maggiolo in 1996, followed by Carlos Esteban Deive, Franklin Domínguez, Andrés L. Mateo, Diógenes Valdez, Mateo Morrison, and José Alcántara Almanzar.

4. For example, in Ignacio López-Calvo's *God and Trujillo: Literary and Cultural Representations of the Dominican Dictator* (2005), in Ana Gallego Cuiñas's doctoral thesis "Trujillo: El fantasma y sus escritores (Análisis y sistematización de la novela del Trujillato" (2005), in Rita De Maeseneer's *Encuentro con la narrativa dominicana contemporánea* (2006), and in Nina Bruni's *Letras de la era: Imagen de Trujillo en la narrativa dominicana contemporánea* (2007).

5. The writer and her work's divergence from dominant Dominican literary tendencies are reflected in Contreras's being rarely cited in relation to a specific literary generation or literary tendency in the country. While Ylonka Nacidit-Perdomo and Rafael García Romero name Hilma Contreras as part of the 1930s generation of Dominican narrators, García Romero also remarks on her divergence from this group, suggesting that Contreras "contributes . . . a different voice in the group of narrators from the generation of the '30s" (aporta . . . la voz diferente en el grupo de narradores de la generación del '30) ("Perfil y valores narrativos").

6. Contreras returned in 1933, when she was twenty-three years old, to Santo Domingo from France, shortly after Trujillo's rise to power, and she would remain there for over twenty years. In 1962, briefly after Trujillo's assassination, she left for Paris once more to work for three years at the Dominican embassy and then returned to Santo Domingo in 1965, where she would remain for the rest of her life (Nacidit-Perdomo, "Hilma Contreras").

7. Mora Serrano, "Hilma Contreras Castillo (1913–2006)."

8. For example, her short story "La espera" (The Wait) is thought to offer the first (nonhomophobic) Dominican literary representation of female same-sex desire.

9. Letter reproduced in Nacidit-Perdomo, *Una vida en imágenes*, n.p. "Debo decirle a Ud., con toda franqueza, que es Ud. una escritora . . . Ud. tiene todas las probabilidades de llegar a dominar el cuento."

10. Ibid. "Permítame aconsejarle una cosa: cerca de Ud. debe haber, como cerca de todos nosotros, mucha gente humilde: cocineras, sirvientas, viejas pobres, niños desamparados. . . . Hurgue en esas vidas, extraiga eso que el común de la gente no ve, pero que Ud. puede ver porque está dotada de la facultad de los escritores. . . . No acuda a escenarios extraños."

11. Ibid. "Para esta época Contreras estaba estrechamente vinculada a los escritores dominicanos y a las poetas frecuentando las tertulias de la Librería Dominicana

... el Club de Música ... las reuniones en el Ateneo Dominicano, los conversatorios e interesantes 'Party' que se realizan en el estudio de la exquisita pianista Aida Bonnelly."

12. Indeed, the only two monographs published during this time are a short story collection, *4 cuentos* (which indeed consists of four stories), published in 1953 by Contreras's friend the writer Aída Cartagena Portalatín in the collection *La isla necesaria* (The Necessary Island), and an essay, *Doña Endrina de Catalayud*, published privately in 1955.

13. Barrios Rosario, "Introduction," *Carnada*, 18. "Los cuentos de esta colección caen en la corriente literaria del Realismo Social con un tono criollista como muchos cuentos de Juan Bosch, quien fue el responsable y precursor de esta tendencia literaria." Barrios Rosario defines this literary tendency in the following way:

> Social Realism with a *criollo* tendency meant the portrayal of the reality of the times starting with certain social problems affecting Dominican society at the moment. Taking place in the rural zone, the human tragedy of poverty and workers' exploitation fuse with other central themes like the people's customs and traditions and class, race, and gender prejudices. These make up the thematic spectrum that best characterized Social Realism in Dominican narrative. Many stories in *La carnada* share these characteristics.
>
> (El Realismo Social con una tendencia criolla consistió en retratar la realidad que se vivía partiendo de ciertos problemas sociales que aquejaban a la sociedad dominicana de ese momento. Enmarcados en la zona rural, la tragedia humana de la pobreza y la explotación obrera se unen a otros temas centrales como las costumbres y tradiciones de los pueblos y los prejuicios de clase, de raza y de sexo. Éstos conforman el espectro temático que mejor caracterizó el Realismo Social en la narrativa dominicana. Muchos cuentos de *La carnada* comparten estas características.) (18–19)

14. Poverty figures centrally in the stories "Ocho días" (Eight Days), "Puñados de dolor" (Loads of Pain), "Jesús en vitrina" (Jesus in the Shop Window), and in "El poder de unas lágrimas" (The Power of a Few Tears).

15. Contreras, *Carnada*, 87. "En mi pueblo se estancaba la vida, se cubría de lama, y como bostezante pantano enfermaba a los hombres nacidos para luchar y desplegar energías. Allí todo lo bueno dormía."

16. Ibid., 88. "Casimente muerto.... To lo gueso me duelen, y lo pioi de to e que sin cédula no puedo dir al pueblo."

17. Ibid., 89. "¡Crueles tiempos los modernos!"

18. Terror does not emanate from a specific location or person but rather is mapped out by Contreras as an oppressive atmosphere bearing down on the characters, often through references to menacing natural elements: the sky, the sun, or the

temperature that "naturalize" the oppressive atmosphere of the Trujillato and reflect its pervasiveness. For example, "the sky was bleeding from its crepuscular wounds"; "the day woke up teary. Nature appeared to be in mourning with its colorless sky and its off-color foliage" (se desangró el cielo por sus heridas crepusculares; el día se despertó lagrimoso. La Naturaleza parecía de duelo con su cielo descolorido y sus frondas destempladas) (Contreras, *Carnada*, 44, 65).

19. Contreras, *Doña Endrina de Catalayud*, 39. "[Le] preocupaba por sobre todas las cosas, la honra."

20. Ibid., 28–29. "La honra castellana es un sentimiento extrovertido, esto es, que ante todo se trata de conservar el buen nombre. No reside tanto en la íntima satisfacción de sentir la conciencia limpia, impecable, cuanto en retener el respeto público."

21. Ibid., 27–28. "A ella no le asusta la soledad con su enamorado, sino en cuanto ello pueda trascender al público, pues la gente murmuraría deslustrando su buena fama."

22. Ibid., 40. "que nos trajo España a nuestras tierras americanas: 'Callad, guardad la fama; non salga de so techo.' ¡Por Dios, que no lo sepan!"

23. Johnson and Lipsett-Rivera, *Faces of Honor*, 3.

24. Caulfield et al., *Honor, Status and Law*, 1.

25. Ibid., 2.

26. Piccato, *Tyranny of Opinion*, 255.

27. Caulfield et al., *Honor, Status and Law*, 2.

28. Martínez-Vergne, *Nation and Citizen*, 156–57.

29. Ibid., 157.

30. The collection reflects the shift in Contreras's writing from social realism that strongly bears the mark of Juan Bosch to her own literary style. While half of the stories from *4 cuentos*, both "¿ . . . Polvo?" (. . . Dust?) and "La Virgen del Aljibe" (The Virgin of the Well) follow her earlier social realist style; the other two stories, both analyzed in this chapter, "Viernes Santo sangriento" and "La ventana," signal her new literary path.

31. Contreras, *4 cuentos*, 9, 15, 11. "El chacal"; "funcionario"; "una buena posición."

32. Ibid., 10. "Contentos de romper las amarras."

33. Ibid. "en una torre de marfil, con dos ventanas que simbolizaban su vida"

34. Ibid. "—Aquí vivo—me explicaba—dolorosamente distendida entre los dos horizontes. Aquí, un trozo de cielo, gris, nebuloso, o rabiosamente azul, que me atisba por el ojo anémico de la iglesia. . . . En cambio por la otra ventana, ¡mire qué montañas! Lejanas, azules, como una promesa de verdadera vida al otro lado de sus crestas. ¡Es maravilloso! Aquí es mi vida tal como me la imponen; allá, mi anhelo inextinguible de superarme."

35. The window is often a slippery signifying zone in many of Contreras's short

stories where it functions both as a site of surveillance and a site where other "outlooks" offer the promise of challenging the local semantic and social context.

36. Ibid., 14. "—¡Mira!—señaló María Luisa—. ¡Si hasta a la Virgen engaña! Convertido en sostén de las santas andas, su padre, el chacal, el hombre de atajos, desfilaba con la procession." When she sees her father, the corrupt government official, participate in the Holy Friday procession, she effectively renounces her faith: "How could one have faith? As long as men like him lead the Virgin, God cannot return my faith to me" (¿Cómo creer? Mientras hombres así conduzcan a la Virgen, Dios no puede devolverme la fe) (14).

37. Ibid., 13. "Viernes Santo Sangriento. Mujeres y niños acañoneados, ciudades incendiadas, hogares destruidos por las bombas, y los hombres que se matan, se persiguen y se destruyen como fieras. . . . Viernes Santo, y se matan en Europa."

38. Ibid., 13–14. "Atropellos, insultos, abusos, injusticias, crímenes. . . . Y mientras los menos se horrorizan, los más aplauden y apuestan como en una jugada de gallos. ¿Cuántos admiradores de la fuerza bruta acompañan al Santo Sepulcro? ¿Cuántos embusteros? ¿Cuántos calumniadores? ¿Cúantos ladrones? . . ."

39. Notably, the story "Viernes Santo Sangriento" already alludes in its title to certain lacerating aspects of the church. The complicity between the paternalist abusive authority and the Catholic Church emerges in several stories that link the public space and its controlling "eyes" also to the Catholic Church. Indeed, the Catholic Church has a social surveillance function and figures prominently in each of the four stories published in *4 cuentos*, reflecting accurately the renewed role of the Catholic Church during the Trujillato.

40. Ibid., 15. "con terquedad desesperante.—¡Que perezca el débil! Al justo ¡que lo apedreen, que lo arrastren, que lo crucifiquen si estorba! ¡Qué caray, este es el siglo de la fuerza . . ."

41. Ibid., 15, 16. "a su hija la posee una indignación callada"; "le grito en las narices a Don Milo."

42. Ibid., 16. "De la boca demasiado repleta le salta la comida por las comisuras tensas. Se le desorbitan los ojos grises, lanza un bufido y se calla."

43. Ibid., 27. "Fue una noche clara como mirada de niño, en una terraza, pequeña, silenciosa, flotante, con el aliento del mar sobre las cuatro. Porque éramos cuatro mujeres en cuatro torres de aire."

44. Ibid., 27. "Oíamos música; la música de Liszt y la nuestra; la que cada uno de nosotros lleva en la sangre, únicamente audible a nuestro propio pulso."

45. Ibid., 27, 28. "Un filo agudo de luz cortó el aire"; "una ventana abierta de un tajo en el espesor colonial de la pared, hueco híbrido entre ventana y tragaluz invertido."

46. Ibid., 28. "El torso inverosímilmente desnudo"; "—¿Listo?—preguntó una voz varonil."

47. Ibid. "—Sí—. . . pero un momento todavía; es mi hora de amar"; "Era su hora, como todas las horas de su vida tonsurada. ¡Cómo si un redondel en los cabellos fuera bastante para encasillar una vida; toda una larga vida de hombre velludo!"

48. Ibid. "Yo no quería penetrar tanto en su pecado ni en su muerte. . . . La emoción me retiró los ojos de aquella herida blanca."

49. Ibid., 29. "Sin mirar sabía que en la ventana colgante en la atmósfera luminosamente callada, enrojecía una sotana a la que había llegado su hora."

50. Ibid., 28–29. "Hubo un temblor en el cielo. A pasos lentos comenzaron a descender las estrellas; se alargaron poco a poco en una caída vertiginosa, todas en una lluvia larga, interminable, sobre la tierra."

51. Ibid., 29. "—Mejor—. . . Ahora estamos verdaderamente solas."

52. Indeed, the story begins with the following premonition of the female narrator: "I knew it would happen. Old rumors made me live anticipating it from a long time back" (Sabía que sucedería. Viejos rumores me hacían vivir presintiéndolo desde mucho tiempo atrás) (ibid., 27).

53. Madera, "'Zones of Scandal,'" 124.

54. Ibid., 125–26.

55. The regime's "ever expanding apparatus of espionage" was, in the fifties, brought under the helm of the SIM (Military Intelligence Service), "a body that centralized and coordinated the various intelligence operations that previously had operated in an overlapping honeycomb" (Derby, "In the Shadow of the State," 302). With the creation of the Military Intelligence Service (SIM), and with the infamous Johnny Abbes García "placed at the helm" in 1957, "the regime sank to new levels of savagery" (ibid.).

56. Ibid., 303.

57. Contreras, *La tierra está bramando*, 55. "Doña Eugenia acudió al llamado del timbre de la entrada. Los tiempos habían cambiado. Antes, la puerta de la sala de las casas permanecía abierta. El visitante entraba libremente. Si no había nadie en la sala, soltaba un sonoro '¡Saludo!' o 'Buenos días' o 'Buenas tardes,' según el caso, para que vinieran a recibirlo. Ahora, por miedo a los ladrones pululantes o para tener tiempo de ponerse a salvo de la Policía Secreta, las puertas se trancaban con cerraduras de seguridad, cadenas y pestillos."

58. Ibid., 9. "imprudentemente"; "una de esas reuniones literarias."

59. Ibid., 9–10. "Hay rumores"; "las reuniones a puertas cerradas resultan sospechosas."

60. Ibid., 20. "Toño, el mensajero de la Diego María Motors Co."; "con todo respeto"; "No le conveniene, se lo digo yo, esos muchachos están fichaos."

61. Ibid., 8. "Yo vivo al margen de querellas porque hace tiempo me cosí la boca. Ni canto ni hablo."

62. Ibid., 14, author's emphasis. "Cada uno era un silencio vibrante, tras los

párpados cerrados, aislado y hermanado a la vez con la emoción de los otros. Eugenia se sentía como una esponja que se dilataba inmensa al saturarse de música. . . . Si *la música es el corazón de la vida,* esa noche el grupo se adentró en ella alcanzando por *un instante infinito* la plenitud de sus propias vidas."

63. Ibid., 18. "Únete a nosotros, enrólate en el PACOIN . . . Partido Comunista Independiente."

64. Ibid., 18. "Siglas, ¡qué manía de las siglas!"; "Un partido comunista independiente ¿de qué o de quién? Un disparate."

65. Ibid., 18, author's emphasis. "Yo soy *independiente* de verdad."

66. Ibid., 66. "Son muy jóvenes, andan algo desorientados."

67. Franco Pichardo, *Ensayos Profanos*, 129.

68. Contreras, *Tierra está bramando*, 19–20, author's emphasis. "Con este asunto del PACOIN han herido de muerte a nuestras reuniones. Uno, tuvo que ser Uno el de la idea funesta, tal vez *redentora*, de decapitarnos espiritualmente. Ahora comienza la inseguridad, el temor a la traición, a que nos revienten antes de florecer."

69. Ibid., 20. "Me sentiré mutilada sin esas horas hermosas en que me olvidaba de los siniestros estremecimientos del mundo y me consolaba pensando que todavía en la vida había emociones limpias sin olor a pólvora ni regusto a sangre."

70. Ibid., 66, my emphasis. "un partido responsable, con visión *realista* de los problemas del país."

71. Ibid., 67. "Respeto a los derechos humanos, libertad de reunión, libertad de disentir, de tránsito, derecho de las masas a mejores niveles de vida."

72. Ibid., 67. "Pues haciéndolo público."

73. Ibid., "—¿Ah, sí?—. . . ¿Vociferándolo en las plazas públicas?"

74. Ibid., 69. "Los habían pegado con chicle en los bancos de los parques, en los troncos de los árboles, en las puertas de las casas, de las iglesias, en las señales de tránsito, en las verjas de los edificios públicos."

75. Ibid., 70. "Pasado el primer momento de estupor, muchos casi se ahogaron de risa por el esfuerzo de contener la carcajada."

76. Ibid., 60.

77. Ibid., 71. "a todos los sospechosos de inconformidad." This unfolding of events echoes closely the Trujillato's actual persecution, imprisonment, and killing of many of the group members of the organizations it had allowed to form. Franco Pichardo, *Ensayos profanos*, 129.

78. Contreras, *Tierra está bramando*, 76. "Beatas [que] . . . recorrían distintos sectores de la ciudad."

79. The church's priest, el padre Benigno, observes the crowd of women, and then "blessed silently the immense blossom of the crowd of heads bowed now in prayer" (bendijo silenciosamente la inmensa flor de la muchedumbre de cabezas inclinadas ahora en oración) and then murmurs "may God protect them" (Dios las proteja) as

he withdraws to the sacristy (ibid., 77, 78). This "blessing" of the priest and the active role that religious women play in this manifestation echo the change in position of the Catholic Church toward the end of the Trujillato, when it openly began to critique its oppression.

80. Ibid., 80. "Una sombra de contrariedad en los rostros de muchos. No habían tirado a matar. Las balas, empero, al rebotar en las paredes habían herido las piernas de una decena de muchachas."

81. Ibid., 85–86. "Sueltan algunos mañana para calmar a las feministas esas"; "una nochecita con la familia"; "desaparecen estos pendejos de la circulación y adiós papeles subversivos."

82. In fact, the death in 1960 of the three dissident Mirabal sisters at the hands of the Trujillo regime caused widespread indignation in the country that is thought to have helped bring about the final unraveling of the dictatorship. The Dominican American writer Julia Alvarez retells the story of the Mirabal sisters' lives and deaths in her novel *In the Time of the Butterflies* (1994).

83. Taylor, *Disappearing Acts*, 197–98.

84. The family appeals again to their *compadre* after the arrest of the niece's boyfriend, Juan Carlos. To save his life, Eugenia pays the captain a visit and asks him to arrange for her to visit the boyfriend in prison, since, as she explains, "if I am able to visit him . . . it is very likely that by becoming a witness of his physical presence in protective custody, I avoid his torture with all the consequences you are aware of" (Si consigo visitarlo . . . es muy probable que al constituirme en testigo de su presencia física en la Preventiva, evite que lo torturen con todas las consecuencias que usted conoce) (ibid., 74). The captain, her mother's *compadre*, admires her courage and concedes her request.

85. Ibid., 108. "Miraba . . . un ovni"; "¡Un ovni! Está loca, que circule. Circule."

86. Ibid., 109. "En la primera esquina doblé a la derecha y eché a correr con todas mis fuerzas, impulsada por la desesperación hacia la zona de los rebeldes."

87. López-Calvo, *God and Trujillo*, 139.

88. Contreras, *Tierra está bramando*, 40. "Así, a la hora crepuscular, una hermosa tarde de abril se miraron a los ojos de manera distinta. El se acercó un poco más. Besó una boca virgen cuyos labios dulcemente interrogantes no supieron corresponder al beso ansioso que aleteaba sobre ellos."

89. Ibid., 12. "Linda chica . . . con sus muslos elásticos, sus pechitos turgentes moldeados en el poloshirt y su piel cálida de un color extraordinario de avellana navideña."

90. Eugenia's first longing memory in the narrative of Agustín Fuencarral is interrupted by the arrival of the young niece (11). Later again "Eugenia leaves the waters of the past to look at her niece" (Eugenia sale de las aguas del pasado para mirar a

la sobrina) and tells her "I want to be your friend" (quiero ser tu amiga) (ibid., 14). Her recounting of their first kiss is also interrupted by the niece, entering and asking, "Aunt, am I bothering you?" (Tía, ¿te molesto?) (ibid., 41).

91. Ibid., 43. "Apreciaba su cuerpo aún joven de apretadas carnes, armonioso."

92. The novel's complete avoidance of this gendered and sexualized imaginary of the Trujillato suggests starkly how none of the antihegemonic possibilities detected in other Dominican cultural traditions, despite their appropriation by the regime, is made out in these problematic gender and sexual notions.

93. At the time, the Dominican Republic, like other Caribbean and Latin American countries, was facing the shattering debt crisis of the 1980s. Negotiations with the International Monetary Fund forced the government to renege on many of its political and financial promises. And, as a consequence, living conditions dramatically deteriorated for the masses. As Lozano describes, "Trapped by its financial limitations, the state neglected to cover the indirect costs of salaries. Health services, education and transportation reflected the lack of state attention in the obvious neglect of hospitals, the elimination of the public transport subsidy and the ever more accentuated privatization of education. All this had direct and dramatic repercussions for the deteriorating standard of living of the working class." (Atrapado por sus límites financieras, el Estado descuidó la cobertura de los costos indirectos de los salarios. Los servicios de salud, de educación y transporte reflejaron la falta de atención estatal en el evidente descuido de los hospitales, la supresión del subsidio al transporte público y la cada vez más acentuada tendencia hacia la privatización de la enseñanza. Todo ello repercutió directa y dramaticamente sobre el deteriorado nivel de vida de las clases trabajadoras.) (*Después de los caudillos,* 40).

Chapter 4. Still Loving *Papi*

1. Baud, "Realidades e ideologías," 41. "estaba enraizado en una cultura política en donde el clientelismo y el autoritarismo juegan un papel importante. El gobierno de Leonel Fernández no pudo romper con estas ataduras culturales."

2. "Despite this continuity, the growing interaction with the outside world as a result of migration, tourism, and globalization has definitively changed Dominican society." (A pesar de estas continuidades, la creciente interacción con el mundo exterior como resultado de la migración, turismo y globalización, ha cambiado definitivamente la sociedad dominicana) (ibid., 20).

3. Hoffnung-Garskof, *Tale of Two Cities,* 10.

4. Ibid., 7.

5. Faxas, *Mito roto,* 10, 228. "predominio de los comportamientos orientados hacia lo privado"; "De un sentimiento de pertenencia comunitaria se ha pasado a uno de exclusión, de no integración, y la idea de éxito social ha cambiado de criterio."

6. Ibid., 20. "la incorporación de las mujeres al mundo del trabajo, sobre todo en las industrias de las zonas francas. En 1992 entre 60 y 64% de los trabajadores de las zonas francas eran mujeres."

7. Ibid., 224–25. "con . . . la incorporación de la mujer al mundo del trabajo se comprueba, por una parte, el cuestionamiento a la autoridad masculina en el hogar y cierta reestructuración de las relaciones en la pareja."

8. Ibid., 225. "Aun cuando la mujer, económicamente independiente, haya conquistador mayor autonomía y una revaluación ante sí misma y los demás, no ha llegado a borrar la fuerza de la tradición 'machista.' De esta forma, en los barrios la figura masculina continua dominando a la mujer."

9. Brea and Duarte, *Entre la casa y la calle*, 153. "Tanto en la familia como en la esfera política prevalence la legitimación del predominio masculino en las posiciones de poder y de decisión."

10. Cordero, *Mujer*, 94. "disociación entre los pujos modernos del planteo teórico y la subyacencia de visiones reproductoras del orden patriarcal."

11. Hasbún and Arvelo, *Poder y representación femenina*, 24. "A las mujeres les gusta más la limpieza."

12. Brennan, *What's Love Got to Do with It?*, 131.

13. Ibid., 174.

14. Gregory, for example, discusses, in *The Devil behind the Mirror*, how tourism can help to produce further gender inequalities: "young women—in particular, women who were racially marked and poor—were routinely stopped by the POLITUR [the tourism police] in identity checks on the premise that they were *mujeres de la calle* (streetwalkers) and potential lawbreakers. The hierarchical landscape of the tourism zone, thus, was structured in gendered terms since women were not only more likely than men to be viewed as being out of place there but also more likely to be seen as exploiting their sexuality" (58–59).

15. Baud, "Realidades e ideologías," 37. "Entre los jóvenes de clase media de las ciudades dominicanas existe un discurso sobre género mucho más articulado, en donde la liberación de las mujeres y la igualdad de hombres y mujeres se presenta como una característica básica de la modernidad."

16. Ibid., 20. "Relaciones fuertemente desiguales entre sexos, siguieron siendo elementos básicos de la sociedad contemporánea."

17. Mena, *Poética de Santo Domingo II*, 12. "Estamos perfilando una nueva subjetividad al calor de las migraciones y del peso de los medios de comunicación."

18. Ibid., 17. "Mientras este país de los titulares y del espectáculo se va produciendo, hay otro subterráneo, más movido y más amplio que el primero, más golpeante porque es el más tactil, el de la calle, el del doblar la esquina. Aunque descuidado e incluso minusvalorado por los saberes oficiales, ahí se está tejiendo el alma que somos."

19. Ibid., 12. "Una noción nueva de dominicanidad."

20. Ibid., 17. "Sólo en el arte y en la literatura se ha producido el tratamiento de esta nueva dominicanidad. Pensarla, abrirse a la calle, a su movilidad, a la necesidad de romper con el mundo reducido a la Isla, es parte de la próxima agenda."

21. According to Rodríguez, "arguably, this divergent literature carries out an archeology of Dominican knowledge, a task that the post-Trujillista intelligentsia was unable to perform" (*Divergent Dictions*, 99).

22. Ibid., 9.

23. De Maeseneer, *Encuentro con la narrativa*, 156. "jóvenes sin rumbo que buscan escapes precarios en la droga, la amistad, la música, los (en)sueños"; "poco presentes en la narrativa dominicana."

24. Rodríguez, *Divergent Dictions*, 125–26.

25. Rivera-Velázquez, "Importance of Being Rita Indiana-Hernández," 208.

26. Hernández, *Estrategia*, 16. "de arriba para abajo, haciendo bulla, fumándonos entre diez un cigarro, arrebatándonos cuando podíamos."

27. Ibid., 13. "una jevita muy *cool*"; "Lorena vivía en Naco en un apartamentazo, a unas cuadras de las Galerías, allí se celebraba unos bonches apoteósicos que siempre terminaban en desastre, una riquita intoxicada vomitando por la nariz sobre un violador de quince años que soba a su amigo dormido por el Lorazepan y el Brugal."

28. For example, Silvia describes the following encounters with one of Franco's sexual partners.

> He introduced himself and smiled with a learned faggotry. He must have already fucked him because Franco was tenacious. . . . Leo, this is how he liked to be called, was seventeen from Ciudad Nueva, he had a little girlfriend who gave him good blow jobs, though she did not let him put it in; "because, sweetie, mine is like a donkey's," and he put his hand in his crotch to confirm the comment. Franco prepared papaya milkshakes and caressed his head as if he were a little stuffed dog.
>
> (Se presentó y me sonrió con una mariconería aprendida. Ya se lo habría metido, porque Franco era tenaz. . . . Leo, que así le gustaba que le dijeran, tenía diecisiete años y en Ciudad Nueva, una noviecita que se lo mamaba muy bien, aunque no se lo dejaba meter; "porque, linda, yo lo tengo como un burro" y se ponía la mano en la entrepierna para confirmar el comentario. Franco le preparaba batidas de lechoza con lecha y le acariciaba la cabeza como a un perrito de peluche.) (ibid., 36)

29. "Octaviano had on his conscience two or three minors with their daddies who had gone to report him, little girls from school. An apostolate whom Octaviano enamored, visited, captivated, fucked and stole from" (Octaviano tenía en la conciencia dos o tres menores con sus papis que habían ido a denunciarlo, carajitas del colegio. Apostolado que Octaviano enamoraba, visitaba, fascinaba, singaba y robaba) (ibid., 26).

30. Ibid., 20. "Saber cómo le contabas a una de tus mujeres que era la única y caerle a otra con otro recital de flechas y corazoncitos me parecía asqueroso"; "ante todo, eramos cómplices del absurdo."

31. Ibid. "La gente siempre tan necia y poco delicada, probablemente pensaba, 'mira esa pobre gringuita cayó en las manos de ese sanki.'"

32. Ibid., 18. "El día se sacudía el polvo de encima y se volvía una luciérnaga enorme sobre la que tú y yo recorríamos la ciudad en círculos perfectos e inservibles, escarbando este laberinto de pelusas que es Santo Domingo."

33. Ibid., 19. "como ganándole ventaja a la tristeza, asomándose siempre la maldita bruja."

34. Ibid., 16. "Siempre acababan echándonos de todos lados, no es que fuéramos tan necios, era algo en la forma de sonreír, comi si con nosotros y nuestro entrar en los baños de tres y tres, nuestro besarnos en la boca hombres y mujeres, nuestro reír en la boca llena, salpicáramos a los que nos miraban con una sustancia insoportable, haciéndolas más mortales aún, porque en nuestra irritante cofradía sólo cabíamos nosotros porque nos habíamos matrimoniado sin saberlo, gracias al Brugal."

35. Ibid., 15. "ese ruido de la porra y que no consumimos nada y que irrespeto, que delincuentes dónde están sus papás y amén, lo de siempre."

36. Ibid., 30. "Ya se habían levantado cuando llegué, el tío me miró sin muchas ganas y volvió a clavarse de cuerpo y alma en la televisión, la abuela que no se acostumbraría a mi, a mi poco hablar, poco comer, poco reír, tampoco hizo mucho esfuerzo en sermonearme y se quedó callada con los ojos en el café con leche."

37. Ibid., 32. "Yo nunca estoy en la casa, a lo sumo duermo, aunque el sueño se me pueble de tarareos desagradables en esta cama en la que el abuelo y la abuela hicieron sus ocho hijos."

38. Ibid., 21. "¿Has pensado que todos los días, millones de niños se levantan, se cepillan los dientes y van a la escuela? Hasta yo fui."

39. Ibid., 37. "Llegaría más gente acalorada y la cueva crecería como un globo, feliz purgatorio de goma donde dormíamos unos sobre otros."

40. Ibid., 72. "un mundo nocturno ya definitivamente."

41. Hoffnung-Garskof, *Tale of Two Cities*, 233.

42. Mena, *Poética de Santo Domingo II*, 10. "La revolución de la nocturnidad"; "La noche . . . como espacio para el consumo, y también para la constitución de nuevas subjetividades."

43. Hernández, *Estrategia*, 58. "un muro de cocainómanos, megalómanos, hermanados en la histeria más deliciosa."

44. Ibid., 43. "Me molesta que la gente me hable, me toque, me diga cosas como si me conociera . . . porque a la gente quiero hablarle lo menos possible."

45. Ibid., 31–32. "Un mundo aparatoso y terriblemente árido. Un espacio instalado sobre el movimiento, el infame cabalgar de la gente, gente sola que no va a ninunga

parte, que coinciden meneando la cabeza con la gran sinfonía del desencanto y el escándalo."

46. Ibid., 72–73. "Esta gelatina absurda que nos han dejado nuestros padres, después de tanto que queremos, tanto *we want the world and we want it*, tanta carcajada histórica, tanto Marx y compañero para esto, esta brincadera de pequeñas bestias sin idea."

47. Ibid., 69. "Fiestas eran para elaborar estrategias; aquí van los afiches, aquí los panfletos, aquí las bombas, y ponían sus bombitas."

48. Ibid. "Tenía un tiro en la rodilla que le dieron en la loma, y con to y eso aguantó," "un pesao . . . , un héroe."

49. Ibid. "Don xxxxx ahora trabaja en el gobierno y tiene en la mirada esa cosa rara de los que fueron torturados en los doce años y ahora trabajan con los torturadores."

50. Ibid., 70. "Me daba cuenta de que todo da igual, al final todo es mentira, todos queremos un carrito japonés y una piscina."

51. Ibid., 13. "La ropita nítida, los cd's siempre nuevos y acabados de salir."

52. Ibid., 15, 47. "Hablamos de Cobain y *Meat Puppets* y bla bla bla . . ."; "Madonna y Darwin y la jirafas . . . Y Platón y Plotino y el Conde Saint Germain y Henry Miller y Pollock."

53. Ibid., 48. "No es fácil ser el Octano, hace falta cojón, hace falta una amnesia absurda y consecuente, hace falta *way* para ponérsele al lado en su mundo de él, en su infierno de latex y hormigón armado, sus zapatos . . . habría que ser Chochueca para ir mendigándole un ratito de vida."

54. Ibid., 49. "Un viejo loco que acosaba a los enfermos terminales y a sus familiares todo por una donación de trapos, que le dieran la ropita del difunto después del funeral. Y andaba así vestido con la ropa de los muertos."

55. Ibid. "Esta ciudad de serpientes, cadáveres de nylon"; "Qué cojones Chochueca, todo el mundo llora, se muerde los labios de pena, se hala los pelos, tú tranquilo Chochueca, tú a tu vaina que no hay nadie coño que el mundo se acaba y los muertos con tierra tienen, magia la tuya Chochueca, la de hacer caminar los zapatos de un muerto."

56. Williams, *Other Side of the Popular*, 225.

57. Moreiras, *Exhaustion of Difference*, 294.

58. Hernández, *Papi*, 7. "Papi está a la vuelta de cualquier esquina. Pero uno no puedo sentarse a esperarlo porque esa muerte es más larga y dolorosa."

59. Ibid., 68. "Pongo un número con el que voy organizando las fotos junto a las otras bodas de papi que se acumulan como postalitas de baseball atadas con una gomita verde."

60. Ibid., 38. "Casi siempre termina en casa de una novia suya que es siempre más culúa que la anterior y con más cadenas de oro."

61. Ibid., 71. "Las novias de papi son una vaina. Me llaman, me mandan cartas, mami las quema, mami se hala los cabellos."

62. Ibid., 21. "Vienen como locas, chillando"; "Ha cogido con reunirse en el parqueo y lo llaman y lo llaman y caminan en círculos con pancartas y fotos de papi y me llaman a mí y luego forman una torre humana enterrándose las agujas de los tacos en los hombros para llegar al último piso de la torre que es adonde estamos papi y yo."

63. Ibid., 22. "Nos están alcanzando, . . . papi, . . . saca una pistola . . . y me la pasa diciendo 'dispara.'"

64. Ibid., 16. "Mi papi tiene tanta ropa y tiene tantos clósets para guardarla que a veces cuando quiere ponerse una camisa tiene que comprarla de nuevo porque se olvida en cual clóset es que está. . . . Mi papi tiene más carros que el diablo. Mi papi tiene tantos carros, tantos pianos, tantos botes, metralletas, botas, chaquetas, chamarras, helipuertos, mi papi tiene tantas botas, tiene más botas, mi papi tiene tantas novias."

65. Ibid., 8. "Cuando papi se fue la primera vez para Estados Unidos con una cubana que no quería que papi le mandara dinero a nadie, mi abuelita Cilí dijo: Está muerto para mí. Y cuando papi le dijo a mami que se iba a casar de nuevo, pero no con ella, mami le dijo: te me moriste."

66. Ibid., 12. "La caravana de réplicas de Pontiac Trans-Am que se manejan solos que papi trae para vender. Decenas de trajes de 5,000 dólares que papi trae para ponerse. Miles de relojes, cadenas, anillos y guillos de oro blanco."

67. Ibid., 9–10. "Ya todo el mundo sabe que estás volviendo, que vas a regresar, que vuelves triunfante, con más cadenas de oro y más carros que el diablo. Ya todo el mundo lo sabe. . . . Y se sueñan contigo llenando la maleta con regalos para ellos, sólo vives para ellos, sueñan que tú les debes todo en la vida, en sus sueños. Se imaginan el reencuentro. Tú, con tu traje de plata, tus zapatos de azabache, corriendo desde el aeropuerto, no, pagando un avión del aeropuerto a sus casas para, antes que nada y primero que todo, tocarles la puerta, y despertarlos con una ducha de billetes verdes que saben a azúcar de pastelería."

68. Ibid., 65. "Acuérdate de los tuyos."

69. Ibid., 66. "Cili chequea sobre el hombro de papi que estén los nombres de todos. Dinero, neveras, carros, hasta casas para algunos en nombre de los viejos tiempos."

70. Ibid., 10. "Algunos han hecho una lista en sus mentes de cada cosa que les debes y por cada cosa escriben, también en sus mentes, lo que vas a traerles, la forma en que ellos creen que debes pagarles. . . . la lista es muy larga (porque ha anotado hasta las veces que te dirigieron la palabra)."

71. Ibid., 88. "Está entronado papi"; "montaña-castillo-torre de mil pisos"; "la fuente de todo sufrimiento y felicidad aquí en la tierra y mundos adyacentes."

72. Ibid., 90. "La Familia Real, que somos yo, mi abuela, mis tías y los mellizos

Puchy y Milly, además de mi mamá a quien las familia real de papi reconoce como la única mujer de papi porque fue la primera y se casaron como dios manda por la iglesia."

73. Ibid., 64. "Yo pienso que es como decir Compadre, o sea que papi le bautiza las criaturas a sus socios y por eso es que los hijos de sus socios vienen y a modo de saludo le meten una mano en el bolsillo a papi y sacan dos, tres billetes."

74. Ibid., 88. "Papi se hace más poderoso gracias a la energía emitida por todos los que desean un carro nuevo en el mundo. Los poderes de papi florecen cuando el espíritu de los deseantes vibra al máximo, haciendo que éstos le alquilen sus mujeres a los guachimanes y vendan por piezas a sus hijos para comprarse un carro en el dealer de papi, adonde se les entrega la llave mágica con la que se puede volar, conseguir mujeres, y eventualmente, más llaves."

75. Ibid., 73–74. "Y papi está creciendo, y sus socios con él, echando pa'lante tan rápido que ya casi ni se ve."

76. Ibid., 99. "Feria de la Confraternidad y el Mundo Unido . . . ese nombre se lo puso papi y que cuando papi le pone un nombre a una cosa nadie se lo puede quitar."

77. Ibid., 96. "Y frente a cada nuevo proyecto un letrero que dice: 'ESTO LO HIZO PAPI.'"

78. Ibid., 97. "Por dondequiera, en vallas, en cruzacalles, en letreros electrónicos, en murales sobre los muros salitrosos del Malecón la cara de papi, con los colores de la bandera, debajo una lema que reza: TODOS SOMOS FAMILIA."

79. Ibid. "Las viviendas son repartidas a partir de un examen de orina que compruebe la filiación con papi, el resultado de este examen puede falsificarse bebiendo sangre de papi o vinagre y a continuación llenando un formulario de treinta páginas en las que el solicitante debe exponer toda clase de anécdotas con papi, con fechas y lugares exactos."

80. Ibid., 145. "el gran poder que es papi."

81. Ibid., 147–48. "Muy pronto estaba integrado en todos los rituales."

82. Ibid., 144. "Pero a la gente lo que más le gustaba era que la nombraran y yo . . . distribuía títulos a troche y moche: delegado de la circuncisión telepática en papi, Virrey del estado de sitio que es papi, Comandanta en jefa de todos los desbarajustes de papi."

83. She describes how they dress up and act alike: "he dresses me up with his suits and we comb our hair with gel and use brushes as microphones" (me viste con sus trajes y nos peinamos con gelatina y usamos cepillos como micrófonos) (ibid., 32).

84. Ibid., 61. "María Cristina y yo nos despegamos del suelo y de papi muy deprisa, mientras nos besamos con ojos cerrados y yo soy tan fuerte que mi brazo de ocho años nos sostiene a ambas."

85. Ibid., 64. "Se ven igualitos, con sus trajes, sus anillos, sus cadenas, sus casetes regados debajo del asiento del carro."

86. Ibid., 7.

87. Ibid., 155. "Mis amigos eran casi todos hijos de otras enfermas."

Chapter 5. How Not to Read Junot Díaz

1. "By the middle of the 1980s, migrant remittances had surpassed agricultural and mining exports as the leading source of foreign exchange in the national economy" (Hoffnung-Garskof, *Tale of Two Cities*, 220).

2. Ibid., 6.

3. Ibid., 7.

4. Ibid.

5. Baud, "Realidades e ideologías," 25. "Los 'dominicanos ausentes' trajeron estilos nuevos de vida y de vestir y percepciones diferentes de las relaciones de género."

6. Levitt, *Transnational Villagers*, 55.

7. Ibid., 61.

8. Ibid., 97.

9. Díaz, *Brief Wondrous Life of Oscar Wao*, 1.

10. Ibid., 2.

11. Ibid., 2–3.

12. Ibid., front matter, n.p.

13. Ibid.

14. Ibid.

15. Ibid.

16. Also, Julia Alvarez's novel *In the Time of the Butterflies* (1994), about three women murdered by the Trujillato, was picked up for a 2001 Showtime television movie production, featuring Salma Hayek, Edward James Olmos, and Marc Anthony.

17. López-Calvo, "Postmodern Plátano's Trujillo," 79.

18. Díaz, *Brief Wondrous Life of Oscar Wao*, 301.

19. For a discussion of Dominican military masculinity and other types of masculinity, see Elena Valdez's "Masculinities in Crisis: A *Tíguere,* a Military Figure, and a *Sanky-panky* as Three Models of Being a Man in the Dominican Republic."

20. Díaz, *Brief Wondrous Life of Oscar Wao*, 323.

21. López-Calvo, "Postmodern Plátano's Trujillo," 85.

22. Díaz, *Brief Wondrous Life of Oscar Wao*, 283.

23. Ibid., 326.

24. Ibid., 334, author's emphasis.

25. Machado Sáez, "Dictating Desire, Dictating Diaspora," 540.

26. Hondagneu-Sotelo, "Gender and Contemporary U.S. Immigration," 565.

27. They declare, "We chose to focus on Mexico-Costa Rica and Nicaragua-Dominican Republic as contrasting cases, indicating migration processes that prevail

at opposite poles of a societal continuum running from patriarchy to matrifocality" (Massey et al., "International Migration and Gender in Latin America," 77).

28. Ibid., 69–70.
29. Decena, *Tacit Subjects*.
30. Díaz, *Brief Wondrous Life of Oscar Wao*, 326.
31. Wroe, "Junot Díaz."
32. Díaz, *Brief Wondrous Life of Oscar Wao*, 326; Díaz, *This Is How You Lose Her*, 175.
33. Díaz, *This Is How You Lose Her*, 212.
34. Wroe, "Junot Díaz."
35. Ibid.
36. Anderson, "Junot Díaz Hates Writing Stories," 28.
37. Díaz, *This Is How You Lose Her*, 191.
38. Díaz's writing here speaks to the assessment of scholars such at Jonathan Hartlyn and Rosario Espinal who point out that generational change alone is not sufficient to change ingrained gender patterns and beliefs.
39. Díaz, *This Is How You Lose Her*, 171.
40. Renda, *Taking Haiti*, 71.
41. Méndez, *Narratives of Migration and Displacement*, 6.

Conclusion

1. Brea and Duarte, *Entre la calle y la casa*, 121. "Cualquier intento de estudiar los procesos de jerarquización de los sexos y de subordinación femenina . . . no podría pasar por alto la extraordinaria función de la ideología, de los mecanismos estatales, y del sistema escolar durante los treinta años del regimen autoritario de Trujillo."
2. Hartlyn, *Struggle for Democratic Politics*, 4.
3. Espinal and Morgan, *Cultura política de la democracia*, 2008, 155. "En el primer lugar hacia la derecha en la escala ideológica."
4. Ibid., 132.
5. Espinal, *Autoritarismo y democracia*, 96. "Discurso político hegemónico"; "por tres décadas se había estructurado en torno a dos polos antagónicos, uno divino (el de orden, paz y progreso) y otro malévolo (el de desorden, guerras y miserias)."
6. Brea and Duarte, *Entre la calle y la casa*, 135. "el principio de la preeminencia masculina."
7. Scott, *Conscripts of Modernity*, 6.

Bibliography

Alcántara Almánzar, José. *Los escritores dominicanos y la cultura*. Santo Domingo: Instituto Tecnológico de Santo Domingo, 1990.
Alexander, M. Jacqui. *Pedagogies of Crossing: Meditations on Feminism, Sexual Politics, Memory, and the Sacred*. Durham: Duke UP, 2006.
Alvarez, Julia. *In the Time of the Butterflies*. New York: Penguin, 1995.
Álvarez, Soledad. "Oposición y similitudes en los personajes de *Materia Prima* de Marcio Veloz Maggiolo." *Arqueología de las sombras: La narrativa de Marcio Veloz Maggiolo*. Ed. Fernando Valerio-Holguín. Santo Domingo: Patronato de la Ciudad Colonial de Santo Domingo, 2000. 27–32.
———. "La poesía de los sesenta." *Coloquios* (2000): 311–18.
———. "Un siglo de literatura dominicana: Modernismo y postmodernidad, libertad y vasallaje." *El siglo XX dominicano: Economía, política, pensamiento y literatura*. Ed. José Rafael Lantigua. Santo Domingo: CODETEL, 2002. 341–405.
Anderson, Sam. "Junot Díaz Hates Writing Stories." *New York Times Magazine*. September 30, 2012. 26–29.
Aparicio, Frances R., and Susana Chávez-Silverman, eds. *Tropicalizations: Transcultural Representations of Latinidad*. Hanover: UP of New England, 1997.
Asturias, Miguel Ángel. *El Señor Presidente*. Mexico City: Costa-Amic, 1946.
Avelar, Idelber. *The Untimely Present: Postdictatorial Latin American Fiction and the Task of Mourning*. Durham: Duke UP, 1999.
Ayuso, Juan José. "La Generación del 60: Hacia la definición del ser y la literatura dominicana." *Coloquios* (2000): 303–10.
Báez, Clara, and Denisse Paiewonsky. *Género y ciudadanía*: Recomendaciones para incorporar la perspectiva de género al programa FOSC. Santo Domingo: Instituto Tecnológico de Santo Domingo: Banco Interamericano de Desarrollo, 2002.
Balaguer, Joaquín. "El principio de la alternabilidad en la historia dominicana." Ciudad Trujillo: Impresora Dominicana, 1952.

Barrios Rosario, Sheila. "Introduction." *La carnada*. Santo Domingo: Letra Gráfica Breve, 2007. 17–26.

Baud, Michiel. "Patriarchy and Changing Family Strategies: Class and Gender in the Dominican Republic." *History of the Family* 2.4 (1997): 355–78.

———. "Realidades e ideologías de la modernidad en la República Dominicana del siglo XX." *Estudios Sociales* 34.124 (2001): 9–50.

Beasley-Murray, Jon. *Posthegemony: Political Theory and Latin America*. Minneapolis: U of Minnesota P, 2011.

Bederman, Gail. *Manliness and Civilization: A Cultural History of Gender and Race in the United States, 1880–1917*. Chicago: U of Chicago P, 1996.

Benítez-Rojo, Antonio. *The Repeating Island: The Caribbean and the Postmodern Perspective*. Durham: Duke UP, 1992.

Betances, Emelio. *The Catholic Church and Power Politics in Latin America: The Dominican Case in Comparative Perspective*. Lanham: Rowman and Littlefield, 2007.

———. *State and Society in the Dominican Republic*. Boulder: Westview Press, 1995.

Beverley, John. *Latin Americanism after 9/11*. Durham: Duke UP, 2011.

Brea, Ramonina, and Isis Duarte. *Entre la calle y la casa: La mujeres dominicanas y la cultura política a finales del siglo XX*. Santo Domingo: Editora Búho, 1999.

Brennan, Denise. *What's Love Got to Do with It? Transnational Desires and Sex Tourism in the Dominican Republic*. Durham: Duke UP, 2004.

Briggs, Laura. *Reproducing Empire: Race, Sex, Science, and U.S. Imperialism in Puerto Rico*. Berkeley: U of California P, 2002.

Bruni, Nina. "El trujillismo en *Uña y carne* de Marcio Veloz Maggiolo." *Revista Mexicana del Caribe* 7.13 (2002): 153–79.

———. *Letras de la Era: Imagen de Trujillo en la narrativa dominicana contemporánea*. Santo Domingo: Secretaría de Estado de Cultura, 2007.

Calder, Bruce J. *The Impact of Intervention: The Dominican Republic during the U.S. Occupation of 1916–1924*. Austin: U of Texas P, 1984.

Candelario, Ginetta E. B. *Black behind the Ears: Dominican Racial Identity from Museums to Beauty Shops*. Durham: Duke UP, 2007.

Cartagena Portalatín, Aída. *Escalera para Electra*. Santo Domingo: Brigadas Dominicanas, 1967.

Cassá, Roberto. "Algunos componentes del legado de Trujillo." *Iberoamericana* 1.3 (2001): 113–26.

———. "Intelectuales: Creencias y poder (debate)." *Xinesquema* 2 (2002): 17–20.

Castillo, Carlos, Javier Mota, and Amanda Mullaney. "Propaganda del régimen de Trujillo." Thesis. Universidad Iberoamericana, Escuela de Comunicación Publicitaria, Santo Domingo, 2002.

Castillo, Efraim. *El personero*. Santo Domingo: Editorial Manatí, 2000.

Caulfield, Sueann, Sarah C. Chambers, and Lara Putnam, eds. *Honor, Status, and Law in Modern Latin America*. Durham: Duke UP, 2005.

Collado, Lipe. *Anécdotas y crueldades de Trujillo*. Santo Domingo: Editora Collado, 2003 [2002].

———. *El tíguere dominicano: Hacia una aproximación de cómo es el dominicano*. Santo Domingo: Editora Collado, 2002.
Connell, R. W., and James W. Messerschmidt. "Hegemonic Masculinity: Rethinking the Concept." *Gender & Society* 19 (2005): 829–59.
Contreras, Hilma. *4 cuentos*. Ciudad Trujillo: Editorial Stella, 1953.
———. *La carnada*. Santo Domingo: Letra Gráfica Breve, 2007.
———. *Doña Endrina de Calatayud*. Ciudad Trujillo: Impresora "Arte y Cine," 1955.
———. *Entre dos silencios*. Santo Domingo: Editora de Colores, 2002 [1987].
———. *La tierra está bramando*. Santo Domingo: Editora de Colores, 2002 [1986].
Cordero, Margarita. *Mujer: Participación política y procesos electorales (1986–1990)*. Santo Domingo: CIPAF, 1991.
Crassweller, Robert D. *Trujillo: The Life and Times of a Caribbean Dictator*. New York: Macmillan, 1966.
Dalleo, Raphael. *Caribbean Literature and the Public Sphere: From the Plantation to the Postcolonial*. Charlottesville: U of Virginia P, 2011.
Decena, Carlos U. *Tacit Subjects: Belonging and Same-Sex Desire among Dominican Immigrant Men*. Durham: Duke UP, 2011.
De Maeseneer, Rita. *Encuentro con la narrativa dominicana contemporánea*. Madrid: Iberoamericana, 2006.
De Moya, E. Antonio. "Power Games and Totalitarian Masculinity in the Dominican Republic." *Caribbean Masculinities: Working Papers*. Ed. Rafael Ramírez, Victor Garcia-Toro, and Ineke Cunningham. Puerto Rico: HIV/AIDS Research and Education Center, University of Puerto Rico, 2003. 105–45.
Derby, Lauren. "The Dictator's Seduction: Gender and State Spectacle during the Trujillo Regime." *Callaloo* 23.3 (2000): 1112–46.
———. *The Dictator's Seduction: Politics and the Popular Imagination in the Era of Trujillo*. Durham: Duke UP, 2009.
———. "In the Shadow of the State: The Politics of Denunciation and Panegyric during the Trujillo Regime in the Dominican Republic, 1940–1958." *Hispanic American Historical Review* 83.2 (2003): 295–344.
Díaz, Junot. *The Brief Wondrous Life of Oscar Wao*. New York: Riverhead Books, 2007.
———. *Drown*. New York: Riverhead Books, 1996.
———. *This Is How You Lose Her*. New York: Riverhead Books, 2012.
Edmondson, Belinda. *Caribbean Romances: The Politics of Regional Representation*. Charlottesville: U of Virginia P, 1999.
Espinal, Rosario. *Autoritarismo y democracia en la política dominicana*. San José: CAPEL, 1987.
———. "El siglo de las tinieblas: El país sigue patinando en un lodazal de corrupción, nepotismo." *Hoy* [Santo Domingo] April 7, 2010: opinion section.
Espinal, Rosario, and Jana Morgan. *Cultura política de la democracia en la República Dominicana: 2006*. Nashville: LAPOP: Vanderbilt University, 2006.
———. *Cultura política de la democracia en la República Dominicana, 2008: El impacto de la gobernabilidad*. Nashville: LAPOP: Vanderbilt University, 2009.

El fantasma de Trujillo: Antología de cuentos sobre el tirano y su Era. Ed. Miguel Collado. Santo Domingo: Ediciones Cedibil, 2006 [2005].

Faxas, Laura. *El mito roto: Sistema político y movimiento popular en la República Dominicana, 1961–1990*. Mexico City: Siglo XXI, 2007.

The Feast of the Goat. Dir. Luis Llosa. Lolafilms and Future Films, 2005.

Ferguson, James. *The Dominican Republic: Beyond the Lighthouse*. London: Latin American Bureau, 1992.

Fischer, Sibylle. *Modernity Disavowed: Haiti and the Cultures of Slavery in the Age of Revolution*. Durham: Duke UP, 2004.

Flores, Juan. *The Diaspora Strikes Back: Caribeño Tales of Learning and Turning*. New York: Routledge, 2008.

Foucault, Michel. *The History of Sexuality*. Vol. 1. New York: Vintage Books, 1990 [1976].

Franco Pichardo, Franklin. *Ensayos profanos: Sobre racismo, pesimismos y izquierdismo*. Santo Domingo: Sociedad Editorial Dominicana, 2001.

———. "Presentación." *El tigueraje intelectual*. Santo Domingo: Centro de Información Afroamericano y Sociedad Editorial Dominicana, 2002. 11–16.

Galíndez, Jesús de. *La Era de Trujillo*. Santo Domingo: Letra Gráfica Breve, 2006 [1958].

Gallego Cuiñas, Ana. "La novela del Trujillato en los ochenta o cómo escuchar el silencio." *Hipertexto* 6 (2007): 3–13.

———. "Trujillo: El fantasma y sus escritores (Análisis y sistematización de la novela del Trujillato.)" Diss. Universidad de Granada, 2005.

———. "La venganza del pueblo: La novela del trujillato tras el tiranicidio." *Anales de Literatura Hispanoamericana* 37 (2008): 303–19.

García Marquéz, Gabriel. *El otoño del patriarca*. Barcelona: Plaza y Janes, 1975.

García Romero, Rafael. "Perfil y valores narrativos de Hilma Contreras." *Escritores dominicanos*. February 23, 2013. http://www.escritoresdominicanos.com/contreras estudios1.html.

Gobat, Michel. *Confronting the American Dream: Nicaragua under U.S. Imperial Rule*. Durham: Duke UP, 2005.

Goldman, Dara E. *Out of Bounds: Islands and the Demarcation of Identity in the Hispanic Caribbean*. Lewisburg: Bucknell UP, 2008.

Gregory, Steven. *The Devil behind the Mirror: Globalization and Politics in the Dominican Republic*. Berkeley: U of California P, 2007.

Gutmann, Matthew C. *Changing Men and Masculinities in Latin America*. Durham: Duke UP, 2003.

Hartlyn, Jonathan. *The Struggle for Democratic Politics in the Dominican Republic*. Chapel Hill: U of North Carolina P, 1998.

Hasbún, Julia, and Josefina Arvelo. *Poder y representación femenina: Estudio cualitativo acerca de la participación de la mujer en la política*. Santo Domingo: Participación Ciudadana, 2002.

Hernández, Rita Indiana. *La estrategia de Chochueca*. Santo Domingo: Riann Editorial, 1999.

———. *Papi*. San Juan: Ediciones Vértigo, 2005 [2004].

Hoffnung-Garskof, Jesse. *A Tale of Two Cities: Santo Domingo and New York after 1950*. Princeton: Princeton UP, 2008.
Hondagneu-Sotelo, Pierrette. "Gender and Contemporary U.S. Immigration." *American Behavioral Scientist* 42 (1999): 565–76.
Iglesias Utset, Marial. *A Cultural History of Cuba during the U.S. Occupation, 1898–1902*. Chapel Hill: U of North Carolina P, 2011.
In the Time of the Butterflies. Dir. Mariano Barroso. MGM, Showtime, and Ventanarosa, 2001.
Jackson II, Ronald L., and Murali Balaji, eds. *Global Masculinities and Manhood*. Urbana: U of Illinois P, 2011.
Jimenes Grullón, Juan I. *Una Gestapo en América*. Havana: Editorial Lex, 1947.
Jiménez Polanco, Jacqueline. *Los partidos políticos en la República Dominicana: Actividad electoral y desarrollo organizativo*. Santo Domingo: Editora Centenario, 1999.
Johnson, Lyman L., and Sonya Lipsett-Rivera. *The Faces of Honor: Sex, Shame, and Violence in Colonial Latin America*. Albuquerque: U of New Mexico P, 1998.
Kimmel, Michael. *Gendered Society*. New York: Oxford UP, 2004.
Kitschelt, Herbert, and Steven I. Wilkinson. *Patrons, Clients, and Policies: Patterns of Democratic Accountability and Political Competition*. Cambridge: Cambridge UP, 2007.
Kitschelt, Herbert, Kirk A. Hawkins, Juan Pablo Luna, Guillermo Rosas, and Elizabeth J. Zechmeister. *Latin American Party Systems*. Cambridge: Cambridge UP, 2010.
Krohn-Hansen, Christian. *Political Authoritarianism in the Dominican Republic*. London: Palgrave, 2009.
Kryzanek, Michael J., and Howard J. Wiarda. *The Politics of External Influence in the Dominican Republic*. New York: Praeger, 1988.
Kutzinski, Vera M. *Sugar's Secrets: Race and the Eroticism of Cuban Nationalism*. Charlottesville: U of Virginia P, 1993.
Laclau, Ernesto. *Emancipation(s)*. New York: 2007 [1996].
———. *On Populist Reason*. New York: Verso, 2005.
Laclau, Ernesto, and Chantal Mouffe. *Hegemony and Socialist Strategy: Towards a Radical Democratic Politics*. New York: Verso, 1985.
Lago Graña, Josefa. "Nombrar(se) o no nombrar(se): Martha Rivera y la narrativa dominicana actual." *De márgenes y adiciones: Novelistas latinoamericanos de los 90*. Ed. Jorge Chen Sham and Isela Chiu-Olivares. San José, Costa Rica: Perro Azul, 2004. 161–80.
Larsen, Neil. "¿Cómo narrar el trujillato?" *Revista Iberoamericana* 54.142 (1988): 89–98.
Levitt, Peggy. *The Transnational Villagers*. Berkeley: U of California P, 2001.
López-Calvo, Ignacio. *God and Trujillo: Literary and Cultural Representations of the Dominican Dictator*. Gainesville: U P of Florida, 2005.
———. "A Postmodern Plátano's Trujillo: Junot Díaz's *The Brief Wondrous Life of Oscar Wao*, More Macondo than McOndo." *Antípodas: Journal of Hipanic and Galician Studies* 20 (2009): 75–90.

Lozano, Wilfredo. *Después de los caudillos*. Santo Domingo: Ediciones Librería La Trinitaria, 2002.

———. "Development Opportunities: Politics, the State, and Institutions in the Dominican Republic in the Twenty-First Century." *Institutions Count: Their Role and Significance in Latin American Development*. Ed. Alejandro Portes and Lori D. Smith. Berkeley: U of California P, 2012. 113–29.

Machado Sáez, Elena. "Dictating Desire, Dictating Diaspora: Junot Díaz's *The Brief Wondrous Life of Oscar Wao* as Foundational Romance." *Contemporary Literature* 52.3 (2011): 522–55.

Madera, Melissa. "'Zones of Scandal': Gender, Public Health, and Social Hygiene in the Dominican Republic, 1916–1961." Diss. Binghamton University, 2011.

Maingot, Anthony P., and Wilfredo Lozano. *The United States and the Caribbean: Transforming Hegemony and Sovereignty*. New York: Routledge, 2005.

Maíz, Ramón, and Requejo, Roberto. "Clientelism as a Political Incentive Structure for Corruption." Chile: University of Santiago de Compostela, 2001.

Manley, Elizabeth S. "'Poner un grano de arena': Gender and Women's Political Participation under Authoritarian Rule in the Dominican Republic, 1928–1978." Diss. Tulane University, 2008.

Manzari, H. J. "Violence and the Seduction of History in *Musiquito: Anales de un déspota y de un bolerista*." *Ciberletras* 14 (December 2005). http://www.lehman.cuny.edu/ciberletras/v14.html.

Martínez-San Miguel, Yolanda. *Caribe Two Ways: Cultura de migración en el Caribe insular hispánico*. San Juan: Ediciones Callejón, 2003.

Martínez-Vergne, Teresita. *Nation and Citizen in the Dominican Republic, 1880–1916*. Chapel Hill: U of North Carolina P, 2005.

Massey, Douglas S., Mary J. Fischer, and Chiara Capoferro. "International Migration and Gender in Latin America: A Comparative Analysis." *International Migration* 44 (2006): 63–91.

Mateo, Andrés L. *Mito y cultura en la Era de Trujillo*. Santo Domingo: Librería La Trinitaria e Instituto del Libro, 1993.

Mayes, April J. "Why Dominican Feminism Moved to the Right: Class, Colour and Women's Activism in the Dominican Republic, 1880s–1940s. *Gender & History* 20.2 (2008): 349–71.

McClellan, Edwin North. "Down in the Dominican Republic." *Marine Corps Gazette: Professional Journal of U.S. Marines*, May 1932. April 29, 2011. http://www.mca-marines.org/gazette/down-dominican-republic.

Mena, Miguel D. "Los dominicanos no somos tan malos." *Clavedigital* [Santo Domingo] March 24, 2010: opinion sec.

———. *Poética de Santo Domingo II: Identidad, poder, territorios*. Santo Domingo: Ediciones Cielonaranja, 2005.

Méndez, Danny. *Narratives of Migration and Displacement in Dominican Literature*. New York: Routledge, 2012.

Miller, Jeannette. "La Generación del 60." *Jeannette Miller Arte y Literatura*. October 26, 2011. http://jeannettemiller.blogspot.com/2010/02/la-generacion-del-60.html.

Mora Serrano, Manuel. "Hilma Contreras Castillo (1913-2006): Premino Nacional de Literatura, 2002." *Pontificia Universidad Católica Madre y Maestra*. February 23, 2013. http://rsta.pucmm.edu.do/biblioteca/html/Dominicanos2/hilmacontreras/hilmacontreras/biografia.htm.

Moreiras, Alberto. *The Exhaustion of Difference: The Politics of Latin American Cultural Studies*. Durham: Duke UP, 2001.

Morgan, Jana, Rosario Espinal, and Jonathan Hartlyn. "Gender Politics in the Dominican Republic: Advances for Women, Ambivalence from Men." *Politics & Gender* 4 (2008): 35-63.

Nacidit-Perdomo, Ylonka. *Hilma Contreras: Una vida en imágenes, 1913-1993*. Santo Domingo: Inmetro, 1993.

NACLA. "Feminismo balaguerista: A Strategy of the Right." *Latin America and Empire Report* 8.4 (1974): 28-31.

———. *Newsletter* 4.7 (1970): 1-10.

Nolasco Cordero, Francisco. *Papaján*. Santo Domingo: Editora Educativa Dominicana, 1973.

Núñez, Manuel. *El ocaso de la nación dominicana*. Santo Domingo: Editora Alfa y Omega, 1990.

Oviedo, José. "Los intelectuales y la dictadura de Trujillo." *Coloquios '98*. Ed. José Chez Checo. Santo Domingo: Comisión Permanente de la Feria Nacional del Libro, 1999. 145-51.

Pacini Hernandez, Deborah. "Dominican Popular Music under the Trujillo Dictatorship." *Studies in Latin American Popular Culture* 12 (1993): 127-40.

Padilla, Mark. *Caribbean Pleasure Industry: Tourism, Sexuality, and AIDS in the Dominican Republic*. Chicago: U of Chicago P, 2007.

Peguero, Valentina. *The Militarization of Culture in the Dominican Republic: From the Captains General to General Trujillo*. Lincoln: U of Nebraska P, 2004.

Peña, Ángela. "Reportaje Robert D. Crassweller." *Hoy*, December 18, 2010. February 20, 2013. http://www.hoy.com.do/areito/2010/12/18/354671/REPORTAJERobert-D-Crassweller.

Pereyra, Emilia. "Intelectuales: Creencias y poder (debate)." *Xinesquema* 2 (2002): 26-27.

Piccato, Pablo. *The Tyranny of Opinion: Honor in the Construction of the Mexican Public Sphere*. Durham: Duke UP, 2010.

Prestol Castillo, Freddy. *El masacre se pasa a pie*. Santo Domingo: Ediciones de Taller, 1973.

Puri, Shalini. *Caribbean Postcolonial: Social Equality, Post/Nationalism, and Cultural Hybridity*. New York: Palgrave, 2004.

Renda, Mary A. *Taking Haiti: Military Occupation and the Culture of U.S. Imperialism, 1915-1940*. Chapel Hill: U of North Carolina P, 2001.

Rivera-Velázquez, Celiany. "The Importance of Being Rita Indiana-Hernández: Women-Centered Video-, Sound- and Performance-Interventions within Spanish Caribbean Cultural Studies." *Globalizing Cultural Studies: Ethnographic Interventions in Theory, Method, and Policy*. Eds. Cameron McCarthy, Aisha S. Durham, Laura C. Engel, Alice A. Filmer, Michael D. Giardina, and Miguel A. Malagreca. New York: Peter Lang, 2007. 205-27.

Rodriguez, Jenny K. "The Construction of Gender Identities in Public Sector Organisations in Latin America: A View of the Dominican Republic." *Equality, Diversity and Inclusion: An International Journal* 29.1 (2010): 53–77.

Rodríguez, Néstor E. *Divergent Dictions: Contemporary Dominican Literature*. Florida: Caribbean Studies Press, 2010.

———. *Escrituras de desencuentro en la República Dominicana*. Mexico: Siglo XXI Editores, 2005.

Roorda, Eric Paul. *The Dictator Next Door: The Good Neighbor Policy and the Trujillo Regime in the Dominican Republic, 1930–1945*. Durham: Duke UP, 1998.

Rosario Candelier, Bruno. "Tendencias, ciclos y valores de la novela dominicana." *Academia Dominicana de la Lengua*. http://www.academia.org.do/content/blogsection/37/102/.

Rosenberg, Emily S. *Financial Missionaries to the World: The Politics and Culture of Dollar Diplomacy*. Durham: Duke UP, 2003.

Sagás, Ernesto. *Race and Politics in the Dominican Republic*. Gainesville: UP of Florida, 2000.

Sagás, Ernesto, and Orlando Inoa. *The Dominican Republic: A Documentary History*. Princeton: Markus Wiener, 2003.

San Miguel, Pedro L. *The Imagined Island: History, Identity, and Utopia in Hispaniola*. Trans. Jane Ramírez. Chapel Hill: U of North Carolina P, 2005.

———. "Intelectuales, sociedad y poder en las Antillas hispanohablantes." *Revista Mexicana del Caribe* 11 (2001): 253–59.

Scott, David. *Conscripts of Modernity: The Tragedy of Colonial Enlightenment*. Durham: Duke UP, 2004.

Segal, Susan. "Gender Equality." *Americas Quarterly* (Summer 2012): 60–61.

Sheller, Mimi. *Citizenship from Below: Erotic Agency and Caribbean Freedom*. Durham: Duke UP, 2012.

Sommer, Doris. *Foundational Fictions: The National Romances of Latin America*. Berkeley: U of California P, 1991.

———. *One Master for Another: Populism as Patriarchal Rhetoric in Dominican Novels*. Lanham: UP of America, 1983.

Stephens, Michelle Ann. *Black Empire: The Masculine Global Imaginary of Caribbean Intellectuals in the United States, 1914–1962*. Durham: Duke UP, 2005.

Suárez Findlay, Eileen J. *Imposing Decency: The Politics of Sexuality and Race in Puerto Rico, 1870–1920*. Durham: Duke UP, 1999.

Taylor, Diana. *Disappearing Acts: Spectacles of Gender and Nationalism in Argentina's Dirty War*. Durham: Duke UP, 1997.

Thomas, Deborah A. *Exceptional Violence: Embodied Citizenship in Transnational Jamaica*. Durham: Duke UP, 2011.

Tinsley, Omise'eke Natasha. *Thiefing Sugar: Eroticism between Women in Caribbean Literature*. Durham: Duke UP, 2010.

Torres-Saillant, Silvio. "Dominican Literature and Its Criticism: Anatomy of a Troubled Identity." *A History of Literature in the Caribbean*. Vol. 1: *Hispanic and Francophone*

Regions. Ed. A. James Arnold, with Julio Rodriguez-Lui and Michael Dash. Amsterdam: Benjamins, 1994. 49–64.

———. *Intellectual History of the Caribbean*. New York: Palgrave Macmillan, 2005.

———. "Marcio Veloz Maggiolo." *Modern Latin-American Fiction Writers*. Second series. Ed. William Luis and Ann González. Detroit: Gale Research, 1994.

———. *El retorno de las yolas: Ensayos sobre diáspora, democracia y dominicanidad*. Santo Domingo: Librería La Trinitaria/Editora Manatí, 1999.

———. *El tigueraje intelectual*. Santo Domingo: Centro de Información Afroamericano y Sociedad Editorial Dominicana, 2002.

———. "The Tribulations of Blackness: Stages in Dominican Racial Identity." *Callaloo* 23.3 (2000): 1086–1111.

Trujillo, Rafael L. *Discursos, mensajes y proclamas*. Vol. 1. Santo Domingo: Editorial El Diario, 1946.

———. *La Era de Trujillo: 25 años de historia dominicana*. Santo Domingo: Impresora Dominicana, 1955.

———. *Evolución de la democracia en Santo Domingo*. Santo Domingo: Impresora Dominicana, 1950.

———. *Trujillo Speaks: A Series of Four Articles Expressly Written for and Published by the* Miami Herald *on April 3–6, 1960*. Ciudad Trujillo, 1960.

Turits, Richard Lee. *Foundations of Despotism: Peasants, the Trujillo Regime, and Modernity in Dominican History*. Stanford: Stanford UP, 2003.

Ugalde, Sharon Keefe. "Veloz Maggiolo y la narrativa del dictador/dictadura: Perspectivas dominicanas e innovaciones." *Arqueología de las sombras: La narrativa de Marcio Veloz Maggiolo*. Ed. Fernando Valerio-Holguín. Santo Domingo: Patronato de la Ciudad Colonial de Santo Domingo, 2000. 199–228.

Valdez, Diógenes. *Retrato de dinosaurios en la Era de Trujillo*. Santo Domingo: Edita-Libros, 1997.

Valdez, Elena. "Masculinities in Crisis: A *Tíguere*, a Military Figure, and a *Sanky-panky* as Three Models of Being a Man in the Dominican Republic." *Queering Iberia: Iberian Masculinities at the Margins*. Ed. Josep M. Armengol-Carrera. New York: Peter Lang, 2012. 113–32.

Valerio-Holguín, Fernando. "Bolero, historia e identidad en *Ritos de cabaret*." *Arqueología de las sombras: La narrativa de Marcio Veloz Maggiolo*. Ed. Fernando Valerio-Holguín. Santo Domingo: Patronato de la Ciudad Colonial de Santo Domingo, 2000. 229–46.

———. *Presencia de Trujillo en la narrative contemporánea*. Santo Domingo: Editora Universitaria-UASD, 2006.

Vargas Llosa, Mario. *La fiesta del chivo*. Madrid: Alfaguara, 2000.

Vega, Bernardo. *Domini canes: Los perros del Señor*. Santo Domingo: Fundación Cultural Dominicana, 1989.

———. *Unos desafectos y otros en desgracia: Sufrimientos bajo la dictadura de Trujillo*. Santo Domingo: Fundación Cultural Dominicana, 1986.

Veloz Maggiolo, Marcio. *De abril en adelante (Protonovela)*. Santo Domingo: Ediciones de Taller, 1984 [1975].

———. *Los ángeles de hueso*. Santo Domingo: Arte y Cine, 1967.
———. *La biografía difusa de Sombra Castañeda*. Caracas: Monte Ávila, 1980.
———. *Ritos de cabaret*. Santo Domingo: Editora Cole, 1999 [1991].
———. *Uña y carne: Memorias de la virilidad*. Santo Domingo: Letra Gráfica, 2006 [1999].
Vergés, Pedro. "Challenging the Silence: A Dialogue with Pedro Vergés." Interview with Margarite Olmos Fernández. *Callaloo* 23.3 (2000): 1068–75.
Walker, Malcolm T. "Power Structure and Patronage in a Community of the Dominican Republic." *Journal of Interamerican Studies and World Affairs* 12.4 (1970): 485–504.
Wiarda, Howard J. *Dictatorship and Development: The Methods of Control in Trujillo's Dominican Republic*. Gainesville: U of Florida P, 1968.
Wiarda, Howard J., and Michael J. Kryzanek. "Dominican Dictatorship Revisited: The Caudillo Tradition and the Regimes of Trujillo and Balaguer." *Revista/Review Iberoamericana* 7.3 (1977): 417–35.
Wiarda, Howard J., and Margaret MacLeish Mott, eds. *Politics and Social Change in Latin America: Still a Distinct Tradition?* Westport: Praeger, 2003.
Williams, Gareth. *The Other Side of the Popular: Neoliberalism and Subalternity in Latin America*. Durham: Duke UP, 2002.
Worldbank. Table, "Vulnerable Employment, Total." *Worldbank*. February 16, 2013. http://data.worldbank.org/indicator/SL.EMP.VULN.ZS.
World Values Survey. http://www.worldvaluessurvey.org.
Wroe, Nicholas. "Junot Díaz: A Life in Books." *Guardian*. September 9, 2012. http://www.guardian.co.uk/books/2012/aug/31/life-in-books-junot-diaz.
Wucker, Michele. "Election in the Dominican Republic: A Break with the Past?" *NACLA Report on the Americas* 30.2 (1996): 2.
Zeller, Neici. "The Appearance of All, the Reality of Nothing: Politics and Gender in the Dominican Republic, 1880–1961." Diss. University of Illinois at Chicago, 2010.

Index

Abbes García, Johnny, 170n55
Abril en adelante, De (Veloz Maggiolo), 63–64; class in, 69, 161n62; critiques of, 159n44, 160n54; end of, 159n43; era depicted in, 71; experimental aspects of, 61–63; letrados in, 51, 62, 63–64, 70, 99; masculinity in, 20, 68–69; race in, 161n62; relationships in, 160n53; Trujillo and Trujillato in, 51, 65, 66; as turning point in Dominican literature, 61–62; women and sexuality in, 66–68, 161n65, 161n67
Academia Dominicana de la Lengua, 57
Acción Feminista Dominicana (AFD), 38
Agriculture, 40, 41, 152n76, 152n78
Alcántara Almánzar, José, 48, 56, 76, 159n40, 166n3
Alexander, M. Jacqui, 13
Alfonseca, Miguel, 157n161
"Alma" (Díaz), 134
Almánzar Rodríguez, Armando, 76, 162n75
Alvarez, Julia, 172n82, 180n16
Álvarez, Soledad, 55, 60–61, 73
Anécdotas y crueldades de Trujillo (Collado), 57
Ángeles de hueso, Los (Veloz Maggiolo), 61
Anthony, Marc, 180n16
Anti-hegemonic: in Contreras's writing, 21, 100; and gender, 79, 142; in Hernández's writing, 115, 116; and Laclau, 8; and post-dictatorship letrados, 50, 60, 64, 70, 79; and Trujillo's national-popular discourse, 37
Antorcha, La (literary group), 56
Aparicio, Frances R., 17, 149n26
"Appearance of All, the Reality of Nothing: Politics and Gender in the Dominican Republic, 1880–1961, The" (Zeller), 27
Argentina, 48, 56, 58, 97, 141, 157n25
Ariel (Rodó), 26
Arqueología de las sombras: La narrativa de Marcio Veloz Maggiolo (Valerio-Holguín), 173
Asturias, Miguel Angel, 158n29
Avelar, Idelber, 58, 59, 157n25, 158n30
Ayuso, Juan José, 60, 157n16

Báez, Frank, 126
Balaguer, Joaquín: exile of, 51; and masculinity, 53–55; and national literary prize, 53; physical condition of, 102; presidential terms of, 20, 53, 71, 80, 101, 102, 107, 111, 155n3; public image of, as president, 53–55, 120; repression and human rights violations during presidencies of, 52, 140, 155n4, 156n5; and Trujillo and Trujillato, 20, 32, 36–37, 49, 51, 53; and United States, 52–53, 155n3; as writer, 53
Balaguerato, 52, 53, 64
Balaji, Murali, 15

194 · Index

Balcácer, Ada, 157n16
Barrios Rosario, Sheila, 83–84, 167n13
Bartolomé, Raúl, 165n1
Baud, Michiel, 39, 41, 102, 106, 124, 153n89
Beasley-Murray, Jon, 22
Bederman, Gail, 148n9
Beijing conference on women, 10
Benítez-Rojo, Antonio, 2, 6–7
Betances, Emelio, 155n4
Beverley, John, 5, 22, 146n14
Bhabha, Homi, 114
Biografía difusa de Sombra Castañeda, La (Veloz Maggiolo), 158n29
Black behind the Ears: Dominican Racial Identity from Museums to Beauty Shops (Candelario), 148n4
Blacks. *See* Race
Blanco, Delia, 164n109
Bolivia, 4, 56
Bonasso, Miguel, 59
Bosch, Juan: as exile, 53; and Hilma Contreras, 82–83, 84, 168n30; as president, 51, 53, 54–55, 155n1, 156n15; as writer, 51, 84
Brazil, 48, 56, 58, 157n25
Brea, Ramonina, 104, 139, 141
Brennan, Denise, 105–6
Brief Wondrous Life of Oscar Wao, The (Díaz), 22, 124–31, 132–33, 134, 137
Bruni, Nina, 19, 57
Buen ladrón, El (Veloz Maggiolo), 159n42

Candelario, Ginetta, 148n4
Caribbean: challenges in, 15; cockfighting in, 88–89; cultural discourses in, 8; economy of, 173n93; gender in, 14; history of, 2; masculinity in, 35; migration from, 2, 131, 145n6; national identity in, 145n6; patriarchy in, 14; postcolonial politics in, 2–4, 8; scholarship on, 2–4, 8, 145n6; standard of living in, 2; and United States, 24, 147n52
Caribbean Pleasure Industry: Tourism, Sexuality, and AIDS in the Dominican Republic (Padilla), 11
Carnada, La (Contreras), 83
Cartagena Portalatín, Aída, 161n65, 167n12
"Cartilla Cívica," 42, 43
Cassá, Roberto, 155n3, 164n109

Castillo, Efraim, 69, 76, 99, 162n75
Catholic Church: and Juan Bosch, 51, 155n1; and Communism, 155n1; and Dominican nationalism, 149n15; strengthening of, 49; and Trujillato, 59, 89, 168n39, 171n79; in works by Hilma Contreras, 88–89, 168n39
Caudilloism, 1, 17, 23, 30, 31–32, 33
Caulfield, Sueann, 86
Cedeño de Fernández, Margarita, 141, 146n25
Cestero, José, 157n16
"Challenging the Silence" (Vergés), 50
Chambers, Sarah C., 86
Changing Men and Masculinities in Latin America (Gutmann), 14
Chávez-Silverman, Susana, 17, 149n26
"Cheater's Guide to Love, The" (Díaz), 134–36
Chile, 48, 56, 58, 157n25
Cibao valley, 41
Citizenship: in the Dominican Republic, 1, 141; in the Caribbean, 2, 3
Citizenship from Below: Erotic Agency and Caribbean Freedom (Sheller), 3
Class: and clientelism/patronage, 41, 42, 43; and *compadrazgo*/co-parenting, 41, 42; and gender, 10; ideologues and, 49; and masculinity, 40; middle, 92; and patriarchy, 39; and post-Trujillo politics, 51; and *respeto*, 43; rural population and, 40–41; and sexual relations, 39; and tíguere, 45–46, 154n103; Trujillo and Trujillato and, 36, 139; in works by Hilma Contreras, 84; in works by Rita Indiana Hernández, 108, 114, 115; in works by Marcio Veloz Maggiolo, 66, 161n62
Clientelism: Balaguer and, 55; Bosch and, 55, 156n15; and class, 41, 42, 43, 153n89; as component of political leadership, 55; and differential relations, 6; discontent with, 15; Fernández administration and, 102, 141, 146n25; forces supporting, 103, 104; literary depictions of, 71; and masculinity, 9, 139; Medina administration and, 142, 146n25; Mejía and, 146n25; pervasiveness of, 9, 103, 139; Trujillo and, 41–42, 152n80; in works by Rita Indiana Hernández, 112, 113, 119, 121; writers and, 21, 79
Colette, 82
Collado, Lipe, 45, 57

Columbia University, 146n25
"¿Cómo narrar el trujillato?" (Larsen), 66
Compadrazgo/co-parenting, 41, 42, 97–98, 119, 152n79
Confronting the American Dream: Nicaragua under U.S. Imperial Rule (Gobat), 149n23
Connell, R. W., 11–12
Consumerism, 120
Contreras, Darío, 91
Contreras, Hilma: archives of, 165n2; and Juan Bosch, 82–83, 168n30; on Catholic Church, 88–89; characteristics of works by, 81–82, 166n5, 168n30, 168n35; depiction of terror by, 167n18; depiction of Trujillo by, 99; on gender, 84, 85, 87; on homosexuality, 82, 90–91; on honor, 85, 86, 87; on letrados, 92, 98; life and literary career of, 80, 81, 82–85, 83, 91, 165n2, 166n6; on paternalism, 89; on poverty, 84; reclusiveness of, 80, 81; on resistance, 92, 94–98; scholarship on, 21, 81, 100, 166n5; on Trujillato, 84, 87, 89, 90, 91–94; on women, 90
Co-parenting. See Compadrazgo/co-parenting
Cordero, Margarita, 105
Corollary to the Monroe Doctrine (Roosevelt), 24
Corruption: in the Caribbean, 2; in the Dominican Republic, 9, 15, 102, 103; and masculinity, 139
Costa Rica, 131, 180n27
Crassweller, Robert D., 16, 29, 30, 31, 32, 149n31
Creólistes, 6
Creonte (Veloz Maggiolo), 159n42
Crime, 26, 42, 128, 148n11
Cuba, 7, 37, 53
Cuban missile crisis, 7

Dalleo, Raphael, 2
Decena, Carlos U., 11, 132
Decline of the Dominican Nation, The (Nuñez), 77, 78
Deive, Carlos Esteban, 78, 166n3
De Maeseneer, Rita, 19, 57, 69, 107, 108, 162n83
De Moya, E. Antonio, 11
Derby, Lauren: on 1916–1924 U.S. occupation, 19, 25–26, 27; on Dominican nationalist mythologies, 149n15; on isolation of Dominican Republic, 47; on tíguere, 45–46; on Trujillo and Trujillato, 16, 40, 47, 92, 93–94
Devil behind the Mirror: Globalization and Politics in the Dominican Republic, The (Gregory), 106, 174n14
Diaspora, Dominican: and Dominican culture, 123–24; and Dominican economy, 123; Dominicans' perceptions of, 123; and gender, 124, 132, 133; as globalizing force, 21; and homosexuality, 132; in literature, 118–19, 122, 125, 132; and masculinity, 22, 131, 132, 134
Diaspora Strikes Back: Caribeño Tales of Learning and Turning, The (Flores), 125
Díaz, Junot, 22, 124–25, 131, 135–36. See also Brief Wondrous Life of Oscar Wao, The (Díaz); This Is How You Lose Her (Díaz)
Dicent, Juan, 126
Dictatorship and Development (Wiarda), 149n31
Dictator's Seduction: Politics and the Popular Imagination in the Era of Trujillo (Derby), 16
Divergent Dictions: Contemporary Dominican Literature (Rodríguez), 19
Domínguez, Franklin, 166n3
Domini Canes: Los perros del Señor (Vega), 33
Dominican Republic: 1963 elections in, 51; 1965 uprising in, 51, 55, 155n4; 1966 elections in, 52; 1980s protests in, 100–101; 2012 presidential elections in, 1; colonial past of, 16, 23; consumer culture in, 103; cultural forces in, 103; economy of, 4, 103, 123, 145n9, 146n24, 173n93, 180n1; education in, 4; femicide in, 128; and Haiti, 16, 23–24, 49, 140–41, 148n1, 158n33; information flow into and within, 47; leadership criteria in, 156n13; media in, 103; migration from, 16, 123; military in, 51, 128; and modernization, 103; national cultural identity in, 4, 16, 149n15; nightlife in, 111; opposition in, 51, 52, 70; opposition within, 48; political conservatism in, 140; political corruption in, 15, 102, 103; political hierarchy in, 9; political stagnation in, 103, 139; public sector of, 10–11; rural nature of, 39, 40–41; social developments in, 13, 103; socioeconomic development in, 139; standard of living in, 4, 173n93; state's role in, 4; travel from, 47

Dominican Republic, and United States: and 1916–1924 U.S. occupation, 1, 19, 23, 25, 26–28, 33, 34, 35, 36; and 1965–1966 U.S. occupation, 51–52, 56; during Balaguer administrations, 52–53, 156n6; and Dominican customs operations, 23, 24; impact of, 129; and impact on Dominican masculinity, 14–15; and race, 148n4; scholarship on, 16, 19, 23–24, 25–26; Trujillato and, 16

Dominican Resistance Memorial Museum, 56

Doña Endrina de Calatayud (Contreras), 21, 81, 85, 87, 92, 167n12

"Doomsday Book, The" (Díaz), 135

Drown (Díaz), 127, 134

Duarte, Isis, 104, 139, 141

Ecuador, 56

Edmondson, Belinda, 2–3, 6

E. León Jimenes company, 77

El Puño (literary group), 56

El Salvador, 56

Eltit, Diamela, 157n25, 158n30

Emancipation(s) (Laclau), 6

Encuentro con la narrativa dominicana contemporánea (de Maeseneer), 57

Entre dos silencios (Contreras), 81, 90, 99

Entre la calle y la casa: La mujeres dominicanas y la cultura política a finales del siglo XX (Brea and Duarte), 104–5, 139

Escalera para Electra (Cartagena Portalatín), 161n5

"Espera, La" (Contreras), 166n8

Espinal, Rosario, 9, 10, 140, 155n1, 181n38

Estrategia de Chochueca, La (Hernández), 22, 107–16, 122

Exceptional Violence: Embodied Citizenship in Transnational Jamaica (Thomas), 3

Exhaustion of Difference: The Politics of Latin American Cultural Studies (Moreiras), 114

Faces of Honor: Sex, Shame, and Violence in Colonial Latin America (Johnson and Rivera-Lipsett), 85–86

Fantasma de Trujillo: Antología de cuentos sobre el tirano y su Era, El, 100

Faxas, Laura, 103–4, 156n6, 156n15

Feast of the Goat, The (Vargas Llosa), 129

Feminism: Trujillo and, 37–38, 49, 135, 137

Fernández, Leonel, 102, 141, 146n25

Fernández, Pedro Pablo, 165n1

Fiesta del chivo, La (Vargas Llosa), 127

Fischer, Sibylle, 148n2

"Flaca" (Díaz), 134

Flores, Juan, 125

Foundational Fictions: The National Romances of Latin America (Sommer), 18

Foundations of Despotism (Turits), 42

Franco Pichardo, Franklin, 77

Galíndez, Jesús de, 47, 149n31, 153n92

Gallego Cuiñas, Ana: on dictatorship novels, 57, 66, 69, 160n55; on homophobia in Dominican literature, 19; on literary depictions of Trujillo, 160n56, 160n57; on misogyny in Dominican literature, 19; on new generation of writers, 165n1

García, Iván, 157n16

García Márquez, Gabriel, 59, 158n29

García Romero, Rafael, 166n5

Gender: and 1916–1924 U.S. occupation, 19–20, 26–28; and class, 10; Hilma Contreras and, 84, 85, 87, 173n92; créolistes and, 6; and crime, 26; and democratization, 12; Junot Díaz and, 129, 132, 134, 135, 137–38; and Dominican culture, 142; Dominican diaspora and, 124, 132; and Dominican public sector, 10–11, 141–42; and economic development, 12; and globalization, 12, 21, 22, 104, 105; and health, 26; Rita Indiana Hernández and, 108, 109, 114, 115; and inequality, 104–6; influences on, 13; literary representations of, 68; and marriage, 132–33; and migration, 124, 131; and modernization, 106; and patriotism, 28; and politics, 9–10, 22, 26–28, 70; and power, 12–13; roles assigned to, 38–39, 104–5; scholarship on, 22, 131–32, 181n38; and social structure, 12, 22; and tourism, 105–6, 174n14; Trujillo and Trujillato and, 19, 24, 28, 38, 81, 87, 92, 139; United States and, 25, 131, 133, 138; and voting, 38. *See also* Sexuality; Women

"Gender and Contemporary U.S. Immigration" (Hondagneu-Sotelo), 131

Generation of '48, 61

Generation of the '60s/Generación del 60, 61, 78, 81, 166n3
Glissant, Edouard, 2, 6
Globalization: and gender, 10, 12, 21, 22, 104, 105, 106; impact of, 4, 10, 104, 173n1; and interconnectedness, 3; and masculinity, 22; media and, 21; Mena on, 106–7; and migration, 21; and mobility, 3; and neoliberalism, 21; and politics, 104; and sexuality, 104; state and, 146n14; and tourism, 21, 106
Global Masculinities and Manhood (Jackson and Balaji), 15
Gobat, Michel, 149n23
God and Trujillo: Literary and Cultural Representations of the Dominican Dictator (López-Calvo), 19, 59
Goldman, Dara E., 3, 145n6
Gregory, Stephen, 106, 174n14
Grupo Quisqueyano, 146n25
Guardian, The, 134, 135
Guatemala, 4, 56
Gutmann, Matthew C., 14, 15

Haiti: and Dominican Republic, 16, 23–24, 49, 140–41, 148n1, 158n33; and race, 24; truth commission in, 56; and United States, 24
Hartlyn, Jonathan: on Balaguer, 52, 156n5; on gender, 181n38; on masculinity in Dominican politics, 9, 10; on Trujillo, 41, 152n81
Hayek, Salma, 180n16
Hegemony: and Laclau, 8, 22, 142; and gender, 12, 142; and Latin American cultural studies, 22; of the legacies of the Trujillato, 31; of Trujillo, 40
Hegemony and Socialist Strategy: Towards a Radical Democratic Politics (Laclau and Mouffe), 5
Henríquez Ureña, Pedro, 48
Hernández, Ángela, 80
Hernández, Rita Indiana, 21, 103, 107, 126. See also *Estrategia de Chochueca, La* (Hernández); *Papi* (Hernández)
Heureaux, Ulises, 33
Hoffnung-Garskof, Jesse, 103, 111, 123
Homosexuality: in dictatorship novels, 69–70, 100; in Dominican diaspora, 132; and masculinity, 108–9; in works by Hilma Contreras, 82, 90–91, 100, 166n8; in works by Rita Indiana Hernández, 108–9; in works by Veloz Maggiolo, 68, 73–74, 109
Hondagneu-Sotelo, Pierrette, 131
Honduras, 4, 56
Honor, 85–87, 92, 154n103
Honor, Status, and Law in Modern Latin America (Caulfield, Chambers, and Putnam), 86
Hull, Cordell, 23

Imbert Brugal, Carmen, 80
International Monetary Fund (IMF), 100, 173n93
In the Time of the Butterflies (Alvarez), 172n82, 180n16
"Invierno" (Díaz), 134
Isla, La (literary group), 56

Jackson, Ronald L., II, 15
"Jesús en vitrina" (Contreras), 167n14
Jiménez Polanco, Jacqueline, 52
Johnson, Lyman L., 85–86
Johnson, Sara E., 148n2
Jones, Edward P., 127
Judas (Veloz Maggiolo), 159n42
Juventud Democrática, 95

Kimmel, Michael, 12, 142
Krohn-Hansen, Christian, 9, 43, 54, 55, 152n80, 156n13
Kutzinski, Vera M., 6–7

Laclau, Ernesto: on factors required to challenge status quo, 8, 115, 142; influence of, 5, 22; theoretical framework of, 6, 7, 8, 37, 79, 104, 115, 116; works by, 5–6
Larsen, Neil, 66, 160n54
Latin America: caudilloism in, 1, 30; cockfighting in, 88–89; economy of, 173n93; education in, 4; fiction in, 18; honor in, 85–86; inequality in, 5, 145n13; masculinity in, 1, 14; migration from, 15, 131; patriarchy in, 13–14; politics in, 5–6, 142; resistance in, 97; unemployment in, 4; women in, 97
Latin American Studies Association, 145n13

Letrados: in dictatorship novels, 99; factions of, 56; and Generación del 60/Generation of the '60s, 61, 78, 81, 166n3; post-Trujillo, 20, 50–51, 55–56, 62, 76–79, 164n109; roles of, 19, 20; during Trujillato, 19, 20, 47–48, 49, 56–57; and United States, 52; in works by Hilma Contreras, 92, 98; in works by Veloz Maggiolo, 62, 63–64, 70–71, 163n87. *See also* Balaguer, Joaquín; Bosch, Juan

Levitt, Peggy, 124, 125

Liberia, 24

Libro de buen amor (Ruiz), 85

Linz, Juan, 30

Literature: allegorical, 158n29, 158n30; characteristics of, 58, 59; class in, 66; cycles of, 57; dictatorship novels, 21, 57–58, 59, 65–66, 69, 81, 98–99, 100, 126, 129, 162n83; family depicted in, 18; and Generación del 60/Generation of the '60s, 61, 78, 81, 166n3; heterosexual romances, 18; homophobia in, 19, 69–70; late-20th-century, 21, 107; magical realism in, 158n29; and masculinity, 20–21; misogyny in, 19, 69; modernization of, 61–62, 159n40; nation depicted in, 18; 19th-century, 18; politics in, 60; race in, 66; realism in, 158n30, 167n13; revisionary, 107; Néstor E. Rodríguez on, 107; and Trujillato, 160n55

López-Calvo, Ignacio: on Prestol Castillo's *El masacre se pasa a pie*, 158n33; on Díaz's *The Brief Wondrous Life of Oscar Wao*, 127, 129; on dictatorship novels, 65–66, 98, 162n83; on gender politics, 19; on literary depictions of homophobia, 69–70; on literary depictions of Trujillo, 162n81; on realism, 59; on Trujillato as literary theme, 19; on Trujillo's sex drive, 70; on Veloz Maggiolo's *De abril en adelante*, 62–63

Lora, Silvano, 157n16

Lozano, Wilfredo, 4, 24, 173n93

Lugo, Américo, 48

Machado Sáez, Elena, 130

Madera, Melissa, 26, 28, 38–39, 91, 151n65

Maingot, Anthony P., 24

Manley, Elizabeth S., 19, 26, 37–38

Manliness and Civilization: A Cultural History of Gender and Race in the United States, 1880–1917 (Bederman), 148n9

Manzari, H. J., 160n57

Marine Corps, U.S., 33–34

Marriage, 39, 132–33

Martínez, María, 40

Martínez, Samuel, 148n2

Martínez-Vergne, Teresita, 28, 86, 148n11

Masacre se pasa a pie, El (Prestol Castillo), 158n33

Máscara, La (literary group), 56

Masculinity: Balaguer and Balaguerato and, 53–54, 55; Bosch and, 55; and caudilloism, 1; and class, 40; and clientelism, 139; and corruption, 139; and democracy, 35–36; Dominican diaspora and, 22, 131, 132, 134; forces affecting, 14–15; and globalization, 22; and hierarchy, 47, 54, 55, 69; and homosexuality, 108–9; homosexuals and, 11; in Latin America, 1, 14; and leadership, 50; letrados and, 20, 50; and literature, 20–21; in Nicaragua, 149n23; and patriarchy, 20; and politics, 1, 9, 50; and power, 12–13, 50; and public sector, 10–11; and race, 2, 19, 35; and resistance, 116; and sovereignty, 2, 20, 35; tíguere and, 45, 161n74; Trujillo and Trujillato and, 1, 20, 68–69, 75, 89, 91, 100, 140, 141, 162n84; in the United States, 137–38; U.S. Marines and, 138; and U.S. occupation, 35, 138; and virility, 11, 13, 27, 28, 35, 36, 54, 68, 70, 72, 73, 74, 75, 100, 141; in works by Junot Díaz, 128–31, 133–38; in works by Rita Indiana Hernández, 116, 119, 120–22, 129; in works by Veloz Maggiolo, 20, 66–67, 68–69, 72–73, 74

Massey, Douglas S., 131

Mateo, Andrés L., 47, 49, 78, 166n3

Materia prima (Veloz Maggiolo), 73

Mayes, April J., 19, 26

Media, 21, 106

Medina, Danilo, 141–42

Mejía, Hipólito, 1, 8, 13, 141, 146n24

Mena, Miguel D., 17, 46, 51, 106–7, 111, 115

Méndez, Danny, 138

"Mensaje a la mujer dominicana" (Darío Contreras), 91

Mercado, Tununa, 157n25

Mexico, 131, 180n27

Migration: and gender, 131; as globalizing force, 21; impact of, 106, 173n1, 180n1; scholarship on, 131, 138, 180n27; in works by Junot Díaz, 132. *See also* Diaspora, Dominican

Military, 42, 43, 49, 51, 128, 152n81

Military Intelligence Service (SIM), 98, 170n55

Mirabal sisters, 172n82

Miraflores, Dominican Republic, 124

"Miss Lora" (Díaz), 134

Mito roto: Sistema político y movimiento popular en la República Dominicana, 1961–1990, El (Faxas), 103–4

Moreiras, Alberto, 22, 114, 115

Morel, Bienvenida, 39

Morgan, Jana, 9, 10

Morrison, Mateo, 166n3

Mouffe, Chantal, 5

Mujer y participación política y procesos electorales (Cordero), 105

Museo Memorial de la Resistencia Dominicana, 56

Musiquito: Anales de un déspota y de un bolerista (Sánchez), 160n57

Nacidit-Perdomo, Ylonka, 80, 83, 101, 165n2, 166n5

Narratives of Migration and Displacement in Dominican Literature (Méndez), 138

National Book Fair Prize, 77

Nation and Citizen in the Dominican Republic, 1880–1916 (Martínez-Vergne), 86, 148n11

Nation-state: Caribbean, 2, 3, 4, 5, 8; Trujillo and, 35, 152n80, 158n28

Neoliberalism, 21

Nicaragua, 24, 131, 149n23, 180n27

"Nilda" (Díaz), 134

Nolasco Cordero, Francisco, 162n75

Noll, João Gilberto, 157n25

Núñez, Manuel, 77, 78

"Ocho días" (Contreras), 167n14

Olmos, Edward James, 180n16

One Master for Another: Populism as Patriarchal Rhetoric in Dominican Novels (Sommer), 18, 59, 68, 69

On Populist Reason (Laclau), 6

Other Side of the Popular: Neoliberalism and Subalternity in Latin America, The (Williams), 114

Otoño del patriarca, El (García Márquez), 59, 158n29

Oviedo, José, 17, 48

Oviedo, Ramón, 157n16

Padilla, Mark, 11

Panama, 56

Papaján (Nolasco Cordero), 162n75

Papi (Hernández): analysis of, 116–22, 175n28, 175n29, 179n83; compared to Díaz's *The Brief Wondrous Life of Oscar Wao*, 129; themes in, 116, 125

Paraguay, 56

Partido de la Liberación Dominicana (PLD), 146n25

Partido Revolucionario Dominicano (PRD), 51, 155n4

Partido Socialista Popular, 95

Patriarchy: and class, 39; Dominican nationals and, 27; homosexuals and, 11; and honor, 86; literary depictions of, 68; and modernity, 13–14; and political power, 35, 36, 39; and populism, 68; and social mores, 39; and U.S. occupation, 26–27

Patronage. *See* Clientelism

Peguero, Valentina, 33, 34, 42, 44, 154n107

Peix, Pedro, 76, 162n75

Peña Batlle, Manuel Arturo, 49

Pepín, Ercilia, 27–28

Pereyra, Emilia, 164n109

Pérez, Odalís G., 164n109

Personero, El (Castillo), 69, 99, 162n75, 162n83

Peru, 4, 56

Piccato, Pablo, 86

Piglia, Ricardo, 157n25

"Poder de unas lágrimas, El" (Contreras), 167n14

Poder y representación femenina (Hasbún and Arvelo), 105

Political Authoritarianism in the Dominican Republic (Krohn-Hansen), 9

"¿ . . . Polvo?" (Contreras), 168n30

Populism, 68

Portugal, 30

Postcolonial: politics, 2, 142; nation-state, 3, 5, 8

Presencia de Trujillo (Valerio-Holguín), 158n30
Prestol Castillo, Freddy, 158n33
Puerto Rico, 131
"Puñados de dolor" (Contreras), 167n14
"Pura Principle, The" (Díaz), 134
Puri, Shalini, 3
Putnam, Lara, 86

4 cuentos (Contreras), 21, 87, 167n12, 168n30, 168n39

Race: as Dominican challenge, 15; Haitians and, 24; and inequality, 7; and masculinity, 2, 19, 35; post-Trujillato, 165n117; public image of, 46; and tíguere, 154n103; Torres-Saillant on, 148n4; Trujillo and Trujillato and, 34, 36, 139, 140; United States and, 24–25, 37, 148n4, 148n9; U.S. Marines and, 34; in works by Rita Indiana Hernández, 108, 109, 114, 115; in works by Veloz Maggiolo, 66, 161n62
Racism: anti-, 116; Dominican, 15; imperialism and, 2, 24; Trujillo and, 36
Recuerdo de la muerte (Bonasso), 59
Renda, Mary A., 138
Repeating Island, The (Benítez-Rojo), 6
Resistance: and co-parenting, 97–98; letrados and, 92; and masculinity, 116; women and, 97, 101; in works by Hilma Contreras, 92, 94–98; in works by Rita Indiana Hernández, 113, 115
Respeto, 43
Retrato de dinosaurios en la Era de Trujillo (Valdez), 70, 162n75
Risco, René del, 157n16
Ritos de cabaret (Veloz Maggiolo), 73
Rivera, Martha, 80
Rivera-Lipsett, Sonya, 85–86
Rivera-Velázquez, Celiany, 108
Rodó, José Enrique, 26
Rodriguez, Jenny K., 10–11
Rodríguez, Néstor E.: on National Book Fair Prize scandal, 78; on new Dominican writers, 107, 175n21; on persistence of Trujillato ideology, 79; on Trujillato, 17, 19, 49; on works by Rita Indiana Hernández, 107–8, 115
Rodríguez Demorizi, Emilio, 49

Rodríguez Soriano, René, 165n1
Roorda, Eric Paul, 33–34
Roosevelt, Theodore, 19, 24
Rosario Candelier, Bruno, 57, 159n40
Rosenberg, Emily S., 24, 25
Rossellini, Isabella, 127
Ruiz, Juan, 85

Said, Edward, 149n26
Sánchez, Enriquillo, 160n57
San Francisco Chronicle, 127
Santiago, Silviano, 157n25
Santo Domingo, Dominican Republic, 51, 92, 166n6
Scott, David, 2, 8, 15, 143
Seis relatos (Veloz Maggiolo), 159n42
Señor Presidente, El (Asturias), 158n29
Sexuality: and gender, 135; and globalization, 104; literary representations of, 68, 108, 114, 129, 173n92; and politics, 70; Trujillato and, 81, 139. *See also* Gender; Homosexuality
Sheller, Mimi, 3
SIM (Military Intelligence Service), 98, 170n55
Social structure: and clientelism/patronage, 42, 43, 46; and *compadrazgo*/co-parenting, 42; and hierarchy, 36–37, 43, 46, 47; individual in, 44, 45, 46; and kinship, 43, 44, 46; rural, 43–44; tíguere and, 45; during Trujillo regime, 43–44, 46–47
Sommer, Doris, 18, 19, 59, 62–63, 67–68, 69
Soto, Miñín, 157n16
Sovereignty: gender and, 27, 35, 36; globalization and, 146n14; Haiti and Dominican, 141; international political discourses of, 2, 20; Spain and Dominican, 23; Trujillo and Dominican, 35, 36; the U.S. and Dominican, 20, 25, 27, 35, 36
Spanish-American War, 24
Stanley, Avelino, 76, 77, 164n109
State: the Caribbean, 2, 3, 5, 8; the Dominican, 4, 10, 14, 17, 26, 33, 104, 113, 155n4, 156n5, 173n93; Dominican letrados and the, 51, 76, 77; gender and the, 1, 26, 35, 39, 97, 139, 147n29, 151n65; globalization and the, 146n14; Laclau, 6, 8; Latin American, 5; in Trujillo and the, 39, 40, 41, 42, 92, 159

Stephens, Michelle A., 35
"Sun, the Moon, the Stars, The" (Díaz), 134

Tacit Subjects: Belonging and Same-Sex Desire among Dominican Immigrant Men (Decena), 11
Tale of Two Cities: Santo Domingo and New York after 1950, A, (Hoffnung-Garskof), 103
Taylor, Diana, 97
This Is How You Lose Her (Díaz), 22, 125, 134–37
Thomas, Deborah A., 3
Tierra está bramando, La (Contreras): analysis of, 92–98, 99–101, 171n79, 172n84, 172n90; as dictatorship novel, 21, 81; scholarship on, 81
Tigueraje intelectual, El (Torres-Saillant), 77
Tíguere, 45–46
Tíguere dominicano: Hacia una aproximación de cómo son los dominicanos, El (Collado), 45
Tinsley, Omise'eke Natasha, 6
Torres-Saillant, Silvio: on Balagueratro, 54; on *The Brief Wondrous Life of Oscar Wao*, 125; on Caribbean, 2; on Dominican-Haitian relations, 148n4; on modernism in Dominican literature, 159n40; on National Book Fair Prize scandal, 77, 78; on post-Balagueratro opposition, 79; on post-Trujillo writers, 60; on race, 148n4, 165n117; on relationship between letrados and the state, 76, 164n109; on Trujillato, 17; on Veloz Maggiolo, 159n41, 159n42; on women, 80, 89
Tourism: and Dominican economy, 4; and gender norms, 105–6, 174n14; and globalization, 21, 103, 106; impact of, 173n1; and inequality, 106, 174n14; sex tourism, 105–6
Transnational Villagers, The (Levitt), 124
Tropicalism, 149n26
Tropicalizations: Transcultural Representations of Latinidad (Aparicio and Chávez-Silverman), 149n26
Trujillato: breaking of tradition by, 16; and Catholic Church, 59, 89, 168n39, 171n79; and caudilloism, 17, 30, 31–32, 33; and class, 36–37, 46, 139; and clientelism/patronage, 152n80; and *compadrazgos*/co-parenting, 98; and democracy, 35–36; discourse of, 84, 140; and Dominican national identity, 16; and feminism, 37–38, 49; fictional representations of, 65; and formation of political parties, 95; and gender, 38–39, 81, 91; and Haiti, 49; and hierarchy, 43–44; ideologues for, 49; intellectuals and, 47–48; isolation of Dominican Republic by, 47; literary depictions of, 69–70, 160n55, 160n56; and literature, 19, 56–57, 59–60, 61, 62, 66; Mario Vargas Llosa on, 127; and masculinity, 68–69, 89, 91, 100, 140, 141, 162n84; massacre of Haitians by, 158n33; and media, 47; military during, 128; and national identity, 49; and national-popular and national-populist, 24, 37, 44, 47, 139, 140; opposition to, 53; origins of modern problems in, 15–16; persistence of, 17–18, 19, 20, 31, 36, 139–40, 157n28; and propaganda, 47, 49; and public support, 154n107; and race, 36, 46, 49, 139, 140; scholarship on, 17–18, 19, 29–30, 31, 33–34, 37–39; and sexuality, 81; and surveillance, 92–93, 153n90, 153n92, 170n55; suspicion and isolation during, 43–44, 153n94; and violence, 92–93, 170n55, 172n82, 180n16; in works by Hilma Contreras, 84, 87, 89, 90, 91–94; in works by Junot Díaz, 125–26; in works by Veloz Maggiolo, 64, 65, 71–72
Trujillo, Angelita, 40
Trujillo, Radhamés, 40
Trujillo, Rafael Leónidas: assumption of presidency by, 33; biography of, 16; and caudilloism, 32; characteristics of, 29, 34, 65, 70, 72, 120; and class, 36, 40; and *compadrazgos*/co-parenting, 42, 98; death of, 36, 50; discourse of, 140; family of, 40, 51; and gender, 38; and honor, 154n103; literary depictions of, 65, 66, 70, 99, 126, 129, 160n57, 162n81; marriages and relationships of, 39–40; and masculinity, 1, 20, 75; and military, 152n81; motivations of, 149n31; and 1916–1924 U.S. occupation, 1; and order, 140; as patriarch, 35; as patron, 41–42, 43; public image of, 17, 32–33, 34, 35–37, 40, 41; and race, 34, 40; relationship of, with Dominicans, 32; rise to power of, 32–34, 39; scholarship on, 19, 29–31, 32, 33, 34, 38, 149n31; support for, 40–41; and U.S. Marines, 34

Trujillo, Ramfis, 40
Trujillo: The Life and Times of a Caribbean Dictator (Crassweller), 16, 29
Turits, Richard Lee, 40, 41, 42, 43, 93–94
Tyranny of Opinion: Honor in the Construction of the Mexican Public Sphere (Piccato), 86

Ugalde, Sharon Keefe, 159n44
Una vida en imágenes, 1913–1993 (Nacidit Perdomo), 165n2
Uña y carne: Memorias de la virilidad (Veloz Maggiolo), 20, 51, 70–76, 113
United States: and Balaguer, 52–53, 155n3; and Caribbean, 24; and dollar diplomacy, 24–25; and gender, 25; and Haiti, 24; marriage in, 133; and Nicaragua, 149n23; and race, 24, 25, 34, 37, 148n4. *See also* Dominican Republic, and United States
United States and the Caribbean: Transforming Hegemony and Sovereignty, The (Maingot and Lozano), 24
Untimely Present: Postdictatorial Latin American Fiction and the Task of Mourning, The (Avelar), 58
Urbanization, 103
Uruguay, 56

Valdez, Diógenes, 69, 76, 162n75, 166n3
Valerio-Holguín, Fernando, 57, 69, 73, 158n30, 164n109
Vargas Llosa, Mario, 127, 129
Vásquez, Rafael, 157n16
Vega, Bernardo, 33, 48
Veloz Maggiolo, Marcio: awards won by, 159n41, 166n3; career of, 61–62; and homosexuality, 73; and magical realism, 158n29; and National Book Fair Prize scandal, 78; stature of, 18, 51; works by, 61, 73, 158n29, 159n42; as writer, 20, 61, 62, 75, 158n29, 159n42. *See also Abril en adelante, De* (Veloz Maggiolo); *Uña y carne: Memorias de la virilidad* (Veloz Maggiolo)

"Ventana, La" (Contreras), 89–91, 92, 94, 168n30, 170n52
Vergés, Pedro, 50, 58
Vicioso, Chiqui, 80
"Viernes Santo sangriento" (Contreras), 87–89, 168n30, 168n36, 168n39
"Virgen del Aljibe, La" (Contreras), 168n30

Walker, Malcolm T., 39, 43, 152n76, 152n79, 153n94
What's Love Got to Do with It? Transnational Desires and Sex Tourism in the Dominican Republic (Brennan), 105
Wiarda, Howard J., 30, 149n31
Williams, Gareth, 22, 114, 115
Women: and crime, 26; and economic parity, 14, 104; and education, 14; and gender norms and roles, 38–39, 91, 104–6, 105, 133, 151n65; and health and healthcare, 14, 26; and honor, 86, 92; and marriage, 105; and migration, 124, 131; murders of, 128; and politics and public sphere, 9–10, 10–11, 13, 14, 97, 105, 141, 146n29, 151n63; and private life, 86; and resistance, 97, 101, 171n79, 172n82; Torres-Saillant on, 80, 89; and tourism, 105–6, 174n14; and U.S. occupation, 26–28; and voting, 38; in workforce, 12, 14, 104; in works by Hilma Contreras, 90, 92; in works by Junot Díaz, 129, 135, 136, 137; in works by Veloz Maggiolo, 67, 74–75; as writers, 80, 81. *See also* Gender
World Bank, 4
Wroe, Nicholas, 134

Zaglul, Antonio, 44
Zeller, Neici, 19, 26, 27, 37, 38, 151n63
"'Zones of Scandal': Gender, Public Health, and Social Hygiene in the Dominican Republic, 1916–1961" (Madera), 26

MAJA HORN is associate professor of Spanish and Latin American cultures at Barnard College.

The University Press of Florida is the scholarly publishing agency for the State University System of Florida, comprising Florida A&M University, Florida Atlantic University, Florida Gulf Coast University, Florida International University, Florida State University, New College of Florida, University of Central Florida, University of Florida, University of North Florida, University of South Florida, and University of West Florida.

www.ingramcontent.com/pod-product-compliance
Lightning Source LLC
Chambersburg PA
CBHW020838160426
43192CB00007B/700